TOM ATKINSON has had a very interesting life. After serving in the RAF throughout WWII, he spent the next twenty years in the diplomatic service of the Republic of Indonesia, having been in a position to help the young Republic to become established, during the latter part of his RAF service. This is described in his contribution to this book.

Luckily, he left Indonesia just before the horror of the military take-over in 1965, when a million or so Indonesians were slaughtered. Since then he has been a hotelier in the remote North-West of Scotland, followed by ten years on a small self-sufficient farm in West Wales.

Returning to Scotland, he founded Luath Press, and wrote a series of guide books to his beloved West and North of Scotland.

Later he helped his herbalist daughter to breathe new life into Napiers of Edinburgh, a herbal consultancy established in 1860, and he operated Napiers Mail Order business for three years, before retiring for the third time.

By the same author:

Napiers History of Herbal Healing, Ancient and Modern

LUATH GUIDES

Southwest Scotland
Northern Highlands: The Empty Lands
North West Highlands: Roads to the Isles
West Highlands: The Lonely Lands

Spectacles, Testicles, Fags and Matches

The untold story of the RAF
Servicing Commandos in World War Two

TOM ATKINSON

Luath Press Limited

EDINBURGH

www.luath.co.uk

First published 2004
Reprinted 2005, 2006, 2008, 2013, 2024, 2026

ISBN: 978-1-906307-85-1

The paper used in this book is recyclable. It is made from low-chlorine pulps
produced in a low-energy, low-emission manner from renewable forests.

Printed and bound by Robertson Printers, Forfar

Typset in 11 & 12 point Sabon by 3btype.com

Contents

Spectacles and Testicles

Spectacles and Testicles??? Whatever can it mean?

It was an irreligious ritual that we followed after any hairy (that is, frightening) episode. This might have been a close escape from the Service Police after a midnight raid on a camp coal dump. Equally, it might have been an expression of heart-felt gratitude on reaching a beach in Malaya, after wading ashore for four hundred yards through four feet of water, and with every step hoping no enemy was taking a sight on us.

The ritual was to cross ourselves whilst saying the mantra 'Spectacles, Testicles, Fags and Matches', and touching the appropriate places 'If they're OK, I'm OK'.

To be honest, I don't really know how widespread this ritual was. Certainly my own group of friends used it – and I almost said 'Used it religiously.' It doesn't really matter. It makes an excellent book title, and perhaps it was that title that encouraged you, the casual reader, to pick it up. So now go ahead and buy it!

An Historical Note

ORIGINALLY IT WAS MY intention to add no kind of editorial comment to the stories told by these survivors of the RAF Servicing Commandos.

However, I have now concluded that this will be a better book if each of the three campaigns in which the SCs participated (North Africa, Sicily and Italy, then Western Europe and last of all South East Asia) is introduced by a brief description of its historical context.

I was driven to that conclusion by talking to classes of young people. I previously had no idea that the episodes I talked about were taught as history! How could it be history, I thought: I was there, I am not a part of history, I am here and now. History is about Robert the Bruce, William Wallace, Prince Charles Edward and, out on the periphery, some remote English king who burned some cakes.

But No, I was assured, I was talking about history, not current affairs, as I thought. So how much did those young people know about this 'history'? Not, I discovered, a great deal. And nor did their teachers. I will give two examples. When mentioning the Falaise Gap, I was interrupted by a young woman who asked if that was some kind of old-fashioned clothes shop. There was immediate laughter from one group when I mentioned The Battle of the Bulge. It seems that was their way of referring to those girls unlucky or careless enough to get pregnant.

So I decided that if I was viewed as part of history I would play the part, and put the things I talked about into their historical context. Hence the short articles on the background to each section of this book.

It is done briefly and is by no means complete, but I greatly hope it removes some ignorance and misunderstanding from young minds. For anyone who is really interested, I suggest finding that very complete and authoritative one-volume book called *Second World War* by Martin Gilbert.

Preface

There are two histories of every land and people – the written history that tells what it is political to tell, and the unwritten history that tells everything.

Calum Maclean

IT WAS WINSTON CHURCHILL who named them The Few. They were the RAF fighter pilots who fought, and largely defeated, the till-then victorious German Luftwaffe – air force – in the dark summer of 1940.

The Allied forces, the British and the French, had been soundly defeated by the Germans on the ground. The blitzkrieg tactics of the Germans were eminently successful, and left virtually all the mainland of Western Europe occupied by the Nazis. France, Britain's main ally, was divided, with most of the country occupied and the rump governed by a satellite of Germany.

Thanks to the heroic and sacrificial rearguard action of the 51st Highland Division, the majority of the British troops in France were successfully evacuated in great disarray from Dunkirk and other Channel ports, leaving behind virtually all their arms and equipment. The Highlanders were not amongst them. Those who remained alive on the perimeter at Dunkirk, exhausted, out-gunned and short of ammunition, were taken prisoner.

The outlook was indeed dark and drear. Only the narrow English Channel and the RAF, it seemed, stood between the British mainland and the obvious horrors of occupation by the seemingly unbeatable and irresistible German armies.

Then began what has come to be known as The Battle of Britain. If the Germans were to mount a successful invasion, they needed to have control of the skies over the Channel and southern England. Such control was an integral part of the blitzkrieg tactic. The 'Lightning War' depended upon close air cover of armoured troops who were the spearhead of the advancing army. Luftwaffe airfields and air strips had to be established and operated immediately behind the advancing armour. It was the task of the Luftwaffe to protect their own armour from air attacks and to destroy the armour of the enemy. It was a tactic which had proved eminently successful in Poland, Holland, Belgium and of course France. There was no reason to suppose it would not be successful in England.

Plans for the invasion were drawn up – it was to be called Operation Sea Lion. However, there was one problem for the Nazis. This was Fighter Command of the RAF. It had to be destroyed or rendered harmless before the blitzkrieg troops and their armour could cross the Channel. There was, of course, also the hope that the RAF itself could be rendered powerless, and thus Britain's last defence destroyed, then perhaps the country and its leaders would accept the hopelessness of their position and come to terms with Germany.

And so began The Battle of Britain, between the Royal Air Force and the German Luftwaffe. The RAF was in fact heavily outnumbered, by more than two to one aircraft, and in addition most of its aircraft were outdated and obsolescent. The exceptions were the Spitfires and Hurricanes, which were at least the equal of anything operated by the Luftwaffe. Other advantages for the RAF were the effective use of radar, or Radio Location, as we knew it then, and effective Very High Frequency Radio ground control.

The RAF had one other thing in its favour, and it was decisive. The battle was fought over southern England, and that was where the RAF fighter squadrons were stationed. The pilots could take off, and within minutes would be engaged with the enemy. That enemy had to cross the Channel twice for each sortie. Their time in the battle area was much less. Up to then, Luftwaffe fighters had always flown from airstrips close up to the German armoured spearhead. Now they had the Channel to cross, and it took up a vital few minutes of their flight time. There were those in the British High Command who noted this, and drew the correct and appropriate lessons. Airfields and airstrips close behind the forward troops in an attack were vital ingredients of success. Out of that observation the RAF Servicing Commandos were born.

The Battle of Britain was a finely balanced battle and no easy victory. No-one who observed it will ever forget those young lads (and they were young) who took off in their Spits and Hurries time after time, day after day, to face considerable odds and a very good chance of dying in a chaos of flames and twisted metal. Day after day we read the figures of enemy and friendly losses – figures which we now know to have been considerably exaggerated, or 'sexed up', in today's vernacular. The most reliable figure is that the Luftwaffe lost over 1,700 aircraft and the RAF over 900.

From July to September of 1940 the Battle of Britain continued, and perhaps it really should be known as The Battle For Britain. On 20 August, Churchill pronounced that the battle had been won, and in his inimitable way praised The Few. In fact, the fighter air war continued until well into September, when the Germans tacitly acknowledged defeat and switched tactics to the blitz on British cities rather than attacking Fighter Command airfields. They also stood down the troops, boats and barges which had been assembled for the invasion in Operation Sea Lion.

So The Few had triumphed, and most certainly those young pilots deserved every word of the praise that has been heaped upon them ever since. However, it took a great deal more than the gallantry of a few hundred young men to win that battle. For every pilot there had to be ten or a dozen more airmen and airwomen to keep that pilot flying. The planes had to be re-armed and re-fuelled, serviced, inspected and repaired. Radar and radio services had to guide the Few into battle and back again. They had to be fed and housed, patched up when necessary, picked up from crash landings in the sea and on land. No-one who helped in providing those essential if unglamorous services through the summer months of 1940 will ever forget the strain, the deadly weariness, the mental trauma of learning that your kite had not returned from a sortie.

However, lessons were learned from it all, and fortunately those lessons were learned well, for had they not been, the future tactics of the RAF and army might well have been very different, and not necessarily successful.

When war began in 1939, without doubt the German forces were better trained, better led and better equipped. They were also experienced. They had devised, practiced and perfected the tactics of blitzkrieg, which was something the Allies were ill-prepared to face. Blitzkrieg depended upon close co-operation between heavy armour and dive bombers. It was a lightning-fast military attack designed to defeat the enemy quickly, and it was successful. The blitzkrieg troops first smashed through, destroyed or isolated the opposition and were then followed immediately by lighter troops, fast-moving and well supplied.

This was a new and highly effective tactic, although military historians have pointed out that in fact it was not much different in principle to the cavalry attacks of the Mongols or the use of armoured elephants by the Moghuls. Its success lay in the ability of the Luftwaffe to keep aircraft in the air over the battlefield for long periods, while they were in constant contact with the armour, and both could be directed to wherever opposition was found. The concept was simple enough, and even obvious, but the Allied High Command had failed to understand it, or to absorb the lessons of its successful use in Spain, Czechoslovakia, Austria and Poland. There was no way, though, that they could avoid the fact that blitzkrieg had resulted in the Allies in France being totally overwhelmed, and to the gallant but humiliating evacuation of the British from Dunkirk. And in warfare to lose a battle and be humiliated in the losing of it, is more than halfway to losing the war.

Unlike the Germans, the Allied command had no recent experience of battle. Nor were they open to new ideas. Their reliance on The Maginot Line for the defence of France was almost medieval. The Maginot Line was a great defensive fortification stretching the whole length of the French border with Germany, from Switzerland to Luxembourg. It was generally considered to be impregnable, and a complete defence against another German invasion into France. It might indeed have been impregnable, and the Germans did not even try to breach it. Instead, they simply went round it, moving through Luxembourg and the Low Countries into northern France, leaving the Allied Commanders dismayed and knowing not what to do. The Maginot Line had proved to be a total irrelevance.

Too many of the Allied leaders, military and civilian, still thought in terms of trench warfare, as in WWI, when most of them began their careers. They were the advanced thinkers: many still hankered after the glory of the cavalry charge!

The co-ordinated use of tanks and aircraft had been considered during WWI, but it had never been implemented. Of course, many officers in both army and airforce had given thought and voice to such co-operation, but nothing came of it, and the concept played no part in strategic planning. Not, at least, until the German blitzkrieg tactic most convincingly showed the error of their purblindness. It was blindingly obvious that any hope of victory depended upon close co-operation between forces on the ground, in the air, and at sea.

Clearly, it was necessary to have a force of combat planes capable of flying from airfields and air strips close to the battle zones. That was obvious, but equally obvious were the problems of doing that. An airstrip close to the battle zone would be vulnerable to attack by both land and air. The RAF ground crews were technicians and tradesmen, not trained or equipped nor indeed psychologically prepared to defend an airstrip against attacks. This was unlike the Luftwaffe, whose ground crews were all trained and armed as infantrymen, as well as technicians.

The blitzkrieg tactics of the Germans as they rampaged through France, driving the French and British armies before them, very convincingly showed the errors in Allied thinking. Clearly, any strategy for winning battles against the very efficient Germans had to include a mobile force of aircraft flying from airfields or airstrips near the battle zone. The advantages of this were obvious. So were the difficulties of doing it.

Any airstrip very close to a battle zone would be open to constant attack by air and land. Men would have to reach those forward airstrips, and so would very considerable amounts of fuel, ammunition, spares, oxygen, oil, coolant, bombs and of course food and water.

Much thought was given to finding solutions to the many problems. Many in both the army and the RAF were sceptical about the whole concept, but nevertheless, after eighteen months of discussion and argument, on 31 January 1942, the Director of Organisation at the

Air Ministry issued orders for the formation of three Servicing Commando Units.

There is little doubt that much of the impetus for this came from Louis Mountbatten, later Lord Mountbattten of Burma. He was at the time a Naval Commodore and chief of Combined Operations, and clearly not afraid of lateral tactical thinking. He himself claimed to be the father of the RAF Servicing Commandos, although, strangely, on one occasion he denied having had any part in their formation.

Each SCU consisted of RAF tradesmen, most of them Group One, the highest grade of training and skill. In theory, every man was a volunteer, although in practice some were idlers or troublemakers posted from Units glad to get rid of them. Most of those misfits were discarded in the early days of training. The volunteers were not told what the job was, but only that they were volunteering for 'arduous and dangerous duties'.

There were two or three officers, including the Commanding Officer, in each Unit. The CO was to be a technician. Each Unit had about fifteen three-ton trucks, a jeep, and two motor bikes. They were meant to be self-sufficient, able to exist and work in the field for long periods. The Units carried in their trucks a fair supply of spare parts for aircraft, and toolkits and equipment enough to carry out routine servicing. Fuel, ammunition, bombs etc were not carried by the Units: these were to be ferried forward as required by the advanced airstrips.

The men were expected to sleep in tents, and to carry a minimum of personal kit. If it became necessary to lighten the load on the trucks, the heavy old bell tents were usually the first thing to be discarded, and then the men slept under makeshift tents made from a blanket and sticks cut from the hedgerow. There was usually some string available for guy ropes, but if not then signal wire from the wireless equipment truck could be 'borrowed'. Those blanket tents, using gas capes as a groundsheet, were surprisingly rainproof, so long as you took great care not to to touch the sides.

The alternative to the blanket tent was to dig a slit trench – what our American allies insisted on calling a foxhole. That was harder to do, of course, but was necessary if there was likely to be night strafing or sniping. Being so naturally ingenious, and quickly learning how to make the most of whatever might be available, the troops often made comfortable homes from home of their slit trenches. It was found very early that the entrenching tools we all carried were very inefficient in digging what was essentially an enlarged grave-like hole in the ground. Mysteriously, an adequate supply of picks and spades appeared on the trucks, and the entrenching tools were used only for the digging of personal latrines – not that any but the most fastidious called them that! And many a farmer found, after the Unit moved on, that half the corrugated sheets had disappeared off a barn – used for covering the slit trenches – and a goodly supply of hay or straw had also disappeared – used as a soft bed on which the weary airmen had rested their tired bodies.

The organisation of the Commando was simple and efficient. The Units were divided into Flights, three technical and one administrative or Headquarters. A Flight Sergeant would be in charge of each, and a Sergeant responsible for each trade – engine fitters, airframe fitters, armourers etc. The Flight would be split into four Sections, with a Corporal in charge of each. It never, I believe, worked out as neatly as that, but the organisation never varied much from the plan laid down from on high.

Then came the training. It was assumed, almost invariably correctly, that the men, volunteers all, were already technically proficient; the training was to be in the arts of soldiering, not aircraft servicing.

Of course, the men were already reasonably physically fit, but were far from the standard of fitness demanded by the Commando instructors. So the rigorous training began with route marches, cross country running, battle tactics, full-pack forced marches, unarmed combat, bayonet practice, swimming, PT, compass and map reading exercises and much else.

The few men who did not measure up to the high standards set by the Commando trainers were quickly posted away.

Every member of the Unit had to learn to drive and be instructed in vehicle maintenance and the water-proofing of the vehicles. This was so that, if necessary, the trucks could be dropped into four or five feet of water when making a landing, and still have engines running long enough to get onto the beach, and into the interior.

Most of the men survived that stage of training, and indeed it was very obvious that a remarkable degree of pride and esprit de corps was developed and nurtured during those weeks of hard physical work and learning.

The next stage was the amphibious training, which in the UK was centred in Inveraray, Argyll, in those days a remote place at the head of Loch Fyne, and a small town which seemed to exist only for the pleasures and purposes of the Duke of Argyll, whose castle dominated the area. There we underwent our Combined Operations training, and were introduced to the various types of Landing Craft and their uses.

Combined Operations was just what the name implied: operations by a combined force of land, sea and air troops. This simple concept was in fact quite revolutionary in its thinking, and was established only after overcoming the resistance of senior officers in all three services, who fought a long rearguard action to retain the autonomy of their own services and resisted handing over command to some-one probably from another service altogether. Fortunately, those remnants of the past did not prevail.

The Combined Operations Training Centre at Inveraray trained all three services in this new type of warfare, and for the RAF SCs this concentrated on the operation of Landing Craft. We were taught how to load our trucks on to Tank Landing Craft (LCTs) in the correct order and with the correct load of men and materials. Those Landing Craft were flat-bottomed craft with an opening ramp at the front, designed to either run ashore and lower the ramp for the trucks to make a dry landing, or to drop the ramp in a few feet of water and unload the trucks there. Those LCTs were sea-going craft, carrying ten or a dozen trucks, but being flat-bottomed and blunt bowed, were hellish uncomfortable in any sort of rough sea. They had no sort of accommodation for passengers, and normally only the truck driver and second driver would accompany the trucks. In training, the trucks carried their full load of men and equipment.

Again in training, the men were carried in a Landing Ship Infantry (LSI). These were bigger vessels, with rudimentary accommodation for a couple of hundred men. The LSIs carried several smaller landing craft slung on derricks and ready to be lowered into the water. Those smaller vessels were Landing Craft Infantry, designed to carry perhaps fifty fully armed and equipped men, sitting on benches, three abreast, and facing forward to the ramp at the bow. The idea was that those LCIs were lowered into the water from the LSI mother ship, and then the men went down into them, going over the side of the LSI and down scrambling nets into the waiting LCI.

The LCIs were of very shallow draft, and after loading the assault party, would make for the shore, which was not meant to be very far ahead. They were run ashore, or at least as near to the shore as they could get, and then the order 'Ramps Down. GO!' was the signal for a sailor to drop the ramps, and for the men to run for the beach, fan out, and do whatever their orders instructed from then on – which was usually to get off the beach and into a defensive position as quickly as possible, overcoming whatever opposition they met.

Well that was the theory, and very simple and straightforward it was, at least in daylight and with a calm sea and with no opposition. In practice, it was never so simple. It was very different on a coal-black night with a heavy sea running and the prospect of an opposed landing. We knew that, really, the opposition was friendly, or was meant to be, but was well-armed – as were we – with blank ammunition, thunderflashes (large, loud and bright fireworks) and smoke bombs, and a determination to drive us back off the beach into the water, using any dirty trick they could think of. But then, so were we.

If there was any sort of sea running, the small LCIs were not sitting quietly in the water, but were jumping wildly up and down and rolling. The gap between the Landing Ship and the Landing Craft kept opening and closing, and it would have been very dangerous indeed, probably fatal, to have fallen between them. For me at least, the most heart-stopping moment was when you had to put your leg over the ship's rail, grasp the web of the scrambling net and start going down, thirty feet or more, to where the landing craft was waiting, quietly, or rumbustiously tossing. We were instructed not to look down, but that was difficult, and far below in the darkness was the faint outline of the landing craft. Never has thirty feet seemed to be such a great distance.

We were in battle order, of course, with small pack, gas mask, gas-cape, full water bottle, bayonet, hunting knife, personal weapons and ammunition. The weapons were standard issue short Lee Enfield .303s – the same basically as those carried by our fathers a generation earlier. Some men had Sten guns instead of rifles. These were light automatic weapons, simple, cheap and unreliable, which were fine (when they worked) at a range of perhaps ten yards, but not much more. Most of the lads preferred the rifles, because at least they were effective at two or three hundred yards, and who wanted to be any closer than that!

I was the Bren gunner for my Flight, and so had to carry that as well as my Sten. My second man was burdened with the essential spare barrel and a number of magazines for the Bren.

To top it all, we wore Mae Wests, or Personal Inflatable Devices, a life belt tied close up under the armpits, and inflated by blowing into a tube.

The Unit also had a Boyes anti-tank rifle. This monstrosity was a vastly overgrown rifle, firing .500 armour piercing rounds. It might conceivably have stopped a small saloon car, but the idea of engaging a German Tiger tank with that thing was ludicrous. In fact, I remember seeing it once only, when we were introduced to it at a demonstration, and fell about laughing. It was probably stored away in a truck and forgotten.

Sometimes, just for fun, the fiendish instructors had us put ashore on some sand bank well away from the beach, and we had to wade ashore through several feet of water, perhaps to find a Marine Commando waiting for us, and ready to use all their skills and wiles to throw us back off the beach.

It was all good fun, and by the time we left Inveraray we were certainly toughened up and ready to go.

But ready to go where? Those SCs formed and trained in the Middle East certainly went into immediate and vital action in North Africa, Sicily and Italy. Those formed in the UK had to wait through many long months until even the most dilatory and reluctant High Command and politicians had to accept that if the British and American forces were to participate in overcoming the German forces, then the Continental mainland had to be invaded.

After the Combined Operations training in Inveraray, the Units continued training, but now actually practising what they would be doing in action, that is, servicing aircraft in operational conditions. Initially it had been expected that they would be working with Fighter Command of the RAF, servicing mainly Spitfires and Hurricanes. As the months passed, virtually any sort of aircraft from any service was handled, re-armed, re-fuelled, repaired and sent off again. It had been anticipated that each SC would be capable of looking after three squadrons of fighters, keeping them operational from forward airstrips during daylight hours. That target was soon surpassed, and there were occasions when a SC serviced six squadrons and serviced them so fast and well that pilots (jokingly) complained they hardly had time to stretch and relieve themselves before some disreputable character, unshaven, dressed in filthy overalls and wearing a tin hat, told him his kite was ready and that his hard standing was urgently required for the next job.

So far as possible, the servicing was done in conditions resembling those expected in action. Refuelling was done from four gallon cans, brought by our own transport from some distant dump and lifted two at a time up to the fillercap and poured through a chamois-lined funnel. Meanwhile, ammunition belts were re-aligned right at the aircraft, and fed into magazines straight from the re-aligning machine, which was probably being turned by, apparently, a senior NCO, who was being exhorted in the strongest possible language to get his finger out. Meanwhile the ancillary tradesmen, having finished their jobs, would be lugging the petrol cans out of the trucks and the ammo. belts out of boxes, and dragging the chore horse starter batteries into position for a quick get away.

The petrol, by the way, was at first not in the now familiar jerricans. It came instead in four gallon cans, thin, fragile and liable to leak. The introduction of the jerrican, which was much more robust and of course re-useable and more easily handled, was a great relief. As the name implies, the jerrican was a German invention, but was eagerly copied by the Allies when they were first introduced to them in the Middle East.

Those disreputable characters lived by choice in their own tents, set in some distant corner. They usually fed at their own mess tent, and their cooks seemed to provide excellent meals using improvised equipment and stoves. One such stove I well remember was a long channel made from aluminium panels from wrecked aircraft. Down that channel trickled thin streams of water and used engine oil from four gallon cans and the trickles were regulated by matchsticks stuck into a small hole punched in the bottom of each can. The stream of oil was ignited by using a pint or so of 100 octane petrol, and the cooking pots hung over the smoky flames on aircraft pickets. (For the uninitiated, they were four feet long corkscrews, four inches in diameter, made from iron rods and meant to be used to tie down aircraft in strong winds.)

I well remember that particular cooking experience because the first time it was tried I happened to have the cook house detail, and spent several dreary hours trying to get the soot off the pans.

After leaving Inveraray, and now entitled to wear the cherished Combined Operations badge, the SCs were scattered around the countryside, frequently in detachments of single flights. Experience was gained on many different types of aircraft, British and American, from the lightest of reconnaissance planes to the heaviest of bombers, and always the men of the SCs put every ounce of their skill and strength into the job. The esprit de corps was remarkable. We were Servicing Commandos; we were ready to go anywhere and tackle any job; we were special, and by God, we were proud.

The idea of being different was nowhere shown more clearly than when a detachment was on a traditional bullshit RAF station, and plenty of them still existed, where the men lived a 9-5 existence, and polished their brasses every night, had church parade on Sundays, and wore collars and ties all the time.

I recall one such station where most of our unit drivers had gone on a water-driving and water-proofing course. We spent the time waterproofing old trucks and then driving them down a ramp into something resembling a swimming pool. If the engine stalled, it was the fault of the driver for not doing the water proofing properly, and he had to get into the water and fix tow ropes and once on dry land again, re-do the waterproofing and the drive into the swimming pool.

It was a doddle, and a bit boring, and we decided spontaneously to liven the place up. Instead of marching sedately in ranks to the mess hall twice a day, to the Air Force March blaring over the Tannoy, we invariably lined up and went there at a quick double. Sometimes we would decide to go in full battle order, piling our weapons outside the mess hall and mounting a guard over them. Instead of attending the compulsory Church parade on Sunday, we went for a ten mile route march in battle order, and returned to the camp at the double. On one occasion we mounted an attack on the mess hall at dinner time, with the lads snaking over the grass, the Bren gunners giving (simulated) covering fire and the whole culminating in a fixed bayonet charge and a fusillade of hand grenades – clods of grass and pebbles. We occupied the mess hall with no problems, but the Flt. Sergeant cook refused to serve us because, he said, we were dirty and our mess tins, which we insisted on using, were not clean enough.

So we retired in good order, back to our own tents and opened up a couple of cases of Compo Rations, and fed well.

We felt we were different, free spirits and rather special, and that was a belief accentuated by our uniforms. Instead of the standard old-fashioned RAF blue tunics and shirts with collar and tie, we wore army khaki battle dress with RAF badges and insignia, army ammunition boots and khaki webbing, but with RAF forage caps. We wore different coloured lanyards to distinguish the Flights, and, of course, our khaki sleeves also sported the precious Combined Operations badges, which incorporated insignia of all three services, RAF, army and RN.

Shortly before the D-Day landings in which SC units were amongst the first troops ashore, we were divested of our khaki battle dress, and ordered to revert to standard RAF uniform, even to the extent of wearing collars and ties.

Not surprisingly, morale plummeted. We had been encouraged to believe and know that we were something special and the outward mark of being special was the uniform. We felt that all the work and sweat we had expended in preparing to do difficult and dangerous operations, which we had volunteered to do, was not recognised or appreciated. We had been trained to operate close up to any battlefield, to service any type of aircraft quickly and well, and ensure that those aircraft were available to protect the ground troops. To do, in other words, what the Luftwaffe had done so successfully during their sweep through the Low Countries and France in 1940.

We had volunteered for a task we had been told was special and dangerous. We had been told there was little chance of promotion, yet if we had stayed in the normal RAF organisation, many would certainly have been promoted. Those were some of the emotional reasons why we felt so angry at being deprived of our uniforms. However, there was a very important practical reason, too.

The RAF blue was not so very different from the German field grey uniform. We knew we would be working in very dusty or muddy conditions. We would be working with oil and grease. Inevitably, that RAF blue was going to get dirty and grow increasingly like the enemy field grey. We were going to be up close to battles – that was what we were meant to do – and soldiers have a natural tendency to shoot at anything resembling an enemy.

I thought at the time, and now believe, that this foolish and exceedingly expensive decision was the result of jealousies and the innate conservatism in some parts of the top command of the RAF and the army. They had been in opposition to the very idea of SCs, opposition finally overcome by the direct order of Lord Mountbatten. There had been niggling criticism and petty obstruction all during formation and training.

Even after those SCs in the Middle East had fought and operated so successfully through North Africa, Sicily and Italy, the questioning continued. It did not need the skills of a psychologist to understand that outward trappings – uniforms – are important in delineating and distinguishing special groups. Kings, Queens and courtiers have known and relied on this since time immaterial, and still do. Senior service officers with their broad stripes and gold braid utilise it. Even our American allies with their chests laden with medals – fruit salad, as we derisively called it – after perfectly ordinary service recognised it.

Yet our own RAF commanders ordered us divested of our beloved symbols just very shortly before we were to embark upon the final battles of the war in Europe. It was a short-sighted, morale-destroying decision. It was foolish.

Introduction

Servicing Commando Formation and Training

WORLD WAR II WAS surely the most destructive conflict in human history. More than forty six million people perished, civilians and military, women and children, old and young, the fit and healthy, the halt and the lame. Very many of those teeming millions died in conditions of prolonged and almost unimaginable cruelty and terror. Naked, starving and without hope or weapons to fight back, they were herded to their death.

There were 2174 days of warfare between the initial German attack on Poland in September 1939 and the surrender of Japan in August 1945. It can well be argued that WWII began in fact three years earlier in Spain and whether it has ended even today is doubtful. But in those 2,174 days, forty six million people perished, and with them died all their love and joy, all their skills and creativity, their learning, their hopes and their happiness.

With them also died the innocence of those of us who survived.

In the early years of World War II, after France and the Low Countries had been so quickly overrun by the German military machine, senior officers of the British Army, the Royal Navy and the RAF began to analyse the enemy's success, and to identify the look closely at the reasons for our defeat.

Numerically, at least, the opposing armies were of equal fighting strength, but the German Army was equipped with modern weapons, its troops better trained than any of the Allied counterparts, and many German units had gained valuable experience in the Spanish Civil War and in Poland. The Luftwaffe had also benefited by taking part in those campaigns and was a ruthless modern fighting force with almost twice as many combat aircraft as the combined Allied air forces, whose aircraft, with the notable exceptions of the Hurricane and Spitfire, were mostly obsolescent.

The German forces were also much better led. There was little co-operation between the three arms of the British forces, and many Allied generals still thought in terms of trench warfare. Nowhere was this failure to grasp the modern principle of mobile war more clearly demonstrated than in the Allies' dependence on the Maginot Line for the defence of France, an almost medieval concept which was soon proved to be irrelevant by the Blitzkrieg tactics of the German army.

The word Blitzkrieg means 'Lightning War', an apt description of a technique that depended upon close co-operation between powerful groups of heavy armour and dive bombers. This was a devastating combination that could first smash through or isolate the opposition, promptly followed by fast-moving infantry and well-organised supplies.

The key to the success of Blitzkrieg lay in the Luftwaffe's capacity to keep its aircraft in the air over the battle areas for long periods of time while in constant contact with armoured units on the ground. It was this twofold domination that overwhelmed the Allied armies and led to the traumatic evacuation of Dunkerque.

During World War One the Allies had contemplated the co-ordinated use of tanks and aircraft but had not implemented the idea. Many serving officers in both the Army and the RAF had recognised the need for such co-operation long before the outbreak of World War II, but unfortunately their opinions had no impact on strategic planning. Once the Germans had so convincingly demonstrated the error of our ways it was obvious that any recipe for Allied victory must include close co-operation between our forces on the ground, in the air and at sea. Then things began to change. One important change was the acceptance by the planners that it was desirable to have a mobile force of combat aircraft capable of flying from air-fields near the battle zones. The advantages of such proximity were obvious enough, but so were the drawbacks. Any airfield close to the front line would be vulnerable to attacks by enemy tanks and infantry and to constant strafing from the air, but the military structure of the RAF was not designed to cope with defending its own airfields. Furthermore, every front-line pilot needs a back-up team of several tradesmen to keep his aircraft operational. Transporting men to vul-nerable airfields and keeping them supplied with large quantities of fuel, oil, coolant, spares, bombs and ammunition, not to mention food and water, would present major problems.

Nevertheless, on 31 January 1942 the Director of Organisation at the Air Ministry gave instructions for the formation of three Servicing Commando Units, although the idea was greeted with some scepticism by both the army and RAF. It was not to be the duty of the Servicing Commandos to fight for airfields, rather: 'The object of these units will be the occupation of advanced landing grounds as soon as they are captured by the army.'

This occupation was to operate as follows: the Commando units would be put ashore from landing craft, complete with transport and equipment and make their own way to the airfield. Once the airfield had been captured, the front-line squadrons would fly in, and while the Servicing Commandos attended to the aircraft, convoys of trucks would bring up their supplies. As Fighter Command would be responsible for the deployment of the SCUs, each unit would be trained to service fighter aircraft and to keep those aircraft operational to support the front-line troops until the battle had moved on and Squadron personnel would be brought in. The SCUs would then pack up and move to another forward airfield as soon as it was safe to use. (At the time, 'fighter aircraft' meant Spitfires and Hurricanes, but as the war went on the SCUs were called upon to service almost anything that flew, with or without special training.)

While not primarily intended as a fighting force, all Servicing Commandos personnel would undergo intensive combat training and would be expected to defend their airfields without reliance on the army, who might have neither the time nor the men available to 'wet nurse a bunch of Brylcreem boys'. This mirrored the German system: all Luftwaffe ground crews were combat trained and organised as army units; consequently they were able to defend their airfields without seeking help from front-line units of the Wehrmacht.

The Air Ministry instructions specified that each RAF SC Unit would comprise two officers and 148 Other Ranks. The CO would be a Technical Officer holding the rank of Squadron Leader or Flight lieutenant, while his second in command would be an Admin. Officer with the rank of Flying Officer or Pilot Officer. There was to be a

Warrant Officer responsible for discipline, and the Units were to be divided into Flights, three technical and one HQ Flight, each with a Flight Sgt. in charge. There would be a Sgt. responsible for each trade, and the Flights would be each split up into four Sections, with a Cpl. responsible for each Section.

Each Unit would have fifteen three-ton trucks, a jeep for the CO and one motor cycle. Only the minimum of servicing equipment would be carried in the trucks, which was to be evenly distributed between them to minimise the effect of the loss of or damage to a truck. In practice, the numbers of men and officers varied, as did the number of trucks and other equipment.

Early in 1942 orders were sent to Training Command to form three volunteer SCUs, and notices appeared on Station Standing Orders asking for officers and men in selected trades to volunteer for a dangerous task, which was not specified.

The training syllabus was similar for all the SCUs, whether they were trained in the UK or in the Middle East, so that any Unit could be sent to any theatre of war.

Rigorous training for all ranks began with drills, forced marches, bayonet practice, and unarmed combat classes, swimming, PT and compass and map reading exercises. All these activities were presided over by instructors on loan from the Commandos, and any man who did not measure up to the high standard set was posted elsewhere without delay.

Every member of the SCU had to learn to drive and take a course on motor transport maintenance, together with instruction for waterproofing vehicles which were to take part in invasion landings onto beaches, in case they were dropped into deep water.

In the UK, the survivors of the first stage of training were sent to Inveraray on Loch Fyne where they embarked on the Royal Navy Landing Ship Infantry (LSI) HMT *Etterick*. The Inveraray Combined Services Training Centre was staffed by members of all three services. Naval units were trained on the handling of all types of landing craft, including Landing Craft Tank. The SCUs used these for the transportation and handling of their mobile equipment, and SCU exercises concentrated on embarking, loading equipment, lowering the full-loaded craft into the water, unloading equipment both in daylight and under night-time conditions, and the use of scrambling nets which were dropped over the ship's side for boarding purposes.

The landing of heavy transport on a beach could be a hazardous operation, especially if the vehicles were driven down a ramp into several feet of water, and practices, in full operational kit, often resulted in casualties, although the Navy anticipated the occasional sinking and had small rescue craft and rafts standing by. Final practice landings usually took place using live ammunition and simulated air cover and/or smoke screens .

After fourteen days of day and night training, the SCUs went to sea in an LCT, whatever the weather conditions, later disembarking and undertaking final practice landings on the beaches at Troon, Ayrshire.

After the beach landings the Unit would move off again for training in the servicing of a variety of aircraft currently in use with the RAF and the United States Army Air Force (USAAF), as an SCU would be expected to be capable of looking after three squadrons of fighter aircraft or two squadrons of light bombers, and one squadron of medium bombers, and to keep them operational from a forward airstrip during daylight hours. The more highly skilled tradesmen were trained to become experts on one type of aircraft so that they could instruct other members of an SCU who were not familiar with the type.

The training course was rounded off by instruction in antiaircraft weapons and techniques, and aircraft recognition lectures.

Fifteen SCUs were formed in the UK and the Middle East, and three small units, each consisting of one junior officer and thirty other ranks of various trades were formed in India during the summer of 1943. Although those units were trained along Commando lines, they were not designated as SCUs, but were known simply as Servicing Parties. Two of them were deployed in Burma, where they played a role similar to that of an SCU, keeping RAF and USAAF aircraft flying from remote airfields and landing strips.

War Cabinet Annexe
1a Richmond Terrace
Whitehall S.W. 1
22nd January 1942

To: Air Ministry D.C.O.
   Copy to Air Ministry (D.D.T. (Combined Operations))
                         D.S. Ops.
                         D.B. Ops
                         D.S.C.
                         C. in C. Fighter Command

Formation of R.A.F. Servicing 'Commandos'
For use in Combined Operations

1. In most combined operations the capture as soon as possible of an enemy aerodrome will be essential in order to allow our fighter, tactical reconnaissance and possibly bomber support aircraft to operate at maximum efficiency.

2. During the early stages it is probable that the use of the captured aerodrome would be limited to refuelling, rearming, flight maintenance, minor repairs and the minimum essential communications.

3. It is suggested that special servicing units should be established with the necessary ground personnel to undertake these duties on the basis of say one Servicing unit to look after three squadrons.

4. This matter has already been discussed by Air Commodore Walker with the Director of Fighter Operations who put forward a minute to the Deputy Chief of the Air Staff on 15 January 1942, outlining the various stages in the process of a combined operation as far as fighter squadrons are concerned and recommending the formation of special servicing units of this nature.

5. For easy reference the recommendations put forward to D.S.A.S are reproduced below:-

(a) form 'RAF Servicing Commandos' with their equipment, and make them an essential part of the various fighter groups.

(b) train these Commandos in their specific duties under the control of groups. In this way they will achieve cohesion and raf esprit de corps.

(c) as soon as we have some Commandos trained in their air duties, they should be sent in turn to the Combined Training Centre where they would go through a thorough training in their 'Commando' duties.

(d) each fighter group, whose Commandos were under training at the Combined Training Centre, would then send fighter squadrons in rotation to be trained in combined operations with the other Services.

6. Air Commodore Walker has discussed these proposals with A.O.C. Fighter Command, who expressed his approval of the scheme in principle.

7. If and when such units are formed I suggest that on completion of their air duties training they should be sent to the Combined Training Centre at AUCHENGATE for periods of extensive training in combined operations with the Expeditionary Force. This training would include being put ashore over the beaches and taking part in exercises in which they would be employed at the Combined Operations aerodrome in servicing operational squadrons under war conditions.

8. After training it is hoped that a number of these servicing Commandos would be definitely held in reserve to accompany the Expeditionary Force should they be required.

(Signed)   LOUIS MOUNTBATTEN
Commodore Combined Operations

Chronology of WWII

	1922
7 Oct	Benito Mussolini (Il Duce) established Fascist dictatorship in Italy.
	1933
17 Jan	Adolf Hitler became German Chancellor.
	1936
16 July	Beginning of Spanish Civil War.
	1937
7 July	Beginning of Sino-Japanese war.
	1938
28 July	Russo-Japanese conflict begins in Manchuria.
29 Sept	Munich Agreement concedes Sudetenland to Germany.
	1939
15 Mar	Germany occupies remainder of Czechoslovakia.
28 Mar	End of Spanish Civil War.
7 April	Italy invades Albania.
28 May	Renewed Russo-Japanese fighting in Manchuria.
20 Aug	Russian attack on Japanese at Nomonham.
23 Aug	Soviet-German non-aggression pact signed.
31 Aug	Soviet Army completed the destruction of the Sixth Japanese Army on the Manchurian border.
1 Sept	Germany invaded Poland.
3 Sept	Britain and France declare war on Germany.
3 Nov	US Congress passes the 'Cash and Carry Act', allowing munitions etc. to be bought by Allies.
30 Nov	Russia invaded Finland. Start of Winter War.
14 Dec	Russia expelled from League of Nations.
	1940
12 Mar	Russia and Finland sign peace treaty.
9 April	Germany invades Denmark and Norway.
10 May	Germany invades Holland and France. Winston Spencer Churchill becomes Prime Minister of UK.

26 May– 4 June	Evacuation of British and French troops from Dunkirk.
10 June	Italy declares war on France and Britain.
22 June	In France, Government of Marshal Petain signs armistice with Germany.
23 June	Gen. De Gaulle declares his intention to continue war against Germany.
27 June	Russia annexes the Baltic States – Estonia, Latvia, Lithuania.
3 July	Britain attacks the French Fleet at Mers-el Kebir.
26 July	USA begins partial embargo of trade with Japan.
15 Aug	Battle of Britain begins.
16 Sept	America passes Act to introduce partial conscription.
22 Sept	Japan occupied Indo-China.
28 Oct	Italy invaded Greece.
5 Nov	President Roosevelt re-elected for third term.

1941

22 Jan	British take Tobruk.
11 Mar	Lend-Lease Act signed between USA and Britain.
6 April	Germany invaded Yugoslavia and Greece.
13 April	Russia and Japan sign Neutrality Pact.
27 May	German battleship *Bismarck* sunk.
22 June	German invasion of Russia begins (Operation Barbarossa).
5 July	USA occupies Iceland.
12 July	Anglo-Soviet Mutual Aid Pact signed.
14 Aug	Atlantic Charter signed.
25 Aug	British and Russians occupy Iran.
6 Dec	Soviet forces open counter-attack before Moscow.
7 Dec	Japan attacks Pearl Harbour, the Philippines, Hong Kong, Malaya and other bases, declares war on US and Britain.
10 Dec	Japan sinks *Prince of Wales* and *Repulse*. Germany and Italy declare war on USA.
25 Dec	Hong Kong surrenders to Japanese.

1942

1 Jan	United Nations Declaration signed.
31 Jan	Order given to form Servicing Commando Units
20 Jan	Conference in Germany on 'Final Solution to the Jewish Problem'.

15 Feb	Singapore surrenders to Japanese.
6 May	Corregidor surrenders to Japanese.
8 May	Battle of Coral Sea.
12 May	Russian offensive opens.
26 May	Anglo-Soviet Treaty signed.
30 May	First 1,000 bomber raid (against Cologne).
3 June	Battle of Midway.
21 June	Tobruk falls to Rommel's Afrikacorps attack.
28 June	New German offensive in Russia.
7 Aug	American Marines land in Guadalcanal.
7 Sept	Joint Force of Australians and Americans defeat Japanese in New Guinea.
16 Sep	Battle of Stalingrad begins.
9 Nov	Operation Torch begins (Allied landings in North Africa).
13 Nov	British re-take Tobruk. Vichy France occupied by Germany

1943

14 Jan	Casablanca Conference.
2 Feb	German Commander Field Marshal von Paulus surrenders his army outside Stalingrad.
19 April	Uprising in the Warsaw Jewish ghetto.
12 May	Last of Axis forces driven from North Africa.
24 May	Admiral Doenitz withdraws U boats from Battle of the Atlantic.
5 July	Decisive battle of Kursk begins.
9 July	Britain and USA invade Sicily.
25 July	Badoglio becomes Premier of Italy. Mussolini arrested, and taken to the island of Ponza, but rescued by German paratroops.
24 Aug	Lord Mountbatten appointed Supreme Allied Commander South-East Asia Command.
3 Sept	Britain and USA invade Italy.
8 Sept	Italy surrenders.

1944

16 Jan	Eisenhower becomes Supreme Commander, Allied Expeditionary Force.

22 Jan	Anzio landings in Italy.
20 Mar	Germany occupies Hungary.
17 April	Japan opens offensive against China.
4 June	Allies take Rome.
6 June	D-Day. Operation Overlord, Allied invasion of Normandy, begins.
13 June	Germans use first V1 weapons
19 June	Battle of the Philippine Sea begins.
22 June	Russia opens summer offensive against Germany. Japanese offensive in Burma defeated.
20 July	Assassination attempt on Hitler.
1 Aug	Warsaw uprising begins.
23 Aug	Romania surrenders.
25 Aug	Paris liberated.
8 Sept	Germans use first V2 rockets against London.
20 Oct	Belgrade liberated by Russians.
7 Nov	Roosevelt re-elected for fourth term.
24 Nov	B29 raids on Japan begin.
16 Dec	Battle of the Bulge begins in Europe.

1945

9 Jan	US forces invade Philippines.
12 Jan	Russia begins winter offensive.
17 Jan	Russians take Warsaw.
13 Feb	First air raids on Dresden.
9 Mar	US begins incendiary bombing campaign against Japanese mainland.
12 April	Roosevelt dies, Truman becomes American President.
23 April	Russians enter Berlin.
25 April	American and Russian soldiers meet on River Elbe. United Nations conference opens in San Francisco.
28 April	Mussolini captured and executed by Italian partisans.
30 April	Hitler commits suicide.
2 May	German army in Italy surrenders.
7 May	Germany unconditionally surrenders to Allies.
8 May	VE-Day. Official end of the war in Europe.
16 July	First atomic bomb exploded in New Mexico.

26 July	Labour Party wins British general election.
6 Aug	Atomic bomb dropped on Hiroshima.
8 Aug	Russia declares war on Japan.
9 Aug	Atomic bomb dropped on Nagasaki.
14 Aug	Japan surrenders unconditionally to Allies.
15 Aug	Official VJ-Day.
17 Aug	Sukarno proclaims Indonesian independence.
2 Sept	Japan signs surrender terms.
	Ho Chi Minh proclaims Vietnamese independence.

WE OWE EACH OTHER MUCH, YOU AND I

We owe each other much, you and I.
In the heat of strife our youth passed us by.
We were called from high and low estate,
Moulded in brotherhood by fate.
The strong bonds we forged will always hold.
We're men that were spawned in St. Crispin's mould.

Then we were lean, we were strong and keen.
Look back to those years where no end was seen.
Now our beards have greyed and eyes grow dim.
Our movements are slow and we're stiff of limb.
Passing years brought us triumphs and pains.
We may have achieved much or lowered our aims.

It matters not when we look to those years,
For each knew the others hopes, dreams and fears.
Each day a challenge to the unknown tomorrow.
Our families we shared, each joy and sorrow.
Now toast our comradeship of times gone by,
We were lucky to be there, you and I.

We were lucky to be there, you and I.
Part of history in times gone by.
Limbs straighten, eyes brighten with tales we tell,
Bad times forgotten, memories heal well.
A toast then to friendship from times gone by,
We owe each other much, you, and you, and I.

Copyright JR Burt 1998

PART I

Background to Operations in North Africa, Sicily and Italy

PRE-WAR, THE WHOLE OF North Africa was colonised by European powers. This included Egypt, which, while nominally independent, was under the 'protection' of Britain, who had considerable garrisons there. After the French surrender in 1940, France was effectively divided into two parts, the major portion being occupied by Germany and the rump being under the control of Marshal Petain's government in Vichy. It was that Vichy government which claimed control of the French colonies in North Africa.

Thus, in 1940-42, Vichy controlled Morocco, Algeria and Tunisia, and Italy controlled Libya. Egypt, with the strategically essential Suez Canal, was controlled and garrisoned by Britain.

In September 1940, the Italians in Libya moved against Egypt, and advanced as far as Sidi Barrani, 50 miles into Egypt. They halted there, and Gen. Wavell, the British Commander in Chief, delivered his counter attack, so effectively that he virtually destroyed the Italian army. It was told by Churchill that on being asked to report on the numbers of prisoners taken, one officer said that he had 5 acres of officers and 150 acres of men, but couldn't estimate the actual numbers.

Perhaps to restore his inflated reputation as a military commander, on 28 October 1940, Mussolini declared war on Greece, and marched his army through Albania (which he had already, in 1939, declared to be 'annexed' to Italy) to invade the north of Greece. His invasion did not go well, and the Greeks not only stopped the Italian army, but began forcing it to retreat.

Once more the Italians attacked Egypt, and once more were forced to retreat with the virtual loss of the Italian Tenth Army. The British followed the retreating Italians closely, harassing them constantly, and captured the strategic strongpoints of Sidi Barrani, Tobruk and Benghazi in Libya.

Greece appealed to the British government for aid, and Churchill halted the British advance into Libya and diverted a major portion of the troops from there to Crete and the Greek mainland.

At that point, Hitler, fearful of having an Allied force in the south of Europe, where it could interfere with his plans for the invasion of Russia, decided to intervene. Only a decisive Axis victory could suffice, and that the Italians were unable to deliver, even though the defence of Greece was not in fact going too well. The Italians were not making much progress, but were certainly not being driven back by the combined efforts of the Greeks and the British. In fact, the two were disagreeing over both tactics and strategy.

In order to get troops into Greece to help his Axis partner, the German forces had to pass through Yugoslavia. Germany issued an ultimatum; it was rejected, and Germany invaded in a blitzkrieg that the Yugoslavs were unable to withstand. Within a week, Belgrade fell, and Germany seized the north and east of the country, Italy the south and west, whilst Bulgaria and Hungary annexed other strips of territory. None of them knew what problems they faced. The Yugoslav partisans under Tito were eventually so powerful and successful that it took two German armies to maintain even a nominal control of the country.

The blitzkrieg flooded from Yugoslavia into Greece, and the uncoordinated Greek and British troops were unable to halt it. After a brief campaign , the Germans occupied virtually the whole country, and then promptly launched an air-borne assault on Crete. This too, was immediately successful, although at great cost to the German troops.

Having repeatedly been made aware of the military shortcomings of his Italian Axis partner, Hitler decided to take over the campaign in North Africa, and sent Gen. Rommel, his best tank commander, there, in command of the Afrikacorps, which was composed mainly of tanks and anti-tank weapons.

Thus the stage was set for the North African campaign. For two years the contending forces fought backwards and forwards over the sands of Libya and western Egypt, and in truth neither side gained any real advantage. It was perhaps not a stalemate, but certainly it could have become one.

On 9 November 1942, the pattern was broken. The Allies began a general offensive, which they named Operation Torch, and Allied troops made concerted landings at three points on the north African coast, Algiers, Oran and Casablanca. It took six months, but eventually the German and Italian forces accepted defeat, and the whole of North Africa was under Allied control.

Of course, it must be understood that most of the North African coast was under the control of the Vichy French, and it was not at all clear how they would react to the Allied invasion. Since the Vichy French authorities controlled considerable military forces, land, sea and air, determined opposition by them to the Allied invasion would have been decidedly difficult and embarrassing. France, of course, was still officially regarded as an ally of the British and Americans, in spite of the Franco-German armistice of 1940.

In the event, British and American forces landed at Algiers virtually unopposed. At Oran, the Americans had to face and overcome strong opposition. The French at Casablanca were poised to oppose the landings. However, it happened that Admiral Darlan, the Deputy to Marshal Petain, the Vichy French Head of State, was at Algiers when the Allied landings began, and his first reaction was to order resistance to the Allies everywhere. Wisely, when he realised the strength of the invasion, Darlan ordered a general cease fire on 10 November, when the Allies had overcome resistance at Oran and were preparing to attack the French at Casablanca.

The Germans were quick to respond to this new challenge in North Africa. Troops began to fly into Tunis and Bizerta on 9 September, and many more troops and supplies arrived by sea from 12 September.

The ultimate Axis defeat in North Africa was not in fact due to a military defeat, but was due mainly to the Allied control of the sea and the air. The Axis armies needed 150,000 tons of supplies each month. Month by month the Allies succeeded in cutting off those supplies so that by April 1943 only 30,000 tons got through. The Allied airfields established in Algiers and Tripolitania ensured the destruction of two thirds of the German aircraft in the Mediterranean, and by 4 May the Axis troops did not have enough fuel to supply the essentials of food, water and ammunition. Hitler issued his usual order to fight to the last man and the last bullet. Sensibly, the troops fired off what remained of their ammunition, put their equipment out of action and surrendered. About 50,000 Germans and 90,000 Italians became prisoners. The stage was set for the next campaign.

It had been agreed by the Allies that when Tunisia was under their control, the next move should be the invasion of Sicily, as a vital step to the invasion of the Italian mainland. Operation Husky, as the invasion of Sicily was known, began on July 1943, with the biggest sea-borne assault of the entire war. Two thousand five hundred and ninety vessels landed 180,000 men in the first wave. However, the airborne assault by glider and parachute was a tragic fiasco. Many of the paratroops were dropped in widely scattered areas of Sicily, and some even at sea. The aircraft and gliders were assaulted by concentrated anti-aircraft fire from four armies, German, Italian, British and American. British and American warships blazed away indiscriminately at any aircraft that came into range. When the airborne troops landed – those that did land – many found themselves under attack by British and American troops. Altogether, it was one of the worst cock-ups of the entire war, and surely the worst example of what we now know as 'friendly fire'.

However, in spite of such an inauspicious beginning, the invasion was successful, and the next stage was ready. This, it had been agreed by the Allied leaders, would be a campaign to drive Italy out of the war. In fact, Mussolini was removed from power before the invasion of the Italian mainland began. On 3 September 1943 the British 8th Army, under Gen. Montgomery, went over the Straits of Messina from Sicily to Italy, and thus became the first Allied Troops to fight on the mainland of Europe since the defeats and retreats of 1940.

On 8 September, the new Italian government of Marshal Badoglio announced an armistice, and in mid-October actually declared war on Germany. Reasonably, then, the invading Allies expected to have a friendly reception when they landed on the Italian mainland. But it was not to be. They met ferocious German counter-attacks, and they continued all the time the Allies slowly fought their way up the leg of Italy.

Mussolini was exiled to a remote island by the new Italian

government, but a dramatic night raid by German commandos rescued him, and Hitler then installed his ally as head of a preposterous little Republic of Salo in the north of Italy.

The Allied battles in Italy were accompanied by massive activity by Italian partisans, who did sterling work often far behind German lines by guerrilla and sabotage activity. The British Commander Gen. Alexander reported that at any one time, one quarter of German troops were engaged against the partisans. And the Germans behaved against them and Italian civilians, their erst-while allies, with a ferocity and savagery as evil as they exhibited anywhere. But there was no subduing the partisans, and they achieved perhaps the height of their ambitions when they took Mussolini from his ludicrous Republic of Salo, shot him and his mistress out of hand, and then hung the body of the first fascist dictator upside down by his heels from a telegraph pole.

**MESSAGE FROM LIEUTENANT-GENERAL DWIGHT D. EISENHOWER,
COMMANDER IN CHIEF ALLIED FORCES,immediately before
the Allied landings in North Africa.**

47

TO THE FRENCHMEN OF NORTH AFRICA

Faithful to the traditional and ancient friendship of
the government and people of the United States for
France and for French protected North Africa, against
the menace of an Italian-German invasion, our princi-
pal aim is the same as in 1917, namely, the annihi-
lation of the enemy and the complete liberation of
invaded France. The day when the Italian-German menace
ceases to weigh upon French territories, we shall leave
your soil.

The sovereignty of France over French territories
remains complete. We know we can count on your co-
operation to clear the way which leads to victory and
to peace.

All together, we shall get them!

Dwight D. Eisenhower
Lieutenant-General

Operations in
North Africa, Sicily and Italy

THE BATTLE OF THE BEES
JR Burt

THE NORTH AFRICAN CAMPAIGN was reaching its final stage. 3202 SC were on a forward airfield in Tunisia. By day North American Mitchell B25 bombers flew into this advance airfield from bases at the rear. The SCs then refuelled and re-armed them for continuous bombing sorties around Tunis and Cap Bon during the day. German photo reconnaissance planes flew high above recording the planes on dispersal. At dusk, the Mitchells flew back to their rear bases, while the SCs sat it out during the hours of darkness as German bombers attacked what they assumed to be squadrons on the ground.

It was very hot during the day with little protecting shade from the blazing heat. The planes were ready for take-off for yet another bombing mission when it was discovered that the 'ship' at the end of the line had a swarm of bees completely covering the bombardier's Perspex cabin. There must have been many thousands of them, like a big black smudge of cold tea leaves. There was a danger of them getting into the cabin, and with the mission due to leave something had to be quickly done. We were clad only in shorts, but one of our lads rolled up his socks, borrowed a shirt, put on a gas cape and sun glasses, then tied a green scarf round the lower part of his face, his hands covered with flying gloves. He looked grotesque in this strange garb – rather like an over-sized goblin!

Armed with a fire extinguisher he cautiously approached the plane, while we all stood a safe distance away to give him moral support, but armed with swats just in case. Standing about two yards from the mass of insects he started pumping the foam. It only trickled out of the end. He advanced a pace nearer, the extinguisher started to function and a cloud of bees dropped to the ground rather like a pile of wet tea leaves tipped from a pot. The rest flew up in an angry mass around their attacker. Casting his extinguisher aside he ran in our direction, and we in turn took to our heels. Here was the amazing sight of six almost naked airmen rushing headlong across a field chased by a frantic goblin surrounded by a cloud of bees.

I turned off across the field. Imagine my consternation when the goblin did the same, and he was slowly gaining on me, although I was only in shorts. However, gradually, his pursuers left him. When we regained our breath we cautiously tried again. Once again our goblin gave a short burst of foam and once again we had to make a hasty retreat. When the crews came over to start their mission the bees were still there. Cautiously we turned the props keeping a wary eye on the offenders. The engines fired, but still they remained. The plane turned into position at the end of the runway. Still they remained. Then as the machine gathered speed, took off and started to climb, they dropped away. Evidently they had no wish to meet 'Jerry'!

OUR OWN PRISONER
JR Burt

ON 8 NOVEMBER 1942, 3202 Servicing Commando made a seaborne landing by assault- and tank-landing craft on the Algerian coast at Ain Tyre. Their task was to move forward to the French airfield of Maison Blanche and secure it to provide air cover for the troops still landing. On the airfield they refuelled and re-armed the Hurricanes and Spitfires coming in from Gibraltar and the aircraft carriers out in the bay. After three days the Squadron ground personnel took over, and the SC. Unit divided, half going up country to Bougie and Dijidjelli. A day later the rest of the Unit embarked at Algiers harbour on a Dutch fast armed merchantman, the *Princess Beatrix*, a combined operations vessel that had been used on the St. Nazaire and Dieppe raids. Under cover of a smoke screen laid down by a destroyer it raced up the north African coast to land the troops at Bone way ahead of the 1st Army advancing by road. On their night time dash they had passed a German destroyer, but had not been spotted.

The small airfield at Bone had been seized the night before by a combined force of British Commandos and Paras., only hours in front of the German force with the same intention. The Servicing Commandos were needed to give aircover over the advancing troops. The position was precarious, for the airfield was some ninety miles in front of the main body of the Army, and the Germans were pushing towards them from Tunisia, only about 100 miles away, heavily supported by planes from Sicily and Tunis.

Once the position was consolidated 3202 leap-frogged ahead to a series of advanced airfields until finally the Axis troops capitulated and we entered Tunis.

With the North African campaign over we were ordered to return in convoy along the coast road to Algiers. Once over the Algerian border with Tunisia and way up in the mountains our lorry broke down and we had to transfer to another lorry to join up with the main convoy, leaving two or three chaps behind to attempt a repair. The following morning we went back up into the mountains to help while the main convoy continued its journey. We would then have to make our own way back to rejoin the Unit as soon as we could. When we reached the lorry Bill, Tubby, Tutton and Laurie were already hard at work. As night fell we were still isolated in the mountains so we took turns to mount a guard while two slept on top of the tilt and the others inside the wagon.

About midnight, when Tubby was on guard, he heard someone moving about. He made a challenge and awoke the others. It was an armed German soldier. He was disarmed and made prisoner until we could hand him over to the army.

When the campaign had finished after the fall of Tunis, the roads had been full of German and Italian soldiers chugging back to the prisoner compounds, sometimes in lorries driven by their own drivers. At other places there were long columns of men three deep lightly guarded and led by a single dispatch rider. Now we had our own prisoner! We gave him a blanket and told him to bed down under the tail board, but it was too cold to sleep so we made him some tea and as he could speak good English we spent the night talking.

He said he had walked from Tunis, a distance of about 100 miles, travelling by night and sleeping by day. He told us that just before the German troops had surrendered he had received a letter saying his mother was ill. When German resistance had stopped he decided he would make a bid to reach Spanish Morocco and cross to Marseilles. We told him it was an impossible task. The whole of the country was occupied by 1st Army and American troops right back to Oran and Casablanca. He laughed, saying 'You are wrong. There is no 1st Army. We have been fighting the 8th Army'. We told him we had landed on 8 November 1942 at Algiers and Oran and the whole of the North African coast was in Allied hands. He did not believe us and brushed it away as pure propaganda.

He said they had been told that Coventry and London had been bombed but they did not believe that. As it happened we had a book in the lorry called *Front Line* showing very graphic pictures about the devastation in London and Coventry, and also Bremen and Cologne, and also information about 8000lb. bombs dropped on Bremen. We told him about the bombing of the great dam in Germany. He never really believed it and brushed it aside as propaganda.

In the morning we handed him over to an Army patrol, and as he left he gave us a Hitler salute and said: 'When we have won the war and you are a prisoner in Germany I hope someone will come and speak to you.'

A frightening brainwash!

A HAPPY GENERAL
JR Burt

ON 23 JULY 1943, 3202 SC made a landing with the Americans on the south coast of Sicily at Gela and with their motorised columns made a thrust through the centre of the island to take the capital Palermo, on the north coast.

As we descended into the town we received an unbelievable reception that words could not describe. Its intensity, genuineness and noisy cheering from the massed crowds was totally embarrassing. We were showered with fruit, lemons, oranges, plums and nuts, as families waved frantically from balconies. The streets were packed with civilians held in check by American MPs and Italian police. We sat on top of our wagons smiling and waving back to the crowds and throwing them cigarettes, chocolate and biscuits. At one stage a man clad in a white apron thrust himself to the front and excitedly pushed ice cream cones on us. So it went on, an amazing eager greeting. This from a nation still our enemy! Hanging from a window a large white banner bearing the words 'Welcome at last'.

Eventually we swung through the gated entrance of Palermo airfield past ruined hangers and outbuildings. Out on the tarmac were numbers of destroyed Italian planes and one German Stuka, but also on the tarmac were our own Spitfires, Marauders and Dakota transports. Already it was time for the unit to carry on eastwards along the coast, but one Spitfire needed an engine change, so six of us were detailed to remain behind and get it serviceable before rejoining the others. Six of us, the only British servicemen in a world of GIs.

On the following morning I was in a hangar sitting on the wing of a

Spitfire taking a recoil out of its Browning machine gun when an American padre entered and proceeded to set up a table, altar and portable organ at the far end prior to starting a service. There was nothing for it but to abandon the work and stand at the back of the congregation, shortly afterwards two of our boys joined me. The service was fascinating, with a new slant, at one point we were asked to pray for our 'Buddies'.

Then we had a hymn, which at that time was new to us – 'The Old Rugged Cross'. After the service we spoke to the padre and said how much we admired that particular tune and words. In the evening there was another service, and again we stood at the back of the crowded hanger. In closing, the padre called for requests in selecting the last hymn. Our shouts were in vain, drowned out by scores of GIS. We needn't have worried. The padre waved to us over the heads of the crowd and said 'I heard 'The Old Rugged Cross!' '

The next day of our short stay held another surprise. I went into our room at the back of a hangar and sitting on our make-shift beds was a One Star General, a Colonel and another officer. They seemed to be in a merry state, sharing a bottle of wine between them. As I entered the General rose unsteadily to his feet, saying 'Cheerio' took a swig from the bottle and then offered it to me. Then Bill Mason's trumpet at the end of the bed took his eye and he shouted for a song. 'Come on! Who knows 'The Grand Old Duke of York, He had ten thousand men...' ' His voice trailed off and Bill continued on the trumpet. At the end he was loud in praise. 'Good, Good... Say, that fella sure can play that thing. Let's have another one... 'I got Sixpence'....Do you know it? Let's sing it!' So Bill played while we all joined in. This was followed by 'Bless 'em All'. Then the Colonel took the trumpet and attempted to play it, while the General was talking in a befuddled manner about old soldiers never dying, only fading away.

At that moment an American Captain came in, saluted and said 'Your plane is ready, General'. The three rose and walked out of the hangar, the General shouting over his shoulder 'So long, Boys, Good Luck'.

Later in the day we were told our uninvited guest was Teddy Roosevelt, son of Theodore Roosevelt, the Rough Rider President, and cousin of Franklin D.

THE EGYPTIAN RIOTERS
Jeff Davies

I SPENT AN ACTIVE life for a year with 39 Squadron, first at Aden and then, after moving into Egypt, flying their aircraft from airfields or landing strips in the Western Desert.

For many airmen and other servicemen it was no picnic living and working under desert conditions. Many of us after a few months suffered from desert sores which soon plated my legs and feet. Others, and myself, were spending more time in the sick bay needing medical attention, instead of working on aircraft.

One day I found myself being called to the Orderly Room to be told I was posted to RAF Heliopolis, one of the peace-time stations built between World Wars I and II, located on the east side of Cairo,

So for about 16 months I worked in Station workshops carrying out all sorts of tasks that I enjoyed doing. Prior to joining the RAF I had for five years been working in factories on machine tools making parts, which stood me in good stead, since I was able to make parts for all sorts of things.

Although my official trade was a Fitter II engine, it was a good experience to get involved in doing other jobs. About the mid-summer of 1942 the workshop had a rush job for the Army, to convert a Bristol Bombay transport twin-engine high-wing plane into a 24-seater paratroop-carrying aircraft. The men, together with their equipment, would have a weight of two tons or more. We had seven days to do the conversion. A team of men worked night and day to complete the task, with the workshop making all the required parts, and it was completed within the time limit.

We heard later that this aircraft was used in a paratroop raid on German Headquarters, and also in an attempt to capture General Rommel or other high ranking officers located in Libya. The paratroops destroyed the Headquarters, and took several prisoners, but General Rommel was in Germany at the time, so they missed seeing him.

Among my memories of my stay in Egypt was an opportunity to visit the three Great Pyramids at Gaza, and also the Great Sphinx and surrounding areas. As we visitors reached the site we were split into small parties each with a guide. Our party had two Army Nursing Sisters, two soldiers and two airmen, including myself. We were first taken inside the big pyramid of Cheops, up the corridors leading to the

King's Chamber, then to the Queen's. It was most impressive to visit those parts of by-gone history, seeing things for ourselves.

On our return to outside the pyramid the guide asked us if we would like to climb to the top, as was possible in those days, explaining that there were footholds and handholds carved into the south east edge of the large layers of stone blocks where one could climb up. This was an opportunity not to be missed, and we all accepted the offer.

On reaching the top of the pyramid there is a square of about twelve feet, just enough room for our party to look around with a view covering up to sixteen or seventeen miles in all directions. In the north one sees the Nile Delta spreading out into green fields and tall date palms. South, the river Nile made its way upstream with its fields each side of the river. To the East one saw the whole of Cairo with its city blocks, including the Dead City area etc. In the west lay the vast expanse of the Western Desert, where the main battles for Egypt would be fought, and which also became the grave for many Servicemen.

There were three other memories. Prior to the battle of El Alamein there were many German supporters living in Cairo and Egypt, and many anti-British mobsters started to appear. One morning at RAF Heliopolis we received an alert that a mob was on its way to storm the airfield. All Station personnel had to collect rifles and ammo., then to stand on guard at the perimeter fence, close to the Guard Room and main road leading to the Station Headquarters etc. An armoured car with a machine gun in the turret was also standing in the middle of the road near the Guard Room. This would have been September or October 1942.

After a while a shout went up 'They are coming', and in the distance along the Station road a mob of rioters carrying sticks and banners were making their way towards us, a mass of bodies on the move. Orders were given to load rifles to be prepared then wait for orders before taking any further action. The mob came within a 100 feet from the fence, when the armoured car suddenly let loose a burst of machine gun fire above the heads of the crowd, which was then almost stopped. A couple more bursts and the mob turned around and ran like hell. I have never seen so many men run so fast and disappear so quickly in the distance. If they had not done this, we would have had to defend the Station, which would have caused a massacre for the mob if we carried out orders and fired on them.

Second, within a few days of the riots, as a show of strength, the RAF carried out a display of a thousand aircraft over Cairo, a flypast of lines of aircraft. It was a wonderful sight, and I have never seen so many aircraft flying together before or since. It certainly proved to the Egyptians we could put up a show of strength when called to do so.

Third, towards the end of 1942, I felt that I wanted to get active again, wanting a life more involved with a Squadron or other form of Unit, so when a notice appeared in January 1943 on Station orders 'Volunteers required for a dangerous task', and that gave a list of ranks and tradesmen required, and which I qualified for, I put my name forward. Shortly afterwards three others and myself were posted away from RAF Heliopolis to proceed to Palestine – now Israel.

A Railway Warrant was issued to us to travel by railway from Cairo Main Railway Station to go to a place called Hadria, some 70 miles south of Haifa, which was a military training camp. I was placed in charge of our small party; none of us knew what to expect, or what we had let ourselves in for.

As other men started to arrive for training we learned that we were going to become RAF Servicing Commandos. Three Units were being formed, each needing 150 men of all ranks, plus two officers, a CO, and Engineering Officer, and also an Armament Officer. The Units were to be known as 3230, 3231 and 3232 SCUs.

We were to be trained by Army Commando instructors for about a month, then a week with the Royal Navy learning the art of landings from various craft, then in due course to be issued with fifteen trucks, one jeep and a Matchless 350cc Telefork motor cycle for general duties.

Each Unit was to have four Flights, split up into Sections of fifteen men per section, with a Cpl. in charge. I was put in charge of a Section. For training purposes an Army Commando Sgt. was in charge of each Flight, with an assistant. We were mainly aircraft ground crews, plus two cooks, one medical Cpl. and an Orderly Room admin airman. A WO or Flt. Sgt. was in charge of all the men. We all had to pass a driving test on the trucks, but those with the necessary driving experience were put in charge of a truck and was its driver.

After all the training was finished, my Unit was sent via the port of Alexandria in Egypt to start our travels to Malta, Sicily and Italy. 3232 SCU was the first SC Unit to land in Europe, at Reggio Calabria at the toe of Italy, at about 7 am. on 4 September 1943, to take over the nearby airport, with the first aircraft, a Spitfire, landing about midday to be refuelled, shortly followed by Squadrons.

About early February 1944, the Unit was shipped to England to be disbanded at Blackpool, to be told we were reserves if D-Day was a failure.

DIARY FOR SC 3202 IN NORTH AFRICA

[Keeping a diary whilst in the Armed Forces in wartime was strictly forbidden. It was, in fact, a serious offence. As a result, few were kept, and the few that were are especially valuable since they record the everyday events of life, whilst the official War Diary kept by each Unit was just that – a record of movements and actions. It seems that just two members of SC Units kept personal diaries, and this entry is the first of them. It is hard to imagine that the authorities will attempt to pursue the writers of the two diaries after sixty and more years, but if they do, I promise that they will face the combined anger of all members of the RAF Servicing Commandos, and that will be a fearsome sight.]

We boarded the *Maron* on 21 October 1942, and it rained all day. We sailed on 22 October, and of course nobody knew our destination. We were also unaware that the other half of our Unit had boarded at Liverpool, on a Dutch ship named *Dempo*, and that they had joined a convoy. We also joined a convoy, and eventually sailed past Gibraltar into the Med. On 6 and 7 November we were given briefings and informed we were off the North African coast and would be making a beach landing east of Algiers. On Sunday 8 November we were up well before dawn when it was still dark, and the *Maron* lay off Algiers. A coastal battery in a fort overlooking the harbour started firing on our convoy. There was some delay in disembarking for a number of reasons, one being the difficulty experienced by the army Royal Engineers in loading heavy equipment such as Bofors guns into the landing craft.

Eventually our Unit was instructed to disembark. For me personally it was quite an experience, despite my previous training, to put one's leg over the ship's rail and climb down scramble nets into the assault craft. We were dressed in battle order, which included small pack on our backs on top of which was strapped our tool roll, and we also had to carry our weapons.

I was in the first ALC (assault landing craft) to leave the *Maron*. Our progress was delayed because of some trouble ashore. Eventually our craft made for the beach, but some distance before reaching the beach the ALC ran into trouble, either hitting an underwater obstruction or a depression. The craft went sideways on, and a number of us were thrown into the water.

We were doing our best to get some of the equipment ashore, but we did lose one bit of equipment. This was a Jackson belt-positioning machine which was used to ensure belted .303 ammunition was properly aligned. It was an essential requirement for ammunition belts for the Browning machine guns fitted to fighter aircraft. This very heavy machine had been packed in a nailed wooden box. Two of the lads grabbed this box and threw it over the side. I wonder if they expected it to float. It sank like a stone.

After making the beach and assembling we made our way to the first objective, Maison Blanche aerodrome. Some of our Unit were already on the 'drome when we arrived. Three RAF squadrons who had flown from Gibraltar with overload tanks arrived. There were 242, 154 and 81 squadrons, Hurricanes and Spitfires. I was with green section and we were given the task of servicing Spitfires of 242 squadron. On this day it was reported nine enemy JU88 bombers had been destroyed. We had three damaged Spitfires and one Hurricane pranged on landing. On that first night it was very cold and we had to sleep in the open, having no tents because our transport had not reached us. It had been decided that the transport would await disembarkation until the port of Algiers was captured and in allied hands.

All day **Monday 9 November** we were kept busy rearming and refuelling aircraft engaged with fighting off German bombers attacking the port of Algiers and the allied shipping. We had some nervous moments. During the late evening in the dark we were re-arming some aircraft when enemy aircraft dropped flares and proceeded to bomb us. The main damage was to an Air France hangar on the opposite side of the 'drome.

Tuesday 10 November. Half the Unit left to go to an advance position further east along the coast in an endeavour to get air cover for the forward army troops who were trying to advance to the east. This part of our Unit landed at Djhidjelli/Bougie Bay. I was in the half of the Unit that remained at Maison Blanche and we were kept very busy. The night of the 10th we were changing a wheel on an aircraft when an enemy aircraft dropped flares and proceeded to bomb us.

Wednesday 11 November. Saw off the dawn patrol. Breakfast from stew, sausage and tea. Nobody has washed since we landed and some of the lads had quite a growth of beard. Water is brought round in jerricans for drinking only. During the afternoon we were bombed by a Ju88. We had been sleeping in the open, but tonight we will be sleeping in the back of the trucks, some of which had arrived.

Friday 13 November. Some of the squadrons' ground staff arrive and we get instructions to make an urgent move. We are transported by our trucks to Algiers dock area where we embark on a combined operations ship called *Princess Beatrix*. Before the war this vessel did the ferry run from Harwich to the Hook of Holland. At 6 p.m. we sailed from Algiers under cover of a smoke screen laid by a destroyer. We proceeded unescorted through the Med. until we reached our destination of Bone in Tunisia at dawn of the 14 November. The aerodrome had been occupied by members of the 1st Army Parachute Regiment and the 6th Army Commando. This occupation was some miles in front of the advancing Allied armies and it was deemed necessary to ensure air cover for the advancing troops.

On this first day we were subjected to several air raids. The first was by two ME109S, and later by two waves of four Macchi fighters and then in the evening we had another attack by two ME109S. Our losses for the day were one Spitfire lost, two Spitfires rendered unserviceable and one pilot burned. Reported successes were one JU88 and three ME109S.

Sunday 15 November. Up at dawn doing usual aircraft Daily Inspections (DIS), and while dropping emergency tanks from one aircraft a JU88 dropped a stick of bombs which came uncomfortably close. Everybody is very nervous and keeps one eye on the mountains which overlook the airfield and over which the enemy planes come swooping down. We had no radar in those days, and they were on us firing and bombing before we knew they were there.

Monday 16 November. Very active day. All we do is dive into trenches between rearming and refuelling. Again bombed. Rumoured German parachutists had landed in the area.

Tuesday 17 November. We are being constantly bombed. One very heavy raid on the docks after a diversionary sweep by 15 ME109S. Six Italian Macchi fighters raided our airfield. We are told all six enemy aircraft were destroyed.

Wednesday 18 November. Very heavy raid on dock area. Bombing through low clouds, a German bomber crashes on the airfield. It was ghastly. One of our lads named Wilcock lost his nerve and today was returned to Algiers with a Dakota aircraft which had managed to fly in with supplies of aviation fuel in four gallon cans. Out of eighteen aircraft with which we had started we now have seven serviceable.

Thursday 19 November. The regular squadron ground crews arrive to a ME109 welcome. We leave the airfield and go to a building in Bone.

Friday 20 November. We spend the day delousing and cleaning up. Some of the lads have their heads shaved. Four of them, Lawrence, Bond, Morling (dysentery) and Joe Lee (with a fever) are admitted to hospital. We prepare the wagons for moving out tomorrow.

Saturday 21 November. We travel west and arrive at Philipville. Very muddy airfield. While servicing a four-cannon Hurricane I lost my tunic in which were my papers, pay book etc. A very serious development. I was interviewed by special officers from the Army Military Police. We had seen on old Arab loitering in the nearby orange groves and we did suspect he could have been the culprit.

Monday 23 November. A Blenheim landed carrying Brig. General Anderson, 1st Army General.

Tuesday 24 November. On dawn readiness. Saw off the Blenheim after refuelling.

Thursday 26 November. It has been raining for days and the airfield is virtually unusable. A number of aircraft are bogged down in the mud.

We stayed at Philipville until 5 December 1942.

Friday 4 December. We prepare equipment, vehicles and draw rations for our journey the next day.

Saturday 5 December. We commence our journey to Maison Blanche. Had a meal of sardines and biscuits on the road and at about 4pm we pull into a gorge where we spent the night.

Sunday 6 December. On the road about 10 a.m. and journey along the coast road. Eventually the convoy parked in a cork tree forest where we had a meal before retiring for the night.

Monday 7 December. Up at 4.30am. Had breakfast in the dark. On the move at daybreak. We seem to be leaving the mountainous country behind. Travelling through flat desert-like land, we actually see some camels. We arrive at Maison Blanche about lunch time. So different from when we were here last. There seem to be thousands of men and hundreds of aircraft. We are billeted in an old French barracks, and I sleep in a proper bed for the first time since arriving in North Africa.

Wednesday 9 December. Had a lecture from the CO. He told us we were going to a farm just outside Maison Blanche where we are to rest and re-fit for a future operation. He also informed us that we are now permitted to officially wear the Combined Operations badge. Everything had been done to hide the existence of our Units before this first operation.

Friday 11 December. I get my lost tunic replaced.

Sunday 12 December. Unit got its first mail since leaving the UK.

Saturday 19 December. 150 francs for a cockerel which Davie Tweed cooked.

Sunday 20 December. Cpl. Williams conducted a church service. Our Armaments Officer PO Hatton gave a sermon.

Thursday 24 December. We bought three chickens. Tubby Dunn, a butcher in civvy street, condemned one as unfit for eating due to what he thought was consumption. Tubby, Fred Limehouse and myself had the job of plucking the chickens.

Friday 25 December. Christmas Day. We had a wonderful meal. Jack Burt and Cpl. Dunkason prepared a table complete with serviettes and menus for each person (there were eight of us). The menu consisted of two chickens, tangerines, oranges, dates and figs There was a choice of six wines including champagne. I had never had champagne before. The Unit engaged in a comic football match and then everybody sat down to a high tea. Went to sleep surprisingly early for Christmas night. There was an air raid on Algiers.

Sunday 27 December. Church service conducted by Cpl. Williams. We continue to work at Maison Blanche aerodrome. White Section did a six-day stint from Wed. 30 December.

Monday 11 January 1943. I am 21 today. Cpl. 'Pip' Bentley had to drive the truck to the nearby army supply depot to get the Unit's food ration. At that time we had to draw daily rations. On his return he presented me with a tin of plums and a can of Libby's milk, which he had obviously 'scrounged', and said 'There's your 21st birthday present.'

Monday 1 February. Still at Philipville. Most of my work has been installing armament in aircraft made serviceable by cannibalising parts from wrecked aircraft.

Tuesday 2 February. We are informed the rate of exchange has been reduced from 300 francs to the £1 to 200. Cpl. Pip Bentley is 22 years old today. During the first half of February we worked at the Philipville airfield undertaking various tasks, but I myself was mainly installing 20mm cannons in Hurricanes. On Thursday 18th work was completed on two Hurricanes. They had their final inspection and were ground tested, the engine tests meeting with approval by the engine fitters.

Friday 19 February. Have instructions to dismantle the aircraft which are being taken by road to Jemmapes for test flying.

Saturday 20 February. 40ft low loaders arrive to transport the dismantled aircraft.

Sunday 21 to 23 February. We start moving out. Some of the lads go to Bone. A party, including myself, go to Jemmapes.

Wednesday 24 February. We install cannons in Hurricane number 489. A Canadian WO pilot inspects the aircraft which is to be his. A 'dope basher' paints 'Canada Forever' on his cockpit.

Thursday 25 February. Hurricane 489 is again ground tested and found to be OK. Ironically, we learn that the Canadian pilot has been killed.

Saturday 27 February. We leave Jemmapes and rejoin our Unit at Bone, arriving there on Sunday 28th. We are back to living in tents about a quarter of a mile inland from the sea. Because of the unsuitability of airfields in the area to be used for heavier aircraft it became necessary for the army to construct an airfield near Bone. The airfield was named Tingli after a Major Tingli who commanded the Royal Engineers involved in the construction.

Tuesday 2 March. At Tingli airfield we bombed up a squadron of American B25 Mitchell bombers. We did the same thing on 3 and 4 March.

Friday 12 March. I was in a party which had to cross a swamp to work on a crashed Wellington bomber. While working on the bomber we were urgently called away to rearm and refuel an American squadron of P40 Warhawk fighters which unfortunately did not arrive.

Thursday 18 March. Reveille 5.30am. We are on the move. Going to work with a bomber squadron flying from a desert airfield. Journey through mountainous country mostly in low cloud. Most of the time the other trucks in the convoy are not visible. Arrive Canrobert airfield in driving rain. Sleep in a hanger with American ground crews.

Friday 19 March. Erect tents on airfield uncomfortably close to a bomb dump. We are working B25 Mitchell bombers of the 81st and 82nd Squadron of the American Air Force. Very warm during the day but bitterly cold at night. A bucket of water left outside the tent overnight would have a thick layer of ice in the morning.

Sunday 21 March. Our aircraft on a mission in the afternoon. Bomb an airfield. Slight damage to some aircraft.

Monday 22 March. A lot of air activity, mainly Bostons and Fortresses. Our B25s bomb an enemy airfield. We have had a period of inactivity because of bad weather conditions.

Friday 2 April. Today we are issued with tropical kit and have typhus inoculations.

Saturday 3 April. Our B25s flew a mission today. The weather over the past few days has been very windy and bitterly cold at night.

Monday 5 April. Our aircraft bomb an airfield. Two B25s are shot down.

16 April. White, Red and Green Sections move about 200 miles to a forward area near Souk el Khemis. We are to service the 81st and 82nd B25s, and they will be making daylight raids on German positions. Next few days we were kept very busy. B25s doing at least two raids a day. Bombing up the aircraft was not as per laid down procedure. The bombs would be delivered to each aircraft on the Bedford trucks. They would be kicked off the trucks. After fitting the bomb fins and removing the detonator cavity filling-pieces, we would load the bombs into the aircraft bomb bay. We would then insert the detonators and fit the bomb pistols after the bombs had been secured on the bomb racks. Not as per text book.

Activity increased towards the end of April. Raids increased and they were making at least three a day. Main targets tank and troop concentrations. 5 and 6 May were particularly busy days. On the 7 May we heard the 1st Army had gained possession of Tunis. Bizerta has also been occupied. The German troops have withdrawn to Cap Bon where they have constructed numerous 'Dunkirk Jetties'.

8 May. Our B25s loaded with 500lb bombs attack four merchant ships in Tunis bay.

8 May. B25s bomb the town of Soliman which at the same time was being shelled by the Navy.

10 May. White 3 collect thirty 500lb bombs. After being loaded with these bombs the B25s attacked an enemy airfield. This was followed by several sorties where our aircraft dropped ninety six bombs, seventy four of which had a six hour delay fuse. We hear the Germans are endeavouring to evacuate troops at night by a JU52 transport aircraft. We are on a minute's standby to move to the front, probably Tunis.

11 May. We are on the move. Come across hundreds of German prisoners. One English-speaking guy I spoke to said he was a pilot and had bombed London, Coventry and Stalingrad. A number of the prisoners wear a red ribbon with black border denoting service on the Russian front.

12 May. Red and Blue Sections move up to the Tunis area. Twenty men from Blue Section go to forward areas.

13 May. A party of men which includes myself are detailed to go to forward areas to locate and if possible recover enemy aircraft. We leave at 1 am, making our way forward in the Tunis area. We see evidence of bitter fighting. In one spot covering an area of about two miles I counted twenty German tanks that had been knocked out. There were also numerous British and American tanks that had been destroyed.

We pass through Tunis which is now occupied by 1st and 8th Army troops. On leaving Tunis and making our way east we see evidence that the Germans have been using roads as airstrips. Aircraft bays have been erected at the side of the roads and roads themselves were used as runways. They had been very heavily bombed.

We went through Soliman, which had been devastated. We chanced to meet up with some of the twenty men from Blue Section. The previous evening they had been in an area which was under attack, but fortunately they had not sustained any serious casualties.

We park in a wood overnight and sleep in the truck. Arising about 5.30 we discover we had parked in what had been a German field hospital which had been hurriedly evacuated. There was German transport parked under the trees all over the place. Stores of all description had been abandoned. In erected tents that had been obviously left in a hurry we found beds, sheets, pillow cases, stretchers, food of every description, arms and ammunition. We put an unopened bale containing 300 white sheets on the truck. We proceeded up Cap Bon and about midday located our target, which had been the German Central aerodrome. This proved to be a large fighter station. Although most of the aircraft had been destroyed there were a number of ME109(G)s serviceable. There were air-craft spares of every description. One which interested me was an 'Instrument Gun Aligning' used for harmonising guns on fighter aircraft. This with many other items were loaded on the truck to take back for examination and evaluation. We eventually left, making our way back and terminating our day's journey on a German airfield about six miles from Soliman. There were damaged aircraft all over the place. Stores of every description. Mobile workshops, aero engines. There were five trucks which the Germans had hurriedly tried to make unserviceable. We found a German Storch observation plane which was undamaged and it was decided this had to be dismantled and made ready for transportation by road. We also saw twenty Russian prisoners of war who had been used to work mainly on the repair of roads.

15 May. Arise at 6am and have cold bath before the other lads are awake. After breakfast we start to dismantle the Storch aircraft. About midday we are relieved by an RSU Unit and we leave to rejoin our main party at the Central 'drome.

17 May. Same small party go to Medjez Temin in Cap Bon. We reach a very large German airfield which had been devastated. I think this is the most heavily bombed airfield I have ever seen. JU52 transport planes, ME109 and FW190 fighters damaged and lying everywhere. There was also a graveyard with thirty graves of men killed in the bombing. They must have had an awful time.

18 May. Today we return to the main party who by now have quite a collection of German transport. German prisoners are still being captured in ones and twos.

19 May. Assist in stripping an ME109(G).

20 May. Hundreds of aircraft flying towards Sicily and Sardinia. Hear we are to rejoin the Unit tomorrow.

21 May. Rejoin Unit. CO informs us we are going on another operation and we have six weeks to prepare. Our kit is to be made lighter and our personal stuff stored.

22nd May. Today we have firing practice on a range. I do pretty well with a Bren gun. Unit has a mail delivery. I get fifteen letters.

24 May. Very warm indeed. F/Sgt. Jack Ife is admitted to hospital.

25 May. It's so hot. Jack Burt, Len Carter and myself make frames for mosquito nets.

26 May. Parade at 6am. CO tells us we must be prepared to move at a moment's notice. He does not disclose the destination but says it will entail a journey of about 600 miles.

27 May. We move off early morning. Benny Kincar and Len Carter are taken ill at the last moment. This makes over a dozen in dock. Feeling a bit queer myself, and travelling in the back of a truck does not improve matters. We travel about 200 miles before stopping for the day. We are informed our destination is Blida. We sleep in the open. PO Hatton is taken ill and has to travel in the vehicle which is used as a mobile office/Orderly Room. Two trucks are having problems. The Green 2 truck is having real trouble and they are left to make their own way.

28 May. After a hard day's run we stop about 250 miles from Algiers. Sleep in the open.

29 May. Make a very early start. Extremely warm and some of the lads are being affected by the heat. We park for the night just past L'Arba which means we must be about 22km from Blida. The CO is not with us. Maybe vehicle trouble is the problem. We bathe in a river.

30 May. CO arrives and goes on to Blida for instructions. He returns with further confirmation that we are to prepare for an important operation. We proceed to Blida and camp on a football pitch alongside our sister Unit 3201 Servicing Commando.

31 May. Parade at 6.30am. Work on equipment. I hand in my Sten gun and retain the German 9mm Schmeisser automatic pistol picked up in Cap

Bon. This is of course in addition to my Bren gun. Everybody is kept very busy. Particular attention being paid to the trucks.

22 June. For some time I have been unable to write up my diary, so I will recall some of the happenings. We moved from Blida to Oran (Port Arwez), where we stayed for about nine days. Most of the time we spent route marching dressed in battle order and charging over assault courses. About fifty per cent of the Unit reported sick. Probably due to our rough living and the intense heat. I had a sore foot and suffered from a sunburnt back. This was brought about by my going on a route march after which we were given permission to bathe in the sea. While at the beach I lay down and was so tired I fell asleep. The lads did not realise I was asleep. Result a severely burned back. The lads pointed out that if I reported sick I would be charged with self-inflicted injury. I therefore went unofficially to Doc. Thompson who gave me some lotion to apply. On exercises, carrying equipment and my Bren gun punished my back, so some of the lads carried my equipment as well as their own. We had some replacements posted to the Unit. One of the lads, Morris Berry from Birmingham had left England six weeks earlier. Tony Tory, our 'cook' had an accident. He was refilling very hot stoves with fuel when one of the stoves exploded and Tony was very severely burned. He has been admitted to hospital and will not be rejoining the Unit. Benny Kincar and Len Carter rejoin the Unit after their stay in hospital and they look pretty fit. Mr. Draycott has apparently left the Unit for good, and a new Warrant Officer has arrived to take over his position.

We departed from Port Arzew and arrived at St. Charles very near Algiers where we stayed for a few days.

23 June. The Unit leaves St. Charles in two convoys, Red and White Sections in one, Blue and Green in the other. We spend the night in a forest of cork trees. We had previously stayed in the forest on 6 December.

24 June. On the move again. We are now beginning our journey by marching a couple of miles before being picked up by the trucks. We journeyed until late afternoon when we stopped in what appeared to be a canyon. Baboons appear in the trees and from behind rocks. I was on guard duty and luckily had the first three hours.

25 June. On the move and again we march a couple of miles before boarding the trucks. While travelling along a mountain road our truck which was being driven by 'Pip' Bentley was in collision with an Army truck. Morris Berry sustained a cut head. Len Carter has a painful back, and I feel groggy, plus having a bruised knee. We camp for the night about thirty miles from Bone.

26 June. Today we continued our journey and subsequently camped for the night about 8km. from Tabarka. We are in a clearing surrounded by trees. There has obviously been some action here. In a nearby cemetery there are 130 American graves, six British and a single French graves.

27 June. We make an early start without the usual march. We pass through Bizerta which has been annihilated with the worst bombing I have seen. Not one building is undamaged. Not a civilian to be seen. Just piles and piles of wreckage. In the harbour and docks sunken ships are everywhere, some blown right out of the water on to the quaysides.

We finally reach our destination about 8km. from Tunis (near Protville). We sleep under trees. Nobody bothers to erect tents and just sleep under mosquito nets. Expect to be here about seven days. General feeling is that 'It's the lull before the storm'.

28 June. Very hot and flies are becoming unbearable. We have a mail delivery. I get a letter posted on 16 June.

29 June. Rise 6.30, parade 8am. Doing nothing in particular. Very warm. Attended an open air concert given to American troops by artistes from the States. Jack Burt and Tubby Dunn also go to the concert.

30 June. Armourers are paraded and briefed on the coming operation.

1 July. Today we have a route march. Quite a few of the lads are complaining of sickness.

2 July. Had a terrible night with pain in my stomach. Jack Burt called Doc. Thompson about 3am. He gave me some 'jollop' which made me go to the toilet and then some! After that I fell asleep.

3 July. Still feeling a bit groggy. The Americans set up an open air cinema and we see a film called *Our Lives*, starring Bette Davis.

4 July. We move about six miles to another site adjoining American infantry. Had our first swim for ages.

5 July. Weather is very warm.

6 July. Get my hair cut. About time, it was last cut in Oran. We are experiencing sirocco winds. Temperature 120 degrees. The wind scorches exposed parts of the body. Unofficially some of us wander off to an Arab village. Have iced lemon drinks. Amazingly, Italian prisoners are wandering about the place as if they own it.

7 July. Had a march up a hill. Quite Strenuous. Pack our kit ready for moving.

8 July. Unit divided into three Sections. I am in No. 2 Section.

13 July. Up at dawn. Early breakfast. We march in full order for about three miles before being picked up by the trucks. We dismount from the trucks on the outskirts of the town and march about a mile to the docks and embark on American LCIs (Landing Ships Infantry). After boarding we are assembled on deck and informed we are landing in Sicily with the American 7th Army (under the command of General Patton). As darkness came down we were heavily bombed. Many aircraft were hit apparently by radar controlled anti-aircraft guns supported by radar controlled searchlights. This was the first time we even knew they existed. During one of those raids I was on deck standing under a gun turret. This proved to be an error of judgement because suddenly the gun fired and I was deaf for hours.

14 July. Dawn saw most of us awake. After breakfast we stood around on deck. Eventually we reach Sicily and lay offshore for about an hour before having a wet beach landing at Gela. The only way to leave the beach was up a concrete stairway to the promenade, but progress was hampered by enemy tanks situated on each side of the road leading down to the promenade. Every time an attempt was made to climb the stairway and reach the promenade the tanks would open fire. It took some hours before the problem was eliminated. During that few hours we were frequently bombed from the air. Part of the plan was that parachutists from the British Parachute Regiment were to drop behind the town and attack from the rear. It could have been that the American AA gunners had been made aware of this (at that time we were certainly not aware of it), because a wave of German bombers flying in very low were not challenged with the result that there was heavy damage and many casualties. This resulted in the American gunners becoming extremely nervous and any aircraft in the area immediately after the raid was fired on. In fact when the Dakotas carrying the British parachutists appeared on the scene they were met with a tremendous gun barrage resulting in many aircraft being shot down and a high proportion of the parachutists were killed and wounded. Part of the force did reach their target at the rear of Gela, and to their credit the depleted force attacked the town from the rear and played a big part in its eventual capture. This incident has been well documented, and is regarded as one of the worst tragedies of the Sicilian campaign.

We, after some time, reached our airfield objective, which had been the scene of a bitter battle. The American infantry transported by half-tracks had been engaging the opposition. Our first task was to go through the buildings and ensure there were no booby traps. It was common practice, particularly among the Italians, to place primed 'Red Devil' grenades around, for example on top of partly opened doors so that when the door was pushed the grenade would explode. Another ruse was to put a primed grenade inside a lavatory cistern so that when the chain was pulled to flush the grenade would explode. During the first hour on the airfield we found many American dead.

As was our normal practice, the four Sections, Red, White, Green and Blue, were dispersed around the airfield with our officers and admin. staff occupying part of one of the buildings. Our main initial task was to try and make the airfield suitable for receiving aircraft.

There was quite a lot of damage, bomb craters, etc. It must be appreciated that the battle was still going on and there was frequent gunfire. Suddenly a light Auster aircraft appeared and was obviously intent on making a landing which was achieved. A number of the lads rushed out to the aircraft to assist the pilot, who turned out to be an Army major. He requested to be taken to our Commanding Officer.

While in conversation with our CO he turned to one of the lads and said 'Where's my briefcase?' This was the first our lads knew of the existence of a brief case, and I think in his anxiety the guy had left the case in the aircraft. Anyway, some of the lads were instructed to go and get the case. They returned to say there was no case in the aircraft. It should be appreciated there was quite a lot of activity, with gunfire etc.

The officer's face took on an unnatural hue, and he started to bellow with some really violent language. Our CO instructed a number of parties to search the surrounding countryside. To our surprise one of the parties found three Italian boys (I guess they must have been about eleven years old) hiding in a ditch and in possession of the briefcase.

The Army officer, obviously relieved to get the case back, proceeded on whatever task he had been sent to perform, instructing our CO to keep hold of the boys pending further instructions. I was told that in the briefcase was money to pay Italian partisans who had been active in the area.

The three boys were kept in a square-shaped tent (it was a German tent we had retained from equipment found in North Africa) and they had to be guarded at all times. Some of our lads had sufficient command of the Italian language to question the boys, and it transpired that they lived some miles away from this airfield, and periodically they would come and tend the family vegetable-growing allotment which was in a field alongside the airfield.

Unfortunately for them this day, 14 July 1943 was the day the Allies were to land in Sicily and those boys found themselves in the middle of a battle. I was one of the guard appointed to look after those boys, and I can tell you there was quite a lot of sympathy for them among the Unit, with the result that some of us decided on a plan.

One of the boys told us that in a village about two miles away he had some relatives. Those of us that formed the guard decided that after midnight when most people should be sleeping this one lad would be taken to the village so that he could inform his relatives of his plight and of course that the three of them were alive. We were, of course, taking a terrible risk. If our superiors had found out we would have been in real trouble, and worse than that we could have met up with enemy troops. Anyhow, a decision was made and Jock Watson, Tubby Dunn and myself took this boy to the village. I can tell you I was scared. We reached the village and the boy pointed out the house. We knocked on the door but the residents were too scared to open it. They merely had a conversation with the lad through the locked door. After this we returned the lad to the tent and his companions. Nobody apart from the members of that guard ever knew what took place that night.

Ironically, the next day our Unit received a signal to proceed urgently to Biscari. Being without any further instructions, our CO let the three Italian boys go.

From 15 July to 20 July we were rearming and refuelling aircraft on the Biscari airfield. We left Biscari on 20 July and proceeded to Agrigento. On 21st we travelled by road preceded by American infantry towards Palermo.

On 23 July the aerodrome at Palermo was captured and we were soon making plans to operate and service aircraft. The name of the aerodrome was Boccadifalco. When we entered the airfield it was a shambles. Damaged aircraft were all over the place and a number of fires were blazing, including an ammunition dump. Our first task was to get some order into the place and prepare a strip to enable two Spitfire squadrons from the American 31st Fighter Group to land. On that first day only two Piper Cub aircraft landed. The next day we serviced a number of aircraft like B26 Marauder bombers, Taylorcraft and several Dakotas bringing in American ground crews for handling supplies etc.

Since occupying the airfield I had been working with Bill Dunkason and our bomb disposal expert Sgt. Shepherd locating and making safe unexploded bombs and booby traps. Unfortunately one of the American soldiers killed himself and injured two of his colleagues by tampering with a device instead of reporting it.

26 July. We received instructions to send a party to an airfield near Termini on the north Sicilian coast. After an exciting journey along the Messina road the party reached their objective and found there were twenty nine trucks loaded with petrol that had to be unloaded. They had been previously advised the job would take about two hours. They did not return to base until 11.30pm.

27 July. At 10am saw the arrival of the two American Spitfire squadrons. At 5pm Red and White Sections plus other selected personnel were ordered to go to Termini airfield which was a distance of about thirty miles. Being in White Section I was involved in this move. PO Hatton was the officer in charge of this party.

28 July. We were visited by our CO, who was anxious to learn how things were going, and he was apparently annoyed to learn that the aircraft we had been sent to service were not expected for a couple of days. The guys left at Palermo (Boccadifalco) were having to service two squadrons of Spitfires plus transport planes. He decided to move some of us back to Palermo to redress the balance. To give some idea of the workload, on the 28 July in addition to servicing the two Spitfire squadrons the Unit refuelled forty Dakotas carrying American ground crews plus a Fortress carrying General Eisenhower and General Montgomery. On 29 July there was a further squadron of Spitfires from the 52nd Coastal Group landed, bringing the total to three squadrons which were refuelled by our Unit because the American ground crews were not in a position to take over the work.

30 July. It was decided the Americans would take over the routine maintenance while our Unit would do all the rearming and refuelling plus Daily Inspections, 40-hour Inspections, engine changes and airframe repairs. Our refuelling involved our Unit handling between 6,000 and 8,000 gallons daily. It was difficult and irksome work because the heavier American cans were not so easy to handle as the British 'flimsy' four gallon cans we had been used to handling.

We were at the Palermo/Termini area from 23 July to 15 August 1943, and although we were kept very busy in short spells the general impression among the lads in the Unit was that we were not doing the job for which we had been trained. I guess one of the reasons for this was the fact we were operating with American 7th Army and the chain of communication was different to that when operating in a British controlled sector. Our CO Ft/Lt. Wheadon was far from happy about this situation and this led him to undertake an incredible journey across Sicily to HQ Desert Air Force at Syracuse because no signals had been received from RAF HQ since our landing at Gela. He was to learn that on the 4 August a signal had been sent to 3202 via American channels ordering the Unit back to North Africa for refit. That signal was never received by the Unit. One bonus from the CO's visit to HQ – he brought some long-awaited mail for the Unit. One wonders what would have happened to this mail had the CO not visited HQ. On his return, the CO lost no time in contacting the port authority at Palermo to arrange transport for the Unit to Bizerta in North Africa.

On 13 August the missing signal from HQ was received and it ordered the Unit to leave all its transport plus aero spares behind and proceed immediately to Bizerta in North Africa.

15 **August.** We were advised an American LST (Landing Ship Tank) was lying in Palermo docks and in just over an hour we were on our way to the docks. It was with some regret that the Unit parted with the 3-ton Bedford trucks, which had served us so well, but those trucks together with all our major equipment was left with the American 55th Service Squadron at Boccadifalco.

We boarded the tank landing craft (USS LST 378), and it set sail the following afternoon at 12.00 hours in a convoy of about thirty vessels plus naval escort. Our presence meant an additional work-load for the American crews, and our Unit was asked to assist with some of the duties. I volunteered to work in the galley which I found very interesting, plus the fact I was able to partake of some tasty fare. It was for me quite an experience standing at a hot plate cooking and serving waffles with syrup and crispy bacon for breakfast.

Because we had abandoned our equipment, the general opinion was that we were bound for Blighty, and there definitely was a subdued excitement in the ranks. We reached Bizerta at 18.00 hours on 17 August. The Unit remained on board while the CO went ashore to receive instructions. I well remember his return to the vessel. When he came on board my impression was that he looked very serious. We were paraded on the deck, and the CO informed us we had one other difficult operation to perform. We disembarked from the LST at 19.30 hours and were directed to a very large American Concentration Area known as Texas Camp, which was in the hills. We stayed at this camp until 31 August. During this period we were re-equipped with trucks and aero spares and the Unit strength was increased by a further fifty-six men which included officers, NCOs and other ranks.

31 August. We moved to a concentration area near Bizerta Docks, which was named Houston. Since arriving on 17th we had been experiencing very heavy air raids. They were a lot worse than anything we had experienced during the last couple of weeks in Sicily.

2 September. The Unit is split into three because for the operation we would be embarking on three LSTs, and today our trucks and motorcycles were loaded aboard the vessels. I, with others of my section boarded the LST during the morning of 5 September 1943. The three LSTs moved outside the dock area and joined a large convoy which was at anchor. We remained at anchor for a couple of days during which time we were subjected to heavy bombing attacks.

7 September. The LSTs leave the main convoy and form a smaller convoy which sailed at 14.15 and we were then informed we were attempting a landing very near Naples. We were not advised of our actual objective.

8 September. We are now sailing off Sicily in a fairly calm sea, and we were assembled on deck and informed that Mussolini had been deposed and the Italian government now in power had secretly negotiated an Armistice with the Allies which had been signed on 4 September. This led us to believe our landing in Italy was going to be a formality. We were also briefed on our objective. Our landing was to be on the beaches in Salerno Bay and after the landing we were to proceed to Monte Corvini aerodrome. We could expect light opposition because of the Italian Government surrender and furthermore intelligence reports indicated the area in which we were to land was occupied by an Italian infantry regiment. The nearest German unit was at rest 50 miles away. In fact after the Italian agreement with the Allies, German troops took over all the Italian occupied positions. When the landing was made at Salerno we were met by crack battle-hardened men of the Hermann Goering panzer regiment.

Our Unit landed at beaches in the Central area. This was a five mile stretch covering six beaches. This area was the main target for two British Army divisions. There were also landings in the northern area by US Rangers and British Commandos and the southern area eighteen miles south of Salerno by an American division.

The first assault landings commenced on 8 September at 3.00am. Our

Unit was scheduled to land at H-Hour plus 16 hours, but this was not to be because contrary to expectations, attempts to achieve a landing on the Central Area beaches were met with fierce opposition and our troops suffered heavy casualties.

The three LSTs carrying our Unit moved into their assigned beaches at 10.30am on 10 September. Our LST hit the beach and we hastily disembarked into an artillery duel between German 88mm artillery sited in the hills overlooking the bay, and British 25 pounders which were lined up on the beach. There was plenty of air activity and I witnessed an explosion on the battleship *Warspite*, which was caused by a radio-controlled glider bomb which had been launched from a high-flying German bomber. German troops who had been taken prisoner and who were confined to an area by barbed wire were in as much danger from the shelling by their own guns as we were.

Our immediate objective was to reach the road immediately beyond the beaches. Having achieved this the Section I was with was forced to lie in a ditch at the side of the road because of the very heavy gunfire. A bitter battle between our infantry and the enemy was being being fought for occupation of Monte Corvino aerodrome, which was our Unit's main objective. We occupied the airfield in the early hours of 11 September.

We were constantly under fire from German artillery. The enemy were using a tobacco factory at the nearby village of Battipaglia as an observation post. Any aircraft attempting to land came under heavy shellfire. The airfield perimeter facing the enemy positions was manned by infantry of the 8th Battalion Royal Fusiliers. The first night under cover of darkness the Germans got back onto the airfield.

My personal experience during this episode was this. The various Sections of our Unit were, as was the usual practice, dispersed around the airfield. Many of our lads occupied well-constructed German defence positions. Myself and Len Carter decided to sleep in a two-man tent. We had had an exhausting day and were soon asleep. It must have been somewhere around midnight when I awoke to a tremendous barrage. Len was sound asleep. I crawled out of the tent and was confronted with a real firework display. Flares, shelling and, more worrying, mortar bombs, were dropping on the airfield.

As I got to my feet I saw a truck moving and I ran across yelling something like 'What's going on?' In the cab was Sgt. Garnham. I cannot recall the driver. They stopped the vehicle and asked where I had come from, and added 'It's back to the beach!' I told them that Len Carter was around. I rushed back to the tent to inform Len and we climbed into the back of the truck but not before we had covered our tent with some of the many tree branches that were lying around. The truck left the airfield and made its way down the road to the beach area. We eventually joined some more of our Unit transport parked on the roadside outside a military hospital. Sgt. Garnham was obviously trying to obtain some information and eventually joined us in the back of the truck when there was a general discussion.

During the conversation I was looking back up the road we had come down. It was a dark night but I did spot this vehicle travelling towards us at some speed. At the time there had been quite a lot of German armoured vehicles infiltrating our lines doing a lot of damage. I called Sgt. Garnham and we observed the vehicle for some time and he said 'Its OK. Its one of our trucks.' I continued to watch the vehicle and my blood ran cold when I realised it was not slowing down. It hit the rear of our truck with tremendous force. The impact was such that the fan shaft of the vehicle came right through the radiator. The driver of the truck was injured, but we were OK, although shaken up.

We never did get back to the beaches. At dawn next morning we were back on the airfield preceded by Sherman tanks of the 40th Kings Liverpool Regiment (Monty's Foxhounds). We remained on this airfield until 17 September and during this period we were to have some scary moments. Our main problem was the constant shelling and we were suffering from fatigue. We had a front line view of Allied aircraft bombing enemy positions close by. At about 11am on the morning of 14 September we watched some American P38 Lightning aircraft coming in for what we expected to be a bombing raid on the nearby enemy positions, but to our consternation they started to bomb our positions. Some of the buildings were hit but fortunately we had no serious casualties, although some of the lads were bruised from diving into trenches. The Unit did receive an apology from the Americans, but I can tell you I was shaken up. Air activity can be judged from the fact that no less then 3,400 sorties were recorded for the two days 14 and 15 September.

16 September. was a day to remember. The Germans, in an attempt to retake the aerodrome launched an attack using two Tiger tanks and two companies of infantry. The attack failed and our troops destroyed one of the tanks. The situation was obviously becoming quite serious because the Army commander decided that our Unit was to be earmarked as an infantry reserve unit. Fortunately it was on the 16 September that the main army force, under the command of General Montgomery, who were advancing from the south of Italy, broke through the German lines and relieved the beachhead.

17 September. The Unit received instructions to join 3326 Servicing Commando on the nearby Asa landing strip to assist in the servicing and maintenance of 322 Wing Spitfires. Also on this day we were heavily shelled both in the morning and afternoon.

18 September. During breakfast we were bombed by an FW109. During the afternoon moved to the Asa strip. Scores of Italians were leaving the German positions and giving themselves up at a nearby Allied POW camp.

25 September. We move to the east of the beachhead to Serretelle airstrip which was a few miles from Battipaglia. Our main task was to service Spitfires, but in general the lads are disappointed because they felt that the routine duties now being undertaken were not the specialist tasks for which we had been trained. I remember one interesting day when our CO Flt/Lt. Wheadon organised a party of which I was one and we climbed Mount Eboli. While at the top one could appreciate what a good view of the bay and beaches the German artillery must have had while we were landing on the beaches. We also saw results of the battle – wrecked transport, tanks and many graves.

At the beginning of October we left the Serretelle airstrip, and preceded by American infantry, we moved, travelling on our own trucks north towards Naples. At intervals during this journey literally hundreds of Italian soldiers came down towards the road to surrender. Any of them that were armed we relieved of their weapons. They were then paraded into squads of about fifty men. After establishing who was the senior man, he was instructed to march south and report to the Allied authorities.

We continued to make our way north, and eventually after the capture of Naples we occupied Cappadichino, the city airport. Our first day on the aerodrome was spent trying to get some semblance of order and to be ready to receive aircraft. There was the usual bomb disposal routine and the search for possible booby traps. Despite our vigilance somebody got into the airfield perimeter during the night (we suspected Italians) and set fire to one of our fuel dumps.

Our CO located a convent quite near to the airport. The nuns had fled to Rome during the fighting. It proved to be an ideal billet for the Unit with its two-tier iron beds and mattresses. Shortly after reaching Naples I had a problem with one of my arms which was very swollen. I was admitted to a large hospital in Naples which had been taken over by the military. My problem was diagnosed as blood poisoning, probably a legacy of an incident on the day we occupied Bone in North Africa where during a raid by enemy fighter aircraft I sustained a flesh wound on the arm which was dressed and apparently healed.

29 October. The CO visited me in hospital to advise that the Unit had been ordered to move the next day to the Adriatic side of Italy. He said that if I felt fit enough to travel he would arrange for my immediate discharge from hospital. Alternatively I could remain in hospital but there would be little chance of me rejoining the Unit. I left the hospital with the CO.

30 October. On the road to Gisia del Colle which is about 30km inland from Bari. We are now back to living in tents. We used ridge tents housing twelve men, six to each side. Very cramped and not so comfortable. The Unit was given various tasks, but again it was obvious to all that we were not performing the tasks for which we had been trained. We remained there for about six weeks, and we were very much under-employed. On 5 November ten of our trucks plus 30 men were used to ferry 500 Spitfire long-range tanks from the docks at Taranto to the airfield. On 14 November a number of our men were used to drive vehicles from Taranto to Bari.

5 November. One hundred and forty nine aircraft tyres were collected from Taranto docks. On 14 November a number of our men were used to drive vehicles from Taranto to Bari.

19 November. The Unit was made responsible for servicing 322 Wing's High Altitude Flight consisting of six Spitfire Mk. IX. The workload was increased when the Unit took over the maintenance of all four squadrons comprising the 322 Spitfire Wing. This was to prepare for the Wing's departure from Gioia. During this period we experienced some very wet and stormy weather.

16 December. We move to Foggia. The Unit was assigned a number of duties while at Foggia. One particular job in which I was involved was the preparation and bombing up of 150 Squadron Wellington Bombers. This squadron had been flown specially from England to undertake a bombing raid on the city of Sofia in Bulgaria. Bearing in mind the time of year this was quite a hazardous flight. All the aircraft returned from this raid, but I do remember a young rear gunner on an aircraft to which I been assigned being so frozen stiff we had to use the external 'Dead Man's Handle' to remove him from the turret.

The underemployment of the Unit was certainly having its effect on everybody. The Unit had a first-class show called 'Juffs', and a performance was given in the Flagella Theatre in Foggia., and was appreciated by the audience which consisted mainly of American troops. We had a Christmas Day when we other ranks were served in accordance with tradition by our officers and senior NCOs. During the early part of January 1944 we experienced very heavy gales with some tents and equipment being damaged.

14 January 1944. On this day we were paraded and those of the Unit that qualified, that was the majority, were presented with the Africa Star ribbon.

18 January. The Unit has its first death. Sgt. Vic. Snape while riding one of the Unit's motorcycles (it was a German BMW we had taken possession of in North Africa) was in collision with a British Army truck and was killed. I was a member of the funeral party. It was a moving ceremony with Bill Mason playing 'The Last Post' on his trumpet. This was a tragedy for the 23 year old Sgt. Snape because within two weeks we were to learn the Unit was being withdrawn from the campaign, disbanded, and returned to England. Vic. Snape's grave is No. 15D14 in Bari cemetery on the road from Foggia towards Manfredonia.

At this time there was much discussion among the lads as to our future activity. One of the possibilities being discussed was the possible landing in Yugoslavia to operate a landing strip in the mountains with fighter aircraft to support the Tito partisans. Some of us did meet some men and women Tito partisans in Bari. We got news of the Anzio landings of 22 January which brought fresh hopes that perhaps we would soon be in action again.

It was on the morning of Thursday 27 January 1944 we were paraded and the CO told us the devastating news that the Unit was being disbanded. We found this difficult to accept. After all the actions in North Africa, Sicily and Salerno. Our CO Flt/Lt. Wheadon and our Engineering Officer WO Drayton had both been awarded MBEs and four men in our Unit had been mentioned in Despatches. In addition the Unit itself had been commended for its performance by the Air Officer Commanding Eastern Air Command. Despite this we were being disbanded! What a waste!

28 January. We paraded and goodbye speeches were made because our officers were being flown to Cairo. Our arms and equipment were handed in to a nearby Air Stores Park.

30 January. We were taken by trucks to the local rail sidings where we boarded cattle trucks, twenty five men to a wagon. Our rail journey took us over the snow-clad Apennine mountains which in unheated wagons was not too pleasant. At the end of the rail journey we were transported to Portici, a suburb of Naples. I was billeted in a boarding house with a veranda from which I could stand and admire Vesuvius.

7 February. The Unit having been disbanded, we were now aware that we were being sent back to England. However, some of the lads were disappointed. I think eleven men were informed they were to join squadrons in Italy. I know that one of those to be bitterly disappointed was Cpl. Williams who I had been with since joining the R&R Party at Croydon in 1941. On this day we boarded a troopship, HMT *Lancashire*, in Naples harbour and set sail for Algiers. It was a terrible journey because we experienced some really violent storms. I was told that those storms were the worst experienced for fifty years. All I know is that I, in company with most aboard, suffered from sea sickness for the entire trip.

11 February. Arrive at Algiers and immediately disembarked, walking across the dock to another vessel, the P&O liner *Strathnaver*. As soon as we are aboard we set sail in company with two other ships, the old Cunard vessel *Stirling Castle* and a submarine depot ship. My understanding was that this small convoy was to make the journey unescorted. It was certainly stressed that everybody was to wear their white life jackets at all times. The vessel was packed with troops. Many of the men were being sent home because for various reasons they were unfit for service overseas. It was obvious that a fair number of men were suffering from mental disorders, shellshock etc. Some of the expressions used were 'Bomb happy' and 'Sand happy'.

We were in sight of friendly shores on 20 February, and we lay off Liverpool. On the 21 February a message on the ship's Tannoy reminded everyone of their duty-free allowance in spirits and cigarettes. We were also reminded that it was an offence to take ashore items taken from the enemy, and we were told that everybody would be subject to a search when leaving the ship. That night under cover of darkness many items were thrown over the ship's rail. I myself still had the German Schmeiser machine pistol which I had acquired in North Africa. I threw this over the side. One of my pals had a German radio transmitter/ receiver complete with power pack. This was a very efficient piece of equipment which was also consigned to the deep. As it turned out, only officers from all three services and naval personnel of all ranks were subject to a search on disembarkation.

22 February. We disembarked at Gladstone Dock, Birkenhead, being greeted by a band, and ladies handing out goodies like fruit, chocolate and cigarettes.

I have never smoked a cigarette. While serving overseas each person was given fifty cigarettes a week. I was everybody's best friend – they all wanted my cigarettes. I probably had the largest stock of chocolate, which was always useful in North Africa, Sicily and Italy because a bar of English chocolate was like currency, and useful for getting your washing done or getting information.

After disembarking we were transported to Blackpool where we stayed until 25 February. We all then proceeded on two week's disembarkation leave, with the advice that we would be receiving while on leave details of our new units. Our specialised Commando Unit having been disbanded, we would now be posted to ordinary RAF units.

3232 SC IN MALTA, SICILY AND ITALY
DS (Dougie) Went

While serving in the Canal Zone in Egypt with No. 5 ARU and being thoroughly fed-up with the uneventful existence stripping down pranged Whimpies (wrecked or damaged Wellington bombers) which had been brought in from the desert, and, I suppose, being envious of those who were serving up in the 'blue', and seeing some action, my 'oppo' Johnny Palmer (sadly long deceased) and I responded to a notice on Daily Orders for volunteers to undertake hazardous duties.

Within days we found ourselves on the night troop train from Ismalia to Jerusalem bound for No. 28 PTC. After arriving at Jerusalem we were soon aboard a local bus rattling our way to an RAF Regiment Battle Training School at Hadera on the Mediterranean coast. My main recollection of Hadera was the tragic drowning of two of our lads while swimming near the camp in a very rough sea, one being Cpl. 'Dinty' Moore who I remember well, but I don't recall the other fellow.

As I held a driving licence and had driven 3-ton lorries before joining up, I was keen to be one of the Unit's drivers, and eventually became co-driver with Cpl. Baylis, a Canadian armourer. We drivers were sent to the Combined Operations training establishment at Kabrit in the canal zone for instruction in the water-proofing of our vehicles. I remember a group of us water-proofing a 3-ton truck and when the time came to test our handiwork the vehicle was reversed on to an LCT which was then taken out into a nearby lake. The LCT turned shorewards and the ramp was lowered at what was considered a suitable place. Cpl. Bob Berry, who was the driver, started the engine and proceeded down the ramp and slowly disappeared beneath the water. A bedraggled Bob emerged through the side window, much to everyone's amusement.

Having been equipped with our transport – 3-ton Canadian Chevrolets, I spent time at Helwan south of Cairo and also Aboukir near Alexandria – ostensibly to gain experience on, and pick up spares for, Kittyhawks and Spitfires respectively. The time came to take the trucks full of spares etc. to the docks to be loaded on to the cargo ship only to discover on arrival that the dockside cranes had a maximum weight limit of 5 tons. As the unladen weight of the Chevs. was about four and a half tons, much of the equipment had to be jettisoned – what happened to the excess is any-body's guess.

Subsequently the personnel of 3232 was embarked on a dreadful old French tramp steamer called the Cap St. Jacques bound for Malta. It took seven days to reach Valetta Grand Harbour in a convoy at a speed of about four or five knots, frequently coming to a standstill while the destroyer escort whizzed around dropping depth charges. No sign of any U boats, but the north African coastal waters were littered with wrecks which would have been picked up by the destroyer's Asdic. I spent most of the voyage up on the foc'sle manning a Bren gun. I remember washing clothes by tying them to a rope and hanging them over the side. They soon dried, if somewhat salty in the hot June sun.

After we arrived at Malta we were put into a primitive tented camp on top of the cliffs on the south coast. Maltese civilians were living in caves below. I think the place was called Dingli. Whilst there we worked with No. 322 Wing Spitfires at Taquali airfield which was a few miles from the camp. We were ferried back and forth each day by truck. One afternoon at Taquali two of our lads walking along the perimeter were killed by a McConnachy bomb left over from a Jerry air raid.

On a lighter note, one afternoon having finished work early long before the transport was due to pick us up, eight of us decided to hitch-hike back to camp. We were picked up by an army 3-tonner driven by a Maltese. One of us, I think, Bob Berry, got into the cab with the driver and the rest of us piled on to the back of the truck. It had no tilt but the support rails were in place. We had no sooner got going than the CO's jeep driven by Cpl. Geordie Steele, who was in charge of the MT Section, came up behind us. We signalled him to drive alongside and all seven of us smartly dropped down from the truck into the jeep while in motion. Geordie then accelerated past the truck to the sheer amazement on the face of Bob and driver.

Our landing in Sicily was delayed for a few days because of the failed airborne attack on the Gerbini satellite airstrips near Catania. Eventually we landed on the beach (dry landing) at Syracuse and assembled with our transport on the outskirts of the town, during which time we had a 'shufti' around the nearby houses and came away with various items of clothing – mainly hats! Bowlers, trilbies, ladies' hats – you name it. When we moved off bound for the airstrip at Lentini wearing that headgear, the CO, Flt.Lt. Paton pulled us up and suggested that an end be put to the fancy dress parade.

Not long after we had landed at Syracuse we were standing around our trucks when who should drive up but General Montgomery. Most of us were shirtless. He obviously wanted to know who we were, and after being told he handed round packets of Woodbines and then drove off. Some time later when the Unit was at Bari another incident occurred concerning the General, although I cannot vouch for its authenticity. Sgt. McManus was driving one of the Unit's trucks accompanied by Freddie Pizarro (a Londoner of Italian extraction). As they were driving along a following Staff car was attempting to overtake them, and I gather that Sgt. McManus was not being very co-operative until Freddie P. remarked that the car following contained the General. Sgt. McManus swiftly pulled over to let them pass.

To return to our time in Sicily, I remember going with 'Yank' Bayliss a couple of times up towards where the action was taking place to see what we could find in the way of abandoned vehicles etc. I picked up a Mauser rifle and ammo. from a dead German. It had no bolt but I managed to get one later. We also removed a couple of spring beds from an abandoned farmhouse. I took mine in the back of my truck for the rest of the time I was in Sicily and Italy.

One morning while working with 244 Spitfire Wing at Lentini, I saw two aircraft flying low over the runway. At first I thought they were ours until I saw the German markings. They were two ME109s in fact. They didn't open fire but disappeared over the hills towards Catania. The next night both the Lentini airstrips were bombed – not too much damage was done to our strip but the 322 Wing airstrip was badly damaged, and there were some casualties. Several delayed action bombs were dropped, one not far from flying control. The bomb was marked by a ring of empty oil drums. Next day the pilot of a visiting Whitney which was festooned with radio aerials landed and parked just outside the drums. Soon afterwards the bomb exploded and covered the Whitney with debris. An elderly couple were sitting outside a nearby farmhouse, but neither was hurt. At the time of the raid we were at the camp which was about a mile from both airstrips. While the raid was going on most of us had taken cover except for Yank Bayliss who was standing on top of his truck giving a running commentary.

I remember one night the Unit moving along a very dusty mountainous road to another airstrip. On arrival we were attacked by clouds of mosquitoes. Fortunately next morning we were ordered back to Lantini because we were in range of German artillery. At Lantini we used to get red wine from a local farm and collected it in cleaned-up jerry cans. On one occasion one of the lads whose name was Woolridge was stopped just in time from pouring himself out a mug of cellulose dope. (A special type of varnish used in repairing and renovating the fabric on aircraft)

After the fall of Sicily we moved on to a marshalling area near Catania, then drove up to Messina ready to cross the straits to Reggio Calabria. On arriving at Messina we were told to hang about for a while as the army hadn't arrived! When we landed at Reggio we were accompanied by a newsreel cameraman who filmed us coming off the LST. I thought no more about this until about eighteen months later when with 3210 in India I was watching a newsreel in an open-air cinema outside Calcutta when, lo and behold, there we were (3232) apparently driving off the LST at Salerno, according to the commentator. Somebody somewhere had got their wires crossed. After landing at Reggio we moved on to the airport having met no opposition apart from hoards of Italian soldiers wanting to surrender to us. After a few nights in the open air we were housed in a winery, sleeping amongst the great vats and other wine making machinery. The grape harvest hadn't yet begun.

The airfield being close to the sea, some of the lads would go fishing on a home-made raft fashioned from oil drums and planks of wood tied together with rope. They used Italian hand grenades to stun the fish. When the supply of grenades ran out they used gun cotton instead. On one occasion disaster almost befell them when the raft disintegrated, pitching them into the water. No-one was hurt, but they lost their catch.

We moved from Reggio to Lecci where we operated a Spitfire pool at an ex-Italian airforce base. There were a number of Italian Savoia Machetti planes and also Machetti 202 single engined fighters on the airfield. One day I was detailed to pick up a load of 100 octane petrol in jerry cans from Brindisi. One of the lads named McLaughlan came with me. On the way I was overtaking a slow-moving convoy of South African lorries when I had to brake rather sharply. The road being wet and greasy and very smooth, the result was that the truck skidded off the road and through a low dry-stone wall. There was little damage and I managed to reverse the truck back on to the road, with the help of a passing army vehicle, and continued my journey. My passenger suffered no harm, and the only help I got from the South Africans were cheers and jeers and the two finger sign. The sequel to this incident occurred some weeks later by which time we were in Bari when the steering completely failed as I was reversing. When it was dismantled it was found that the steering column had been cracked through for some time. Needless to say I kept quiet about the earlier incident.

During our stay at Bari we lived in tents among olive trees by the side of the airfield, using a farmhouse as the domestic site. It was there that I drank Anisette for the first and last time. When it was time to go back to the tent I found I couldn't stand and had to crawl back on my hands and knees.

On 2 December 1943 we had a grandstand view of the notorious air-raid on Bari docks, when seventeen Allied ships were sunk. Next day it was rumoured that mustard gas had been released into the harbour from one of the ships. Some years after the war I came across a book about the raid in which the mustard gas incident was the main topic. The Powers-That-Be were severely criticised by the author for refusing to confirm that mustard gas was present. The start of the raid began at roughly 19.00 hrs. when a flare was dropped immediately over the air-field which at the time was jam-packed with US transport aircraft. The whole area was lit up like daylight. Myself and another member of the Unit hoofed it smartly into the surrounding countryside, jumping over what appeared to be a stream. I misjudged and landed in what turned out to be an open sewer. After covering what seemed a safe distance from the airfield we stopped beside an outcrop of rocks and watched the raid take place. There were two massive explosions about an hour apart. Next day when I drove past the docks there was devastation everywhere.

A rather nice house a few miles from the town was taken over by the Unit for use as a sort of rest camp. A local Italian lady was recruited to act as landlady, providing comfort and sustenance for the troops, but not for long as rations began to disappear at an alarming rate.

At the onset of winter in southern Italy we only had our tropical kit, so we were issued with battle dress and greatcoat – mine being second-hand and well worn. By the time we left Italy in February 1944 and ended up in Blackpool prior to disembarkation leave my trousers had split across the seat but that didn't deter me! After a few pints I would go to the Tower Ballroom with my mates, but not daring to take off my greatcoat.

The Unit having been disbanded, I was posted to 13 MU Henlow, not too far from home, but what a contrast! After active service in Sicily and Italy to suddenly be pitched back into a strictly regimented eight – five existence, and having to march back and forth twice a day from the quarters to the hangars. Even more of a contrast was when I was sent on a month's detachment to Hawksley's aircraft factory at Brockworth near Gloucester, working on a production line assembling Albemarles, alongside civilian workers who were of course paid much more than us. By way of a sop we were given an issue of free cigarettes. After my return to Henlow all was to change.

One day when a notice appeared on daily orders asking for volunteers for the Servicing Commandos, I lost no time in responding and soon found myself with No. 3210 at Andover, together with LAC Overton (ex-3226), who had also been in Italy, also Bill Atfield, Bill Pratt and one or two others from Henlow. After two weeks embarkation leave it was on to West Kirby and then on board the troopship Johan van Oldenbarnevelt. After being aboard ten days while various problems with the ship were being sorted out, we missed the convoy and sailed unescorted to Bombay via Colombo, spending Christmas 1944 on board. At Colombo a detachment of WAAF were being disembarked.

After disembarking from the troopship in Bombay we spent a few weeks at Worli transit camp, eventually setting off by train to Calcutta, which took about four days. The train had wooden seats and shutters instead of glass. Sometimes we got off and walked beside the train when it was on uphill gradients.

At Calcutta we lived in a tented camp in Chowringhee in the centre of the city. We were set to work at an MU at Red Road not far from the camp. It was very hot and sticky day and night, and the only respite was the air-conditioned cinema. Because of the climate and conditions I contracted Bullous Impetigo and was smartly whisked off to hospital for a few days, followed by two weeks of very welcome hill leave at Shillong in Assam. After returning to Calcutta VE-Day was celebrated with an issue of British beer.

Some of us went off to various detachments, one of which, at Chakulia in Orissa state, was to deal with damaged Thunderbolts which literally had been sucked up and dropped down again by a passing cyclone. Most of the corrugated iron sheeting from the hangars had also gone, but the thatch on the Indian basha huts in which we were accommodated was left intact. On another detachment at Amada Road I remember being kept awake by wedding celebrations in a nearby village, by the beating of drums and blaring of trumpets.

Back in Calcutta we were engaged in waterproofing our vehicles ready for a landing somewhere when the war with Japan ended. We celebrated in much the same way as on VE-Day. It was decided that we could carry on as planned, and we boarded the troopship *Dunera* at Calcutta. After a few days sailing we were transferred to infantry landing craft and landed on Morib beach in Malaya and spent a wet night in a rubber plantation. We later moved into a nearby kampong (a Malayan village with huts on stilts). The drivers of the Unit were ordered by the CO Flt/Lt. 'Mugs' O'Malley to make our way to Port Dixon where our vehicles would be arriving. How we got there was up to us – we had no transport. However, someone had seen an army 6-ton Mack parked in the vicinity and it was suggested that perhaps we might be able to borrow it. Subsequently the truck was found and arrangements were made with an Indian Havildar (Sgt.) who was in charge of the vehicle. It was agreed that we could borrow it for a short time on condition that it was returned ASAP. It was brought to the kampong and parked off the road a little way. The vehicle identification number was changed with a piece of chalk. It was decided that we would set off for Port Dixon just before day-break. Some apprehension was felt about a bridge that had to be crossed, and which was guarded by Indian sentries. During the evening an army jeep drove past the kampong with a couple of MPs who were looking for the missing Mack. We told them there was one parked along the road: they looked at it but said it wasn't the one they were looking for. It had a different registration number. We set off at the appointed hour with Sgt. Jowett driving, keeping fingers crossed as we approached the bridge. The sentries waved us on, and on we went rejoicing.

On the outskirts of Port Dixon we took over a very nice villa which had probably been a rubber planter's residence. The Mack was then driven into the countryside and abandoned. We learned that our trucks would be coming ashore on LCTs and next day we went down to the shore to wait for them. It was some days before they appeared. In the meantime we unloaded various vehicles belonging to other Units and drove them to a nearby compound. One night, when we were living in the villa in comparative luxury, we were issued with a quantity of Navy rum, which I think was the allocation for the whole Unit. A happy evening was had by all, especially one, who by the end of the evening was quite legless and happy as a sandboy. No names, no packdrill.

Eventually our vehicles arrived and we then picked up the rest of the Unit personnel and drove to Port Swettenham, about 50 miles away where we drove on to LCTs for a very uncomfortable seven-day voyage to Tandjong Priok, where we came ashore and drove to the airfield of Batavia, which was called Kemajoran.

Memories of Kemajoran: Two amply proportioned Dutch sisters (ex-internees) Miep and Fietje, were working in the airport building. Some of us were spending an evening with them and other girls at a dance in one of the internment camps outside Batavia. Transport was provided in the form of one of our trucks. After the dance on the way back to camp the truck stopped to let the girls off. Yours truly, being of a gentlemanly disposition, jumped down from the truck and escorted them to their front door. In the meantime the truck moved off, presumably assuming that I was on to 'a good thing', which unfortunately I was not. So there I was stranded all alone in the suburbs of Batavia. I had left my Sten gun on the truck but still had the magazine and began the lonely trek back to camp in some trepidation, but soon came across another lost soul from another Unit on the camp, which was something of a relief. We eventually found our way back without incident, but it was somewhat scary due to the unstable political situation prevailing at that time.

As a matter of interest I have a match programme for a soccer game between an RAF Eleven and a team of the Batavia Football Union which was played on 2 February 1946. I remember being annoyed at the time because only one player was chosen from 3210, and he was Cpl. Goodwin, a very good half-back. My pal Bill Atfield was an excellent centre half, and the general consensus was that he should have been in the team. Also in the team were two chaps from 3205 – Brown and Fleming. The game was played at Decca Park, Batavia, and the RAF won 2-1. It was quite an affair with the pipes and drums of the 1st Patalia Regiment in attendance.

Other memories of Batavia are of the Japanese POWs who worked like the devil unloading ships at the docks. We used to transport petrol and ammunition etc. in the early days from the docks at Tandjong Priok to Kemajoran. In contrast to the Japs were the Korean POWs – lazy so-and so's. They used to do our dhobi. In the morning, they would take it to the other side of airfield, bringing it back in the afternoon after lounging around in the sun all day.

YOU ARE IN THE ROYAL AIR FORCE, NOT THE ARMY AIR CORPS! AND DON'T FORGET IT!

JR Burt

For much of our time, certainly in North Africa, we were working in forward areas as ground crew to the American Army Air Corps, often with B25 North American Mitchell medium bombers. The co-operation between the two countries was amicable, and air crew and ground crew had a profound respect for the professionalism of the other.

Inevitably Anglo-American compatibility meant that each absorbed the humour and idioms of speech of the other.

At one stage we had a large number of large cylindrical tubes which packaged bomb tail fins. The Americans decided it was a shame to waste them. They were twelve inches in diameter and over three feet long, so they had an idea that they could be used as latrines in place of the 'pit and plank'. They half-buried them in the ground in a vertical position. Complete with lid they made an efficient toilet.

Then they had another bright idea. When the toilets had been in use for some time they unearthed them with their filled contents, replaced the lids and dropped them over their targets. Which was worse for 'Jerry', a bomb or a bucket of …?

Another fun thing for the air crews was to take several cast iron bomb nose plugs, tie them together and attach a label 'Wanted, Pen Friends' and again dropped them over the target.

On a number of German raids on the airfield, the enemy dropped 'crows feet'. These were small cone-shaped triangular metal objects with jagged saw-toothed surfaces. Coming through the air they had the lethal effect of a dagger, and however they fell they always had a wicked upturned edge. Sprinkled on a runway or dispersal point they would play havoc with plane tyres. So, 'tit for tat', they were collected and dropped back over the next target.

All the aircraft had names usually with very artistic cartoon illustrations above them. My particular aircraft was named 'Home For Easter', but as the campaign continued it was re-named 'Home For Thanksgiving', then 'Home For Christmas'. The American crew chief was a full blooded red Indian, indeed both his parents and all his relatives were still on the reservation. The Air Corps was his entire life, and the plane entrusted to him was the centre of his universe; it was his baby. When it was grounded he would sit cross-legged next to it by the hour, playing poker and winning a considerable sum of money. If the plane was on a mission he would fret until it returned. He had a complete distrust of his British ground crew, and viewed them with great suspicion for fear they would harm his protégé.

On one occasion the plane returned from a bombing sortie in pretty bad shape with much of the fuselage and tail riddled with holes. We took a look at it and promised to fix it. One of our skilled riggers set to work with fabric repairs until it was as good as new. During the whole operation our American crew chief followed every move like a hawk; he was far from convinced that the work could be done to bring the plane back to a satisfactory condition. When he saw the final result he was overwhelmed with gratitude. From then on in his eyes the 'Brits' could do no wrong.

As previously mentioned many Americanisms rubbed off on us. A good illustration of this was an occasion when our CO made a visit to Dispersal to see how we were coping. He was a long-service dedicated officer. He approached one of the airmen. 'What are you doing, lad?'

'I'm just gassing up this ship, Sir.'

He received a terse response!

'While you are in the Royal Air Force, airman, you will continue to re-fuel aircraft.'

PART II

Background to Operations in Western Europe

IN SPITE OF HAVING suffered considerable reverses in Russia, North Africa and Italy, by mid-1944 the Germans were still a formidable fighting force, even though to an objective observer, or to a later historian, their situation would seem hopeless.

They had lost Italy, their only European ally of military significance. Moreover, that ally had itself declared war on Germany, and the Italian troops, more suitable for the conditions of mountain warfare on the mainland of Italy, were fighting their former allies well and gallantly. Furthermore, the Allies in Italy were reinforced by a Partisan guerrilla force that was exceedingly effective and growing in strength by the day.

The Yugoslav partisans under Tito were holding down several divisions of crack German troops who were urgently needed elsewhere, but could not be spared.

The Russians were driving westwards steadily and inexorably, and almost everywhere were already west of their pre-war frontiers.

The Luftwaffe, although still theoretically a powerful fighting force, was in fact rarely operational, largely because of lack of fuel.

The U Boat war against Allied shipping had been lost and was abandoned.

Everywhere the Nazi beliefs and principles about Aryan superiority were being shown to be false. The 'untermensch', those 'inferior beings' the Slavs of Eastern Europe, were everywhere driving back and defeating the Aryan forces of The Thousand Year Reich. The Battle of Stalingrad, and the surrender of the proud, battle-hardened Sixth German Army under its commander Von Paulus (who had been appointed Field Marshal by Hitler the day before the surrender) shattered the confidence and destroyed for ever the feeling of omnipotence and superiority which had encouraged the Axis forces since 1940. The battle of Kursk in July 1943 further eroded Axis morale.

At Kursk, six thousand tanks and four thousand aircraft met in combat, and again the Axis forces were defeated. It was the biggest tank battle of the war, and the Germans used some hundreds of the powerful and dreaded Tiger tanks. And still they were defeated.

Much of Europe was ablaze with partisans, resistance and guerrilla activity. In the meantime, the German extermination camps were as busy as ever. It seems inconceivable that at a crisis point in a major war, one of the warring nations should spend so much time and energy in eliminating what presented no threat.

The list of atrocities committed by the Germans and their remaining allies is endless. It was a deliberate policy of terror designed to discourage all support for the partisans. It failed, and much of Europe was ablaze.

Even as late as 15 May 1944, the Germans began a new phase of The Final Solution. After careful planning they began the removal of hundreds of thousands of Jews from Hungary to Auschwitz. Four thousand were to be deported by train every day. The less fit, the old, and young and the sick, were to be gassed immediately on arrival at the camp. From half to two-thirds of every 'consignment' was considered 'unfit', and were immediately slaughtered. The remainder were sent to work in the many factories that had been established around the camp, and which relied on this slave labour. They were not really the lucky ones, for they suffered longer from a regime of incessant and dangerous labour, semi-starvation and irrational cruelty from the guards.

Ten days after the deportations began in Hungary, the ss general in charge of the whole operation proudly reported that 138,870 Jews had been 'despatched to their destination (Auschwitz) in ten days.'

On 31 May the camp administration at Auschwitz reported that it was holding forty kilograms of gold taken from the teeth of Hungarian Jews gassed in the previous fifteen days.

So the Final Solution of the Jewish Problem continued its horrifying activities, and even intensified. For me, nothing shows the horror of the extermination camps so much as a report given to Himmler – the man in charge of The Final Solution – detailing the material collected from those passing into the execution chambers of Auschwitz and other camps in Poland. The list included twenty two thousand pairs of children's shoes, one hundred and fifty five thousand women's coats and three thousand kilograms of women's hair. There was also 'a very considerable amount' of gold. I have no idea of how many gold teeth and worn wedding rings it takes to make up 'a considerable amount', but it must be many thousands, perhaps as many as the 'several millions' of pairs of spectacles stored in a Warsaw warehouse after being removed from victims in the killing sheds.

And of course it must never be forgotten that it was not only the Jews of Europe who perished in those places of horror and terror. Unknown numbers of Russian and other Slav prisoners were also 'processed.' Socialists, Communists, Co-operators, Trades Unionists, homosexuals, Gypsies, 'inadequate' children (the physically or mentally handicapped) – all passed naked into the gas chambers, together with the Jews of Europe.

The myth of the invincible German fighting machine had been shattered at Stalingrad and in the deserts of North Africa. The young men of Hitler's Thousand Year Reich were being driven back out of Russia, almost to the borders of Germany itself. It was time indeed for the Allies to invade Western Europe, to open the Second Front our Russian allies pleaded for. It was time for Operation Overlord, time for D-Day, time for H-Hour.

By dawn on 6 June 1944, eighteen thousand British and American paratroops had landed in Normandy. D-Day had arrived. The paratroopers's task was to capture bridges and disrupt communications. At 6.30 in the morning the first troops landed, Americans in amphibious tanks. At 7.25 the first British troops were ashore, and so were the Canadians.

By midnight of 6 June, one hundred and fifty five thousand Allied troops had landed, and the battle for Europe was well under way.

ALLIED EXPEDITIONARY FORCE

Soldiers, Sailors and Airmen of the Allied Expeditionary Force!

You are about to embark upon the Great Crusade, toward which we have striven these many months. The eyes of the world are upon you. The hopes and prayers of liberty-loving people everywhere march with you. In company with our brave Allies and brothers-in-arms on other Fronts, you will bring about the destruction of the German war machine, the elimination of Nazi tyranny over the oppressed peoples of Europe, and security for ourselves in a free world.

Your task will not be an easy one. Your enemy is well trained, well equipped and battle-hardened. He will fight savagely.

But this is the year 1944! Much has happened since the Nazi triumphs of 1940-41. The United Nations have inflicted upon the Germans great defeats, in open battle, man-to-man. Our air offensive has seriously reduced their strength in the air and their capacity to wage war on the ground. Our Home Fronts have given us an overwhelming superiority in weapons and munitions of war, and placed at our disposal great reserves of trained fighting men. The tide has turned! The free men of the world are marching together to Victory!

I have full confidence in your courage, devotion to duty and skill in battle. We will accept nothing less than full Victory!

Good Luck! And let us all beseech the blessing of Almighty God upon this great and noble undertaking.

Dwight D Eisenhower

Operations in Western Europe

A 'SPROG' GROWS UP

Tom Atkinson

(A sprog was, and perhaps still is, a young, new, inexperienced airman)

Two, four, six, eight, who do we appreciate?
Three, two, one, oh Commando!!!

The war cry of 3210 Servicing Commando

My first posting after training as a Wireless Mechanic was to an Air-Sea Rescue Squadron being formed at Ouston, near Newcastle, and only a few miles from my home.

Our wireless training was at Bolton Technical College, and for the whole six months or so we lived in civilian billets. About six of us were in what was actually a theatrical boarding house, and there was an endless stream of music hall entertainers passing through – vocalists, whistlers, musicians, ventriloquists, and, particularly, chorus girls. The regular chores of potato peeling and washing up were no hardship if some of the girls decided to help. One of the most popular chores was to draw black lines down the back of the girls' legs, in imitation of a stocking seam, before they left for their evening performances, or other engagements.

Altogether, it was a happy time, although, since I had always been useless at any maths beyond the twelve times table, I really had to struggle with the trigonometry and algebra. The last two months was taken up by practical work, and this was taught by grounded wireless operator air crew. We were nowhere near an airfield, but in the basement of the college was the fuselage of a Boulton Paul Defiant, and that old wreck was repeatedly ripped apart and re-assembled. Consequently I at least became proficient at working on VHF – Very High Frequency – radio, IFF (Identification, Friend or Foe) and other bits and pieces used in Fighter Command, although my ignorance of the more complicated items used in bombers was almost total.

Two of us were posted to RAF Ouston, and one of us at least was a very raw airman indeed. My mate, Ginger Johnson, had already served as a GD (aircraftsman, General Duties: a man with no trade) for a year before re-training as a Wireless Mechanic, and was able to introduce me for the very first time to life on a station. The pair of us, both AC2s, found ourselves the only wireless blokes on this new squadron, which was, happily, equipped with Boulton Paul Defiants, and a couple of Walrus Flying Boats. We learned fast.

It was a cushy number, really, and when a couple of WAAF Wireless Operators were posted to us, it became even cushier. They could be left to do the DIS (Daily Inspection of airworthiness) and other routine things, while Ginger and I did repairs and maintenance in the warmth and comfort of the workshop in the hangar. We were also able to help other trades do interesting things like plug changes and even engine changes. Furthermore, we got in quite a bit of flying, acting as lookouts on searches. One chore we could not avoid completely was sitting on the tail planes while the engine fitters ran up the aircraft. The WAAFs simply refused to do that, and I don't blame them.

But the war was going on, and I didn't seem to be doing very much to help. It was all very well fiddling around with AVO meters, oscilloscopes and Meggers in the warmth of the Wireless Workshop, but I wanted something more active. So I began volunteering for anything that might come along. Rejected for aircrew because of a weak left eye, it seemed like a gift from Providence when the notice about Servicing Commandos appeared. I promptly applied, and within days was on my way to Coltishall, where 3210 SC was forming.

After a few days at Coltishall, the Unit moved to Zeals, and, strangely, I have absolutely no recollection of how we travelled. I must say that Zeals was something of a culture shock. Up to then, my life in the RAF had been somewhat sheltered, I suppose, but there was nothing sheltered about life at Zeals.

Of course, we were all supposed to be volunteers, and thus dead keen, and surely the vast majority of us were. Some though, must have volunteered to escape worse things, perhaps a posting to Wick or some other distant and unpleasant post. One Cpl. in my Nissan hut had 'volunteered' as an alternative to fourteen days in the Glasshouse for absence without leave, insubordination, drunkenness and striking a superior officer. He rarely washed, never showered, and was violently drunk every night, thanks to cheap rough cider, the infamous 'Scrumpy'. However, he and a number of his mates soon disappeared, posted back to their Units as unsuitable.

For the rest of us, Zeals was rough, ready and exciting. There was much to learn and much to do. I already held a driving license, although the only vehicle I had driven was my Dad's old Ford Eight. Learning to handle those first three-ton trucks was an experience! They were not the later Bedfords, but battered AECs, with crash gear boxes, a clutch-stop and seemingly no acceleration. Still the MT Sgt., Jerry Jowett, passed me out, and I got my Services Driving Licence.

Our Wireless Section was headed by WO. 'Chick' Taylor, with Sgt. Tony 'Galento' Stanford. Chick was an ex-apprentice, and Tony Galento a long-serving VR. Tony, by the way, got his nickname because he resembled a heavyweight boxer of the day, 'Two-ton Tony' Galento.

I think there were only two other Wireless Mechanics and three or four Wireless Operators in the Unit. As it happened, only two were experienced with the VHF equipment of Fighter Command, and therefore I found myself, as a newly promoted Cpl., in charge of the Wireless Trades Workshop.

After Zeals and our initial toughening-up we headed for Inveraray and Combined Ops. Training. The long trip north, in our own trucks, was enlivened for me, at least, by the incident of the Adj.'s tin hat.

'Timber' Woods, a rather comical hard-drinking lad, was in the truck in front of mine, and during one long stretch, Timber simply had to relieve his over-full bladder. It happened that for some reason the Adj. had left his tin hat in that truck, and, very understandably, Timber used it as a useful, indeed the only, receptacle. Suitably relieved, Timber emptied the contents over the tail board just at the very moment that one of the Dispatch Riders, 'Darkie' Davies, I think it was, accelerated past, and Darkie caught it full in the face.

It wasn't exactly a conversation that ensued between the two of them, more in the nature of a slanging match, with Timber insisting that the ditched liquid was only tea, and Darkie no more than half persuaded. A little later, when the Adj. came down the convoy looking for his tin hat, he, in turn, was no more than half convinced that its dampness was only condensation.

Some time after that came the issue of khaki battledress, and that began a period of serious bullshit. Never had there been so much spit and polish on boots, shining of cap badges and burnishing of brass. Nothing else, in fact could have so cemented our esprit de corps. We bought our own shoulder lanyards, colour-coded to show different Flights, and illicit 'Commando' shoulder flashes appeared, as well as the licit 'Combined Ops.' badges. We carried our sheathed hunting knives on our belts. We were young, proud, fit and anxious to see some action..

What we got was a long series of airstrips and dromes, where we serviced whatever was to be serviced. Rarely together as a Unit, individual Flights were detached here and there, almost as Flying Columns of tradesmen, going happily with our trucks wherever those mysterious Powers-That-Be directed us, and all of us mucking in together to do whatever was necessary, whether it was cooking a meal or changing an engine. Route marches in full battle order, driving trucks through deep water, day and night exercises, using all our different weapons on ranges whenever we could – I think we all knew that those things were preparing us for the real thing, the invasion of Nazi-occupied Europe.

Before that happened, though, there was a serious blow to our morale. We were divested of our khaki uniforms and reverted to Air Force Blue. Our unique uniform, a mixture of Air Force and Army, had distinguished us, we felt, as something different and special. We were almost all volunteers, and we greatly valued the distinguishing marks of our uniqueness. To lose them was quite a blow. Apart from that, there was another serious reason why we should not have reverted to Air Force Blue. We knew well that when The Day came, we would be working in dusty and muddy conditions. A dusty Air Force Blue was not much different from a German Field Grey, and we feared, rightly, that we could be mistaken for the enemy. I don't know whether anyone from an sc Unit was actually shot in error, but certainly there were some anxious cries of 'J'ai Anglais, you stupid buggers', especially when confronted by members of the French Resistance. Two members of 3210 were brought back to our encampment, dusty and dishevelled, and very angry, by the Resistance, who seemed to be quite unhappy at losing their prize of supposed German prisoners.

So, at last, we embarked for the invasion, as others in this book have recorded. At last we were doing the job for which we had trained for so long.

But were we really? Certainly we were in the first few weeks. We re-armed and re-fuelled, repaired and inspected and made countless journeys to the beach head dumps for ammunition and fuel and food. We were busy, hard-worked and happy. However, as the British advance got hung up around Caen, we were given less and less useful work. Indeed, towards the end of June, much of what we were doing seemed to be jobs thought up to keep us busy – salvaging crashed aircraft and gliders, for example. We even had days off and organised trips to Bayeux and Omaha Beach. Chick Taylor and I made a number of unauthorised 'scrounging trips' in the Wireless Workshop truck, usually returning with enough milk and eggs to provide excellent omelettes for the bods. I can recommend omelettes stuffed with diced Spam or Soya Sausages, although I haven't tasted them for the last fifty years.

Not that we needed extra food. Our Compo Rations were acceptable enough, although I could never again face tinned meat – Maconachie's Irish Stew and Oxtail and Haricot saw to that. I remember our Section Sgt., Tony Galento, trying to withhold and hoard the ration of boiled sweets from the boxes, arguing that they should be kept for an emergency. He was told, very strongly, that we were in an emergency, and demanded our full ration. We suspected that Tony had hoped to do a bit of extra personal bartering with the French, who held sweets in high regard, even above chocolate.

For some undiscovered reason, Tony also tried to hold back some of the ration of toilet paper. The ration was three sheets per man per day – 'one to clean your bum, one to polish your bum and one to write home to your Mum'. Tony thought two should be enough and that we should build up a stock 'just in case'. Again, he was disillusioned.

There wasn't a whole lot to laugh about during those last weeks of June and early July. However, I do remember Jock Keable trying to take a shower during a brief rainstorm. At the crucial moment, just when he was well soaped up, the rain stopped, and he was left soap-covered with no water available to rinse off. I suppose it is not really very funny, actually, but it seemed so at the time.

Days were spent playing cards, arguing and sleeping, and growing increasingly restless. And the restlessness was well-founded. We were in the midst of a great war to free the world of an obnoxious terrorism, and we spent days arguing about the relative merits of popular singers, and footballers, and whether we owed a debt of gratitude to Winston Churchill. Morale was really at a very low point, and it was no surprise when one day our very popular MT Sgt., Jerry Jowett, appeared with a list of men volunteering for service in the Far East. I no longer remember how long the list was before it was delivered to the CO, but I do recall that my name was not on the first sheet of names, ranks and numbers.

I have no idea whether our CO, 'Mugs' O'Malley, took any action about our request, but within a week the whole Unit was on the way to Arromanches for embarkation and return to the UK. So ended 3210's part in the battle for Europe.

Well, not quite. Based at Thruxton, the Unit, either as a whole or in detachments, resumed the routine of re-fuelling, re-arming and servicing.

And, of course, a fair amount of route marching and similar exercises. We had a week of disembarkation leave, and then, a great loss, we had to turn in the 3-ton Bedford trucks to which we had grown so attached. I lost the Wireless Workshop, with its benches, cupboards and shelves, and all its elaborate wiring. Chick Taylor was a very proficient scrounger, and had ensured that we were well equipped. At one time, until the smell grew intolerable, we even had a deer skin rug on the floor. That appeared mysteriously one day about a month after we left Inveraray, which just happened to be in the midst of the Duke of Argyll's deer forest.

I believe it was at Thruxton that Pretty Billy Hannaford, our Armaments Officer, had an embarrassing experience. In those far-off days a quite popular contraceptive was Rendell's Tablets. One of these was meant to be inserted into the appropriate orifice before action commenced. The tablets were the choice of those fastidious types who, while properly wishing to use a contraceptive, yet refused to 'wash their feet with their socks on'. And if you don't understand the expression, then you have led a sheltered life.

The occasion was a Friday night dance to which a number of WAAFs and nurses had been invited. The time was just after ten, when the pubs. had closed, the floor was crowded and the band swinging merrily. Dougie Blair was on the door – and this is really his story. Dougie, the Orderly Room clerk, was perhaps the only man in the Unit who could be completely trusted to stay sober and also keep a strict check on the takings – sixpence admission.

Pretty Billy appeared at the door in some perturbation, and demanded that Dougie leave his post and immediately produce a mug of tea. This of course he did – and I am pretty sure that Dougie would have been able to produce a mug of tea if anyone had asked him as we went ashore from a Landing Craft. Taking it outside, and into the bushes, Dougie discovered a young nurse in tears and quite literally foaming very liberally at the mouth. A frustrated Pretty Billy stood by while the universal panacea of tea was administered and the girl cleaned up. It appeared that Pretty Billy had taken the girl outside, for what purpose I know not, given her the Rendell's tablet and asked her to use it whilst he went further into the bushes, perhaps to admire the stars.

The girl, obviously an innocent, did use the tablet. She chewed it, and immediately began liberally foaming at the mouth. Having got her cleaned up, Dougie was instructed to say nothing to anybody about the incident, and Pretty Billy disappeared back into the hall, at least temporarily frustrated.

Of course the story could not be kept a secret, and very soon the Irishman Paddy Bridges, 'The Bard of B Flight' had added two more verses to his Ballad of 3210. This was sung to the tune of 'Phil the Fluter's Ball', and was entitled 'Mugs O'Malley's Balls' – Mugs O'Malley being our CO. Unfortunately, I cannot now remember much of it, but it recorded in somewhat blank verse the character and doings of the Unit.

Have you heard of 3210,
The Servicing Commando.
Things were going well with them,
They were a happy band O...
With a toot on the flute,
And we're always on the fiddle O,
Now we'll all get brown
Like a herring on the griddle O
Up, down, hands down,
Across and to the wall,
Oh, hadn't we the gaiety
With Mugs O'Malley's Balls...
Pretty Billy Hannaford was skulking round the Waafery,
Mr. Ramsbottom appealing to the men,
Adj. Harry Schofield was sitting in his office chair,
Helping Chicko Taylor tie ribbons in his hair.

And so, interminably, on.
But events were moving on, and so were we, for embarkation and the Far East.

SIGNAL FROM THE AIR OFFICER COMMANDING, 83 GROUP

TO:- 3210 Servicing Commando
FROM:- No 83 Group, Main hq. Signal No. 0.216
28 July 1944

To O.C from A.O.C. (.)
I wish to thank you and all ranks of No. 3210 Servicing Commando for the fine efforts you have all put up in support of the invasion of Europe (.) Both I and my staff are grateful for your loyal and successful work, and we regret much that you should now have to leave us (.) We know that you have often wished for more work than has been given you (.) This reflects great credit on your enthusiasm, esprit de corps and efficiency (.) The best of luck for the future.

Signed A.H. Montgomery, A/CDRE
T.O.O. 282000B

Serial No 11
Page .1
Date 5.5.44

Unit Routine Orders
by
Flight Lieutenant A.O'Malley, Officer Commanding, 3210 Servicing Commando

1.   PERSONAL MESSAGE FROM THE COMMANDING OFFICER

On the Anniversary of our Unit's formation. I desire to express my appreciation for the keenness, willingness and co-operation of all ranks during the past year.

I regret that owing to the operational commitments the anniversary Party has had to be postponed, but it is intended to hold it in the very near future, but at a venue as yet unknown. I hope and trust that the spirit of the Unit will remain at its present level throughout the somewhat grimmer days of the not too distant future, and that all ranks will endeavour to keep up the Commando tradition of being able to "Dish it out and Take it :- repeat "Take it and live up to the Unit motto SPECTEMUR AGENDO = By our deeds are we known.

Signed A. O'Malley F/Lt.

OVERTURE TO OVERLORD
George Revell

I suppose that all those of us involved in that great operation have stories to tell. Mine is that of an 'erk's' eye view, as the RAF were represented on the ground during Overlord, as well as in the air. In fact there were those who remained on the sea in the Fighter Director Tenders, Air Sea Rescue etc. (An 'erk', by the way was the lowest RAF ranking, the equivalent of an Army private.)

For me, it had all begun about 15 months earlier when, as a Leading Aircraftsman Fitter 2A, I had volunteered for duty with the RAF Servicing Commandos, having just recently returned from taking Spitfires on aircraft carriers to Malta during the siege. We had been given some additional military training as well as a wider spread of technical experience, taking care of the various types of fighter, reconnaissance and ground attack aircraft in the 2nd Tactical Airforce which was formed to support the Second Front when it came.

During the year or so leading up to 'D-Day' we had travelled the countryside working in conjunction with the squadrons of Spitfires, Hurricanes, Typhoons, Tempests, Mustangs and Mosquitoes, even getting involved with the Bomber Command 'Heavies' when they were diverted to what were normally fighter stations due to damage or bad weather.

I assume that each of the several Servicing Commando Units were similar to 3207, which was the one I joined when it formed at Tangmere on 1 April 1943. Certainly a number of Units formed about the same time. After a week or two 3207 moved off to start our additional training at RAF Zeals down in Wiltshire. There we were licked into shape by RAF Regiment instructors and learned the basic 'Battle Drill' that had been established as a result of experience gained by the British Army. From this evolved the formation of sections and flights which also constituted our own technical organisation. Each section had a corporal in charge and contained a balanced quota of tradesmen, engine fitters, airframe fitters, electrical and instrument trades. These were represented in smaller numbers in each flight, which consisted of three sections. As each section totalled about twelve, the strength of a flight was about 36 with a sergeant in charge. In addition to four such flights, each pair of which were controlled by a Flight Sergeant, a Headquarters Flight completed the unit, to provide the necessary administrative support, including Orderly Room, Catering, MT maintenance etc.

During our few week's stay at Zeals we were all given some driving instruction by British School of Motoring so that we were capable of moving a vehicle with some degree of safety! The Unit transport was the 3-ton Bedford truck with a couple of 15 cwts, 2 water bowsers, 2 Jeeps and a few motor bikes. Drivers were to be 'B' Class, in other words any tradesman who passed a proficiency test and thus could hold a service driving license. Most of those selected to hold licenses were those who had driven before in civvy street. Thus by the time we had finished at Zeals we had drawn additional kit and a start had been made to get the Unit equipment together. Our additional personal kit included khaki battledresss, denims and greatcoat, army boots and gaiters, khaki webbing in place of our blue and our personal arms – rifles for most, with a Bren per section, and the odd Boyes Anti-Tank Rifle in each half. Although we wore khaki we retained our RAF caps, badges and insignia, as well as the RAF 'Best Blues' for such occasion as required it to be worn.

The Unit transport was put into use to form a convoy to take us north to the Combined Operations Training Centre at Inveraray on Loch Fyne. We staged through RAF Wittering and Carlisle, night-stopping at each one. I remember that after Loch Lomond we reached that climb up the road known as 'Rest and be Thankful', and in our case to off-load from our truck and get out and push!

At Inveraray, on the estate of the Duke of Argyll, we continued our training – assault courses, unarmed combat, demonstrations of various vehicles being developed for use in beach landings etc. After a few days of this we embarked on assault craft and joined a ship at anchor on the loch, using scrambling nets to board.

Once aboard we were allocated to 'serials' and briefed for an exercise which would involve re-embarking into assault craft at first light next morning for an assault landing and forced march inland to an imaginary airfield, being attacked en route by 'enemy forces' on land and from the air. The navy issued us with hammocks and showed us how to sling them, so that when the various lectures and briefings were over we could try to sleep before our 'serials' were called early next morning.

As I remember it the loch was reasonably calm as we went down the scrambling nets fully equipped the next morning and loaded into the assault craft by sections. When the craft was loaded the crew cast off and steamed away up the loch at a good turn of speed to produce enough spray to ensure that all of us were pretty well soaked before heading in for the beach where it was 'Down Doors!' as the craft grounded, and we were away up the beach at the double.

Our journey on foot on land was across open country, through heather and bracken, rocky streams and grassy banks. After several miles of this, with skirmishes with the enemy ('Thunderflashes' and all) we reached our map reference where we were allowed the luxury of a ride back to camp in army trucks that got us back for camp in time for a well-earned meal.

And so it went on for a couple of weeks, getting more strenuous as the days went by. One of the last events arranged for our benefit was a climb to the top of what we called Donna Quaig (actually Dun Cuaich), a high point a few hundred feet above the Duke's golf course, involving the usual assortment of bracken, scree etc. on the way up and a breathtaking scramble down the other side.

At the end of the course it was considered that we were eligible to wear the Combined Operation badge on our khaki battledress, and we then started the journey south eventually arriving on Romney Marsh at Ivychurch where we found Typhoon squadrons operating under 'field conditions' – no runways except wire mesh 'Somerfield Track' and dispersals.

For many of us this was our first experience under canvas and this provided yet another opportunity to sort out the individual sections. From now on each section lived in its own tent – a bit crowded with 12 or so in each. It travelled in its own truck which was loaded with its share of unit equipment as well as the 'bods' and their personal kit. Each section had a 'trolley acc.' and Chore Horse, which to the uninitiated was a set of heavy duty 12-volt batteries mounted on a trolley with 2 rubber-tyred wheels, used to provide electrical power for engine starting and general electrical servicing of many of the aircraft we took care of. The chore horse had a small petrol engine driving a generator to charge the trolley acc. batteries. Some aircraft, like the Typhoon, had cartridge starting and others like the Mustang could be 'wound up' using a starting handle before engaging the starter to turn the engine over.

In addition to travelling together and living in the same tent, the sections worked together – fitters and riggers paired up, armourers formed teams for re-arming, the rest of the trades took up their own and helped out the others as required. There was some cross-training so that each trade could cope with other trades to some extent. The cooks and others who 'volunteered' to prepare meals had to cope with limited facilities and simple rations. Pressure burners, using petrol and cooking utensils, some of which were improvised, were set up under a tarpaulin-shrouded frame out of the wind and rain, and with the magic appetiser of hunger helping, adequate meals were produced for us collectively as a rule. 'Tommy cookers' and 24 hour ration packs were issued on occasion, so that we were individually independent, but generally speaking we were on 'Compo' or bulk rations.

Often the Unit would split into two – one half going to an airfield in one direction and the other half going to another. On arrival we would drive up to the allocated dispersal and off-load the trolley acc. etc., and set up fuel stocks ready for use. The armourers organised themselves with ammo., bombs and rockets, and the 'Instrument Basher' sorted out his oxygen bottles ready for use. A site would be allocated for tents and the cookhouse, and soon the spades would be put to good use providing for the needs of Mother Nature – a good trench, a stout pole, a stretch of hessian and a load of bleach! Comradeship grew out of this situation, and a feeling of well-being with your mates was generated with what seemed no obvious effort.

The art of scrounging is well-known amongst service blokes, especially in war-time and under the mobile conditions we experienced. After all, who would miss a handy-sized bit of coconut matting we 'found' on the morning we happened to be leaving for some place far away? The coconut matting would cover the floor of our tent very nicely, and how about a spare tarpaulin to rig up at the end of the tent to keep some of the gear in?

One particular exercise took place in South Wales with Pembrey Golf Course being used as the Concentration Area. As we waited for the exercise to develop, off-duty time was spent in Llanelly (known as 'Slash' to all and sundry) where we were allowed to visit in khaki battledress complete with Combined Ops. Badges. The local girls were very friendly but somewhat gullible I suppose, as they accepted our story that the badge indicated that we were NAAFI managers!

After a week or so we moved off to Margam and then on to the docks at Port Talbot where we loaded our vehicles and 'bods' on to some merchant ship. We were told that one aspect of the exercise was to try out methods whereby troops would be landed and reach the beach dryshod, so our ship was deliberately beached at high tide in Tenby Bay. We then waited for the tide to go out, the vehicles were off-loaded by the ship's derricks into shallow water and driven ashore without waterproofing. We followed up and off the beach into the Welsh countryside to meet up with the Royal Engineers. They were preparing a wiremesh runway whilst we assembled all the usual fuel and ammunition etc. After a couple of days a

Mustang landed and took off again without much in the way of servicing, but at least it was a token gesture confirming that the army had provided the strip, and the RAF could operate it.

At the end of the exercise we began the journey back to 'somewhere in England' on a Sunday morning. We reached Neath and our vehicle developed a snag which resulted in a stop at the side of the road as the local folk were on their way to chapel. Dave Luckett in our section had his trumpet with him, having been a member of the Salvation Army Band in Coventry, and was having a 'blow', playing 'Bread of Heaven', as I remember. He was doing very well as the local minister approached and asked if he could a chat. The reverend gentleman climbed aboard our Bedford and chatted as we relaxed on the kit in the back of the truck. He complimented Dave on his skill with the trumpet, offered up a prayer and passed round what was left of his pack of cigarettes. He left us to join his congregation as we thought, but came back shortly after with another pack of cigarettes. From then on Jock Murray, who was well known as the section wit, decided that our Bedford would be known as the Hallelujah Chariot, the tent would become the Hallelujah Temple and Dave Luckett was from then on known as Bandsman Luckett. In fact several suitable painted inscriptions appeared over the bedspaces on the tent canvas. I believe Len Cottrell was The Backslider and Jack Edy, our wireless man, whose round chubby fact topped by his tin hat gave him a kind of angelic face, became The Bishop.

And so it went on through the summer and autumn of 1943 – help out at Tangmere or Manston on re-arm and re-fuel, move on to one of the Advanced Landing Grounds among the Kentish marshes and hopfields to take care of the various fighter wings and then away again.

Our section decided we could use a portable radio and as we were all due for leave we each undertook to try and get one. I was fortunate enough to buy a Marconi set complete with dry battery and accumulator, and on return from leave found that no one else had been able to get one, so a day off was organised to allow me to collect the lot. At that time we were operating without our Orderly Room so we had no leave forms 295 or Unit stamp to officially authorise the absence. Our Sergeant (Joe Eyles) told us to write out the necessary on a piece of notepaper and he signed it 'Unit Stamp not available', and away we went, Jock Murray and I, to collect the radio I had organised at my home.

We had 24 hours, from mid-day, and on the way back to Victoria Station we were stopped by the RAF Police. On showing our scraps of note paper the corporal 'snoop' nearly took off and he got more perplexed when we pleaded 'security' when refusing to tell him where our Unit was located. He took us round to his HQ where a sergeant took over and to whom we would only admit that our postal address was 'Blue Group Home Forces', and left him to find out more from his own resources. By midday we were still held by the Service Police but by then they had located the unit and received an explanation. We also got a 6 hour extension and were escorted into the Strand to Catti's Restaurant which was being used as a canteen, to ensure that we got a meal before continuing our journey. This was at the request of the Adjutant of the airfield we were operating from, we later learned.

The 'snoops' were as nice as pie as they saw us on to the train, Jock with the batteries and me with the radio. We got back to the airfield, near Great Chart in Kent, before the extension expired and were glad to hear that Joe Eyles had not got into trouble over the way things had gone.

The radio was much appreciated as a means of entertainment and providing news. It saw service later in Normandy, using accumulators from a German Beetle Tank, I'm told, and later in Burma. I'm told that when 3207 disbanded in Singapore it was decided to raffle the radio among those who had bought it. I wasn't there, but the lads included me in the raffle, and I won, but haven't received the radio yet.

By the autumn we found ourselves living in hutted camps instead of tents at places like Armament Practice Camps (Hutton Cranswick, Weston Hoyland etc.) where Spitfire Squadrons would visit for a couple of weeks. The pilots would attend lectures on the latest techniques and then practice applying them against towed targets. I remember 'Screwball' Beurling, the Canadian 'ace' who had made his reputation in Malta, queuing at a Salvation Army Canteen wagon for his tea and a wad – or bun. He didn't have a mug and the dear lady didn't have one to spare, and was a bit offended by his remark 'Jeez, Mam, what sort of canteen are you running here?' We handled an Australian Spitfire squadron there and the COS kite was damaged on the last day when a trailer bowser (petrol tanker and pump, used to refuel aircraft), parked at the top of a slope in line with the Spitfire, rolled down and damaged a mainplane to such an extent that the mainplane had to be changed by the local Maintenance Unit. 'Sir' was not pleased; evidently the bpwser's brakes were not effective and there was no chock positioned to hold the bowser.

Whilst at Lasham about October/November 1943, servicing Mosquitoes of a Polish Squadron, a new Commanding Officer took over

3207. This was FO Smith, our original CO (FO Ogle) having been found 'unsuitable' by his superiors. The Dutch Navy were operating Mitchells also at the time, and I always remember that their Airgunners were 'erks' like ourselves and had their meals in the cookhouse with us. They had their operational bacon and eggs, which we didn't, but we didn't complain. They deserved good grub.

AN 'ERK' ON D-DAY

George Revell

In trying to write an account of my experiences on D-Day and the days following, my memories are, of course, affected by the passage of time. I have not tried to authenticate any of the details by reference to official sources, and can only offer my recollections of the events.

My Unit, 3207 Servicing Commando of the RAF, had moved into the 'Hotel' during late May. This was the description given to the Concentration Area by Air Vice Marshall Harry Broadhurst. As the AOC No. 83 Group 2nd Tactical Airforce, he had briefed us on the general form the preparations for our part in the 2nd Front would follow. He had visited us in early May and during the briefing had recalled the experience he had with Servicing Commandos in Italy during that campaign. He admired enthusiasm but made the point that, resulting from the attention paid by our contemporaries whilst he was still in the cockpit of his Spitfire, he found it necessary to remind us that there were 'certain parts of his anatomy' that he preferred to be left intact!

Our stay in the 'Hotel' at RAF Old Sarum provided time for water-proofing vehicles, getting things up to scratch and generally relaxing whilst waiting for the next phase of what we thought could be another exercise. We moved out of the Concentration Area down to the Marshalling Area which was also a tented camp, but this time provided by the Army. It was just outside Fareham, I believe – positive location was difficult with signposts etc. removed in support of wartime security. That was the night of June 5/6 and the procedures we followed included the collection of 24 hour personal ration packs, an issue of 20 cigarettes in a flat tin and, in contrast to any previous exercise, picking up a pound's worth of French Francs in new notes.

The following morning started with early breakfast and the move down to the foreshore around Gosport where we were formed into

groups. I found myself with a few others detached from the majority of
3207 personnel, and, together with Mick Ryan, was detailed to board a 3-
ton truck belonging to a Royal Canadian Air Force R&SU positioned in a
side street. Mick and I were both part of No. 2 Section in A (Red Flight)
of 3207 with whom we had trained and operated ever since the day we
formed in April 1943, and this latest situation was completely foreign to
the way we had always exercised. No sign of our Section NCO (Cpl. Taffy
Wetherall) or of Sgt. Joe Eyles, the sergeant in charge of A Flight, as our 3
tonner progressed towards the 'Hards'. Traffic was heavy and a radio
somewhere in earshot provided us with the first advice that this was not
an exercise – the BBC announcement at 0900 to the effect that the
Normandy landing was started.

The 7th Armoured Division (Desert Rats) were moving down to the
Hard with us and when an overhanging motor cycle loaded on one of
their 3-tonners ripped the canvas of our 3-tonner our RCAF Corporal
driver got very upset! He was soon informed that if that was all that could
happen he hadn't much to worry about. One of the Desert Rats
seeing us in RAF Blue remarked that if the RAF were going in, the NAAFI
must be there! Eventually our 3-tonner was driven onto an LCT reversing
on and leading other vehicles so that by the time the ramp was raised and
we cast off our craft was loaded with a selection of vehicles which seemed
to constitute the Air Traffic Control and Operations of a Canadian
Spitfire Wing plus the Coles crane and supporting vehicles of an RCAF
R&SU Salvage Team which would be available for runway clearance etc. I
think the only 3207 vehicle aboard was a 15 cwt driven by Jack Crofts
our MT mechanic, and it was parked about amidships amongst the ambu-
lance, fire tender etc of 127 Wing. We were right aft with the poop of the
LCT reaching up above us.

The LCT moved out into the Solent and anchored in the sunshine with a
view of the mainland and the Isle of Wight. More craft moved in empty,
loaded up and moved out to moor around us. Came midday and Compo
Rations were broken out. I remember the fruit pudding as if were
yesterday! Early afternoon we cast off from our mooring and got under
way. The number of the craft in the convoy was considerable, steaming in
some sort of order. It was not only the quantity of craft that impressed me
but also the strange shapes of some and their loads. In addition to LCTs
and LSTs. and the like loaded with trucks, tanks etc of various shapes and
sizes, there were adaptations with included LCK (Landing Craft Kitchen)
with what seemed to be a selection of Field Kitchens aboard with short
chimneys jutting out at odd angles but eventually pointing upwards. I

assumed these craft would supply hot meals to crews who would be in small craft which had no galley facilities operating off the beach.

I don't remember moving around our LCT very much, but recollect that, in addition to the RCAFelement, I saw a few other 3207 lads on board as well as a few from a sister unit (3209). The evening came and I was wondering what to expect – no officers from either Commando and the only Senior NCO was F/Sgt. Jock Cruikshank, an armourer from 3207, and I didn't see much of him until later on. The crew went about their duties but no indication was given as to how long we would be at sea. There was no instruction on emergency procedures either, although we each had the usual life belt (Mae West, of course) round the waist which you inflated by blowing down a rubber tube connected into the belt.

When darkness came the only noise was engine noise from the craft and the splash of water. I settled down on the kit in the back of the 3-tonner and dozed. About 1.30 I roused and had a look around the convoy. Each vessel was making its own bow wave and leaving a trail with a slight phosphorescent glow. No one had given us any orders – still no briefing, so decided I would load 10 rounds into the magazine of my rifle before settling down on the kit to doze again.

Then it happened – one hell of a bang and a cascade of water followed by flame and shouts of pain. One of the 20mm Oerlikons on the poop of our craft fired a few short bursts and then stopped as I climbed over the tailboard of the 3 tonner and up onto the poop. Looking for'ard the craft was fairly well illuminated by flames which were spreading and increasing in intensity. The LCT slowed down, and I think the engines were stopped. There was obvious heavy damage on the starboard side about midships. The convoy sailed on. A torpedo had struck us, launched from a surface craft – an R boat or E boat, causing the damage and resulting in the fire which very quickly enveloped the vehicles in the area generating heat which was felt throughout the craft. The Coles crane jib glowed, it seemed white hot and began to sag. The forward part of the LCT began to yaw, pivoting about the weakened area.

An MTB (Motor Torpedo Boat) appeared eventually and took off personnel from the for'ard part, before moving out of the way as the for'ard end of the LCT began to break away. I don't know how many got off before the MTB then came round and approached from the stern and on the starboard side. Our craft was pretty low in the water and the fire was still burning. I think it was realised early on that trying to control the fire was out of the question and it was essential to get as many as possible off the for'ard end. The MTB slowed down and was just about hove to on the starboard side, under control about midships but the relative movements in all three planes between us and the MTB was such that getting across the gap to the MTB was a gamble to say the least. A rope was passed from the MTB and made fast aboard us, which helped to keep the separation distance under control to some extent. One or two took the chance of crossing on the rope which meant, as it sagged, they took a ducking but fortunately no-one was crushed as the two vessels came together in the swell. At this point a few more jumped aboard the MTB. One of the first to go was the Canadian Wing Commander Medical Officer, followed shortly afterwards by other officers.

About this time I saw fellows coming back from the midships area and climbing up on to the poop. One of them approached me who I failed to recognise until he spoke. It was Jimmy Wright, an armourer from B Flight of 3207, badly burned and with shoulder and arm injuries. He was wearing a balaclava helmet (cap comforter) which had been some protection but much of the skin of his face was hanging off, but fortunately his eyes seemed undamaged. I found a French Canadian Medical Orderly and brought him to see Jim. He took a quick look, made some remark about not being able to help and took the next opportunity to get across to the MTB. Mick Ryan had been with me throughout and we managed to get Jim into the shelter of one of the gun positions on the poop. The skipper and the rest of his crew mustered on the poop and the MTB cast off. The risk of damage to the MTB and the need for it to pursue its own duties meant she couldn't stay and so we were left to our own devices. The for'ard end finally broke away whilst the rest of the hulk continued to burn though the flames were subdued. As the craft settled in the water wreckage went overboard. The skipper and crew discharged their responsibility by destroying what needed to be destroyed and then broke out the rum, passing a mug full around to warm us up, as by this time we were wet and cold.

We wrapped Jimmy Wright in blankets and gave him a swig and a cigarette whenever he felt like it. Came the dawn and we were well down in the water. The poop remained above water but its deck was awash at times. There seemed to be nothing in sight from our position for some time, until a couple of Lockheed Lightnings flew low overhead and shortly afterwards we saw a small craft approaching. It turned out to be a United States Coastguard cutter which came alongside. We passed Jimmy over and then scrambled over ourselves.

As the Yankee cutter pulled away the skipper of our LCT looked back at what was left of his ship and said to his crew 'There goes the old girl – I knew something would happen to her, just count up her digits.' Her Code Number was still visible – LCT 760 (or was it 670? In any case, it added up to 13!)

The Yanks took us further inshore, making the rounds of various navy vessels which I believe were American, until eventually we were directed to a vessel which was anchored someway off the beach. We went alongside and Jimmy Wright was lifted aboard on a stretcher, and we followed up scrambling nets to find ourselves aboard a Fighter Director Tender. Jim was taken to the sickbay and the rest of us were directed to the mess deck where we lined up for breakfast. This was followed by some form of documentation and a chance to sort ourselves out. In addition to its directing job, the FDT served as a base for Air Sea Rescue and a Calshot based ASR launch was tied up alongside. It was due to be relieved about noon, and we were told we would be returned to Calshot with it. We said cheerio to Jimmy who was to remain in sickbay. I think he had a broken collar bone among other things, in addition to the burns. As the FDT was as Royal Naval vessel we left the skipper and crew of our LCT aboard, I think.

When we boarded the ASR launch we found that we were taking an injured Luftwaffe pilot back with us. He had ditched in a FW190 during the morning and had been picked up with back injuries. The run back to Calshot was uneventful and we were directed to the sickbay on landing. After a check-up we were told that we were staying in sickbay for the night. Of course we only had what we stood up in, and the following morning the Service Police at the Main Gate Guardroom loaned us shaving tackle so that we could clean up before loading on to a vehicle that took us round to a Holding Unit somewhere a few miles away, located in a wood. They didn't want us and we moved to a Holiday Camp near Bognor where we were kitted out and after a day or so went on seven day's Survivor Leave. On return we moved back to Old Sarum to join a Casualty Replacement Pool where we were told we would wait for a Unit to come through the Hotel who needed replacements. During the subsequent weeks I pestered anyone in authority in attempts to get back to 3207, but without success. Eventually I was posted to 420 R&SU as they were coming through and crossed to Mulberry about the time of the Falaise Gap battle and the break-out from the beach, but that's another story. By this time 3207 were back in England being reformed for the Far East.

I lost touch with Jimmy Wright and Mick Ryan. Jimmy recovered sufficiently to be posted back to 2nd TAF on some Rearm and Refuel Unit, I believe. Jock Cruikshank I saw many years later – he stayed on in the RAF and had remustered to MT. Of the others on the LCT I remember Sailor Wright and some others whose names I don't recall. We met up at Old Sarum to learn that one of them, having dived over the side and swam for it, was picked up on the other side of the convoy and was almost charged with desertion.

I also had a letter sometime later from a Mrs. Skegg whose son had not survived, asking for details. I think he was also 3209, and I regretted that I could only advise her of the broadest details, not knowing him personally or where he was when the incident occurred.

Obviously I have always reckoned that every day since D-Day has been a bonus!

'K' RATIONS AND COMPO RATIONS
Bryan (Rocky) Stone

In early June 1944, when 3208 SC arrived at the reception centre from the Concentration Transit camp on Salisbury Plain, to which we had gone on D-Day, we were told that nobody stayed there for more than 24 hours, with most Units being on their way to Normandy the same day. Inflatable life belts were issued to each man, which were to be worn tight up under the armpits. This was most important, as if worn lower down it caused the man to float upside down, which meant he probably drowned. This in fact happened to many American soldiers at the major exercise at Slapton Sands in Devon, where almost a thousand men died when E-boats attacked their convoy of Landing Ships.

American 'K' rations were issued to the men of the Unit. Two 24 hour packs to cover the first two days ashore. They contained dehydrated porridge, concentrated meat, some biscuits, Camel cigarettes, chewing gum, chocolate and boiled sweets. Believe it or not, but after landing in Normandy it was said that one of the airmen took the block of porridge to the wife of a French farmer and asked her to cook it. Having never seen it before she promptly fried it.

In addition to the 'K' rations we were issued with a small metal gadget called a Tommy Cooker, which consisted of a couple of metal plates which interlocked forming a cruciform shape. One then stood it up and placed a solid block of methylated spirits on the top which when ignited could be used for heating up food or water.

We were also issued with a rectangular shaped tin marked 'Emergency Ration. NOT TO BE EATEN UNLESS THERE IS NO OTHER RATION AVAILABLE.

Soon afterwards we were warned to be ready to move at short notice, to travel to the Embarkation Area where we would be embarking on the landing ships. It our case it was an American LST.

After the first two days we were apparently going to survive on British 'Compo Rations', one pack of which, as I recollect, fed fourteen men for one day. As I remember they turned out to be quite good. The sultana puddings were excellent, but the tinned bacon was very fatty. The circular tin of soya bean sausage was cut across the centre a number of times which produced triangular sausages. The tinned potatoes had an odd flavour, but on the whole the packs were quite satisfactory. Whenever we set up our tented encampment at an airstrip our cooks always seemed to manage to produce a wonderful mug of 'char' made with plenty of sugar and evaporated milk.

From the time 3208 SC arrived in Normandy, in June 1944, until almost the end of the campaign in Northwest Europe, men of the Unit served on airstrips in the Normandy beachhead, plus ex-Lüftwaffe airfields as follows: B3, B4, B7, B8, B10, B14, B15 (twice), B16, B17, A12 (American), B29, B37, B51, B56, B58, B59, B60 and B71.

ALWAYS SHOW INITIATIVE

Frank Rye

Early in the Normandy campaign we were moving in convey to a new location when the dispatch rider behind the lorry I was driving, overtook and signalled me to stop, pointing to the back of the lorry. I did so, not knowing what could be wrong until I got out and saw smoke coming from under the canvas tilt. As I raised the corner of the tilt to see what was wrong, by letting the air in, the whole lorry burst into flames.

The lorry was the unit's MT lorry, and was laden with petrol, oil, spares, trolley jack, batteries, our tent, cookhouse equipment and personal kit, and within a few minutes the whole lorry was a blazing inferno. Everything was a write-off, and it posed a severe problem to the unit losing so much operational equipment at that time, not to mention the loss of personal equipment, kit and the tent. All other tents were full to the maximum.

As regards our personal kit, all the lads rallied round and helped out with shaving gear, tooth brushes and tooth paste, soap, writing paper etc.

Within a day or so a couple of the lads arrived at the new site and unloaded a tent from the back of the 15 cwt they had driven in. The tent was erected in much haste and out came the aircraft dope and all available bods helped camouflage the tent to match those others on site. So once again we had sleeping quarters in a tent of our own, but no-one really knew where the tent actually came from.

Some days later I heard on the grapevine that a tent had gone missing from the RAF police post while the police who were manning the post went to investigate an alleged theft of aircrew clothing on the other side of the strip that someone in a 15 cwt had reported taking place.

Whether there was any connection between this incident and our new tent I never found out, but you can draw your own conclusions.

THE STRAY ROCKET ON PAY DAY
JC (Joe) Shepherd

On landing in Normandy during the morning of the 7 June 1944, one of the three-ton Bedfords in front of us had beached from the TLC (Tank Landing Craft), and had turned left along the beach, past the Beachmaster, and hit a shell hole in the sand. Corporal White who was hanging onto the rope fastened to the canopy metal frame, was bounced into the air, and fell on to the beach, and hit an anti-personnel mine. This went off with a loud bang, and Chalky White fell face down in the sand, and then shouted 'I'm hit. I'm hit', and called for help. People rushed to him and noticed his boot heel was blown off and the back of his trousers was soaking wet. On checking him over, we found that a ball bearing from the mine had pierced his water bottle, from the bottom to the top, the water had run out and soaked his trousers, and apart from a very sore foot, he was not injured. What a lucky escape!

After about ten days, we of 3210 were assembled in our Bivouac field for our first pay parade. The CO, the Adjutant and the pay clerks were sat at a table, with all the Allied paper money, when a loud bang came from the strip, where Typhoons were being refuelled and re-armed. There was a loud 'Whoosh!' followed by an explosion at the tree behind the pay table, the tree split in two neatly. Everyone on parade made a dive for the ground or ditch, where the CO. Adj. and table party had retired to, and money was floating in the air like confetti. The Adj. drew his revolver and shouted 'I'll shoot the first person to take a penny!' Strangely, all the money was accounted for when calm was restored. We never really found out how the 6lb Rocket had been set off, but once again no casualties.

Some 14 days after landing, we were told we would be given a half day off, one half of each unit each afternoon.. I was in the half for the first afternoon off, and everyone went into Bayeux. The second afternoon the other half went off. Harry Emsley and Chalky White decided to hitch-hike to Caen, where in the outskirts of Caen they came across some British soldiers sitting and lounging about against the wall of a house. They talked for a while, then asked if it was alright to go down the next street. The soldiers said 'Yeah, go ahead'. So off they went, half way down the street they were greeted by cheering French citizens, and were dragged down into a cellar where they were plied with bottles of wine and cognac. Many hours later the street was liberated by soldiers of the British Army, who found two drunken airmen, who said they belonged to 3210 SC. No one believed them, and they were arrested and taken away by the Red Caps. Next morning Harry and Chalky were delivered back to the CO about 10.00am. They were shackled hand and foot, and stood dejected and sore-headed., but relieved at last and delivered back to their Unit.

(Please excuse my handwriting, but arthritis strikes in the strangest of places. Also, I'm sorry about the delay in getting this to you, but I have been in hospital and also had cataracts removed from both eyes. I am a very lucky 82-year-old now, and reasonably fit.

MY LONGEST DAY — 6 JUNE 1944
(With acknowledgements to the film of that name)
Ben Taylor

When the day dawned I was in the back of a 3 ton Bedford truck on a very slow journey along the roads of Wiltshire and Hampshire from Old Sarum to Gosport. Slow, did I say, it was in fact the largest traffic jam the world has ever seen: talk about the M25 being the largest car park in the country, it was nothing compared with the snarl up we had on all the roads leading to the South Coast. Every road, lane, verge and even some of the fields were full of tanks, armoured cars, with all types and sizes of transport vehicles loaded with a multitude of supplies, fuel, food, ammunition and personnel, all waiting their turn to be loaded for the Channel crossing. Those who lived along those roads were all at the road side, willing to keep us supplied with food and drink even though they were having to feed themselves on the meagre ration available to civilians at that time. I vividly recall the morning papers being handed to us headlining that the great day had arrived. I have here, not that morning's edition but the *Daily Express* for Wednesday 7 June by which time we were lying off the coast of the Normandy Beachhead near Arromanches.

I am racing ahead somewhat, for my story started in January, when I, 1694313 LAC Taylor, B, was posted from RAF Wheaton-Aston, a Flying Training School near Stafford, to RAF Eastchurch on the Isle of Sheppey, to join 3209 Servicing Commando in my capacity of Aircraft Engine Fitter, and I had not the slightest idea what a Servicing Commando was: however, I was soon to find out. When I got there the Unit had gone, but not so far, only to Gravesend, where I caught up with it. As I have said, I had not previously heard of RAF Servicing Commandos, but discovered that the outfits were the brain-child of Lord Louis Mountbatten, and that after a few trial runs with very small parties, mainly in the Middle East, the first major group, numbers 3201, 2, 3 and 4, was organised in March 1942 and went ashore in Operation Torch, the landings in North Africa towards the end of 1943, were adjudged a success and followed up in landing operations in Sicily and Salerno and Anzio in Italy, where they were joined by units which had operated in the Western Desert, numbers 3225, 3226, together with 3330, 31 and 32. Why the numbers did not run consecutively I never found out. Six SCUs, numbers 3205 to 3210 had been recruited and trained to take part in Operation Overlord, the D-Day landings in June 1944.

The basic idea of the Units was they should be composed of RAF tradesmen, Engine and Airframe fitters, Armourers, Wireless Mechanics etc., and a small Administrative staff which included a Medic. and Dispatch Riders. We drove our own vehicles, 3 ton Bedford Trucks carrying all the tools of the trade and a smattering of basic spares.

These units were recruited in the middle of 1943 and had been trained in landing and defence techniques at No 1 Commando training unit at Inveraray on Loch Fyne in Scotland, and originally all were volunteers. I hasten to add that I was no hero and did not look for trouble, however, there I was in the company of a group of daredevils, some even convict types with very little respect for regulations, but just the right lads to have around you when trouble loomed. Following the Commando training, there followed a year during which the Units had to become efficient in landing on beaches, the use of arms for defence, in mobility and particularly the servicing of different types of Fighter aircraft, Hurricanes, Spitfires, Mustangs and Typhoons to mention a few. I was thrown into this halfway through the period, but soon became part of an integrated unit. We were not attached to any squadron, and were expected to get the planes back in the air quickly whatever the type. The theory was that immediately there was a landing strip available, aircraft could land, be refuelled and rearmed and back in the air again, so saving time in returning to their home base for this to be done. During this period we travelled to airfields as far north as Peterhead and down to the south coast and many points in between, having often been given a matter of an hour or two to pack up all our gear and get on the road.

By the end of May we assembled as a complete Unit in a wood near Boxgrove in Sussex (often during training having operated in small groups as each Commando was split into four flights and was able to operate individually or in any combination.) It was here that we had the job of waterproofing the vehicles so that the engine did not stall if it was necessary to run onto the beaches through water which could stop the flow of exhaust gases or interfere with the ignition of the engine. It was realised that our Air Force Blue battle dress when covered with dust could easily be confused with German Grey, and therefore we were issued with khaki, but were allowed to wear the RAF wings shoulder flashes and the oval Combined Operations badge consisting of an anchor crossed by wings and a Tommy gun. We got our pep talk from Air Vice Marshal Harry Broadhurst (later Sir Harry), Air Officer Commanding 2nd Tactical Air Force, and then moved to the assembly Area at Old Sarum on Salisbury Plain, with hosts of Commonwealth troops. Here we were issued with special concentrated ration packs which included a simple device for heating food, this being a block of naphtha which was surprisingly quite efficient, and (specially printed) Invasion French Francs, not that we had much use for them for quite some time. We were also given three pre-printed postcards with a stock statement 'Have landed safely and am fit and well', which could be despatched within a couple of days.

I well remember that we were tented very close to a body of Canadians, many of them being French-speaking, who, of course, were enthusiastic at the prospect of taking part in the liberation of the country of their roots. Their enthusiasm seemed to rub off on us, even though I was probably the last person in the world to be affected in this way. I was certainly not hero material, in fact I joined the RAF to learn something I thought would be useful after the war, and to keep me away from any bullets and shells that may be flying around. I certainly did not envisage becoming part of a Commando Unit which would go ashore so early in a landing operation. Very early in the morning, about 2 o'clock as I recall, of 6 June, we proceeded in an endless convoy to our port of embarkation, Gosport. A very slow journey, a mammoth traffic jam, as I have already said, and during that early morning we got news that D-Day had arrived.

It was late afternoon before we embarked on an American LST (Landing Ship Tank). The vehicles had to be reversed through the bow doors so that we were in position to drive straight off immediately we hit the beach. We set sail round the Isle of Wight as dusk was falling. The sea was very choppy and rain falling as we headed into the Channel. We certainly did some rolling, the flat bottomed LST not being the most stable vessel in a choppy sea. You will recall that D-Day had been postponed for twenty four hours due to the state of the weather. Two or three times during the night our escort hailed our Captain to tell him to keep station in the convoy as enemy E boats were on hand. Our vessel was one of the fortunate ones to reach the coast unscathed. One of the small Landing Craft carrying a Flight each of 3207 and 3209 was hit and sunk. Two of our colleagues (one from each Unit) were lost. Their names are inscribed on the RAF Memorial at Runnymede.

The morning of 7 June dawned, and we were off the coast of Normandy in lovely sunshine and the sea had calmed to almost duckpond conditions. We were surrounded by shipping of all shapes and sizes and the 'block ships' were being manoeuvred into position to form the sea defences of the Mulberry Harbour. In the middle of the afternoon all seemed peaceful and I was sunning myself clad only in gym shorts and lying on the canvas cover of the 3 ton Bedford truck with tin hat and Sten Gun close at hand. All seemed serene until the ship rocked violently. HMS *Warspite*, one of the largest battleships afloat, had opened up with a full broadside with her 18 inch guns at some target ashore; the sound wave hit us on the beam and we rocked to about 40 degrees. I have never moved so quickly in my life. I came down to deck level like a startled rabbit, somewhat shaken.

There was no room on the beaches for us that day, so we were forced to spend another night on board off the Normandy coast. As the Spitfires, Hurricanes, etc headed for England at dusk, the Messserschmits and FWS. came in to cause what trouble they could before light faded away. The deluge of anti-aircraft fire during this period was most intense and we again came through the period unscathed. No great trouble during the short night, but E Boats were active on the fringes of the anchor area.

8 June. By about 9am (as for as I can recall) we drove ashore and I did not even get my feet wet. We were led by a Jeep along a track which was well marked with white tape to keep us to the area which had been cleared of land mines, and finally arrived, without problems, in a field between two Normandy villages, Villiers-le-Sec and Bazonville, about six miles from the beach, where Royal Engineers were laying wire mesh on the strip that they were bulldozing and grading to form a runway. Our first job was to dig slit trenches and cover them with canvas and camouflage for our own protection and to lay in stocks of fuel and ammunition, all manhandled from DUKW amphibious vehicles which had been loaded off-shore from freighters. This was to enable us to start operating, thus saving the aircraft returning to England between each sortie.

The necessary build-up of stores was soon completed and we were turning planes round for further sorties within 2-3 days of arrival. It was a case of refuel, re-arm and do emergency repairs by daylight and as dusk fell, off to the beaches to bring up more fuel in Jerry cans, bombs, rockets and ammunition and rations to keep us going for a further 24 hours. To refuel an aircraft under those conditions the petrol had to be manhandled onto the wings and poured into the tanks through a chamois leather to ensure that the fuel was dust- and water-free. Re-arming was of course just as important as refuelling, the magazines in the wings supplying the eight Browning machine guns, and in the case of Typhoons replacing the four rockets, two under each wing, also smallish bombs slung under the Hurricanes. The rocket-firing Typhoon was the major weapon used to bust the German tanks. Although as tradesmen we had our own spheres of responsibility there was certainly no demarcation. We all mucked in and the esprit de corps was superb, as you would expect when our lives and others were at risk. Due to our efforts the squadrons were able to operate and keep up the intense air offensive until dark. It was estimated that they were able to almost double the numbers of sorties being flown, on what would have been possible if the aircraft had been obliged to re-cross the Channel between trips. This routine continued for about 5 or 6 weeks, but we became unemployed when the regular squadron ground crew took over.

The plan was as the advance continued, and as further strips were constructed or airfields captured, we should move forward and repeat

The watchful guard, with Bren gun, ensuring that the lads have a quiet smoke.

General Montgomerey drops in to see his RAF Commandos.

A Hawker Typhoon being rearmed with eight rockets
before another tank-bursting sortie in Normandy.

Commandos taking their rest.
Where better than on a few hundred gallons of high-octane petrol
and thousands of machine gun rounds.

Typhoon fighter taxying to take off in Normandy.
Note clouds of dust which played havoc with the aircraft engines.

Pete Humphries and
Tom Atkinson of
3210 in Batavia.

RAF Commandos welcomed by villagers in Normandy.

A happy band of lads in Normandy.

A Japanese kamikaze suicide aircraft.

Rearming and refuelling a 'Kite'. No slacking here.

VE-Day celebrations – which seem to have gone on for a long time.

An awkward squad being drilled.
3205 celebrating VE-Day in Burma.

Servicing a spitfire in Normandy.
Everyone is busy but 'Chiefy'.

A Japanese seaplane about to be dismantled in Malaya.

Mac was never without his pipe,
even when posing for a portrait.

Close friends (for today). Mac McQuillan
and Sergeant Tony Galento of 3210 seem
to have become friendly – for once.

Airstrip in Normandy,
showing clouds of chalk dust as aircraft landed and took off.

the operation so keeping the flying time to base to a minimum. This did not happen, as was hoped, for the army got bogged down at Caen, and it was well into August before the breakthrough came and the Falais Gap was closed, thus enabling the rapid advance to begin.

Four of the Units, Numbers 3205,7,9 and 10, were sent back to England, and only 3206 and 3208 stayed on the Continent to do the follow-up job. It was on 3 August that we embarked once again, this time from the Mulberry Harbour, now wholly operational, and again on an American LST. After a hit-and-run attack by an enemy aircraft, the ship's Tannoy blared out 'Fire on the fantail! Fire on the fantail! Will passengers keep clear of the fantail.' It turned out that the garbage bin had caught fire, whether from enemy action I can't say, but there was much activity on the part of the Yanks. They chased all over the deck, fire hoses trailing behind them, until three of our lads picked up the bin and tossed it over the side and we then got on our way, and reached Blighty the following morning, and then temporarily to Thruxton near Andover, now a motor cycle racing circuit.

One of the first things I did was to go into Andover in order to telephone home to advise my parents that I was safely back. It so happened that during the last few days in France, being unemployed we played cards quite a lot, and although it was not one of my usual pursuits, I got involved, and won a matter of 2 to 3 thousand francs, which were in my wallet, and I left the wallet in the telephone kiosk. I reported the loss to the police and was very surprised to find that it had been handed in and was returned to me with the contents intact. I wonder if that would happen today.

Back in England we were used for a number of jobs including the refuelling of the aircraft at Manston in Kent which were used in Operation Market Garden, the dropping of the Air-borne Forces at Arnhem. Soon after this we were re-grouped, the more senior members being posted to other duties and two of the Units, 3205 and 3207 were brought up to strength from the younger element of 3209 and 3210. I went to 3207, and we were shipped out to Bombay, then across India to Burma, which border we crossed on Christmas day. That however is another story.

A FRUSTRATED PILOT

Dennis Munns

This is my story of how and why I joined the Servicing Commandos.

In 1938, when war seemed inevitable, I was only fourteen. I decided to join the RAF as a fighter pilot. I had been reading 'Biggles'! So I visited the local recruiting office and they persuaded me to join as an Aircraft Apprentice and then volunteer for aircrew training after passing out at Halton. So I did.

But it was March 1942 when I left Halton and was told that I was too valuable to be wasted on aircrew. They sent me to Inverness, a long way from all the action. So I went to the Orderly Room and said that as I couldn't be aircrew could I go overseas. They said 'No', because I was still down for aircrew training. Then I was posted to Invergordon, even further away from the fighting.

That winter of 1942-43 was very hard, with many gales. As a fitter-armourer I spent many nights bombing up Sunderlands and Catalinas in the gales. We lost many flying boats sunk at their moorings, complete with storm crews. The storm crews consisted of one aircrew and two ground crew. One night we lost three Sunderlands and one Catalina. Two Sunderlands were never found, not while I was at Invergordon. We had so many funerals one week that we ran out of blank ammunition and had to borrow from the Army.

We had a good Armaments Officer. I was excused all parades and all other duties. He gave me all the gunsmith jobs. I looked after the officers with private firearms, making parts, servicing and supplying ammo. to officers of the RAF, Navy and Army, as well as the other ranks who came to me with problems with firearms. A Canadian captain came to me with the parts of a .280 Ross sporting rifle and six rounds of ammo. He had found them and the engineering machinery to make them in a remote castle. I fitted it all together with iron sights. He would get a night sight fitted when he took it back to Canada. I refused the offer of another set of parts because the ammunition would be very difficult to get.

One day on SROs there was a notice asking for volunteers to be Servicing Commandos. So I wrote a letter to the Station Commander in the usual way, something like 'Number. Rank. Name, I have the honour to cancel my applications for aircrew training and overseas service. I hereby volunteer as today's SROs for the Servicing Commandos. I remain, Sir, Your obedient servant' and all that bull.

Very soon after that they posted me for a three weeks' course on chemical weapons. There we played about with lots of mustard gas and other nasty things. That was on Salisbury Plain.

On the way back to Invergordon I called in at home, near Leicester, for a couple of days. Well, my Dad's club was a man short in the Long-Alley Skittle Team, so I had to play.

When I eventually got back to camp I went into the Orderly Room and they asked me where had I been, and told me I was supposed to be at Exeter. Without waiting for me to answer they gave me my Clearance Chit and told me to nip smartly round the camp to get it signed. So next day I was back on the train going south again.

George Sheldrake was with me at this time. He had been on detachment to Stranraer when he was recalled to Invergordon to get cleared to go to Exeter to join 3209 with me. I don't remember very well, but it is quite possible we got to Euston and had the odd drink in London before going on to Waterloo to get a train for Exeter. I do remember going to the Orderly Room and a nice little WAAF taking down my particulars (don't laugh!) and directing us to three or four huts in a little group a long way from the rest of the camp.

After dumping our kits on some empty beds, I joined a group of blokes talking together around a table, the subject was prisons. They were discussing the pros. and cons. of Dartmoor, Strangeways and various other well-known jails with the glasshouses of Shepton Mallet and Colchester and the like. One young lad spoke up about the hard time he had had, and he mentioned a place. They told him to shut up 'cos that was only a Borstal'. So I didn't mention my few days on jankers at Halton.

We were left to our own devices for a few days. Then one morning someone shouted 'Everyone Out, On Parade.' And then, 'No parade, just come as you are.' It was our new Unit CO, Fl/Lt. Woods and WO Discip. Tommy Blackwell. They told us that we would soon be moving to Zeals in Wiltshire and issued with khaki battle dress. 'Timber' Woods told us that there would be no parades except for battle order and no petty charges. If anyone was found to be unsuitable he would be sent back to the previous Unit. Dress correctly for battle order, we were told, and he didn't mind how we dressed at other times.

At Zeals there was the odd clash of personalities among the men. But not many. Our officers and senior NCOs were very sensible and soon we were all working together like a well-oiled machine. Which we often were in the evenings. I will explain as best I can. Young men, when work for the day is finished, will tend to go out together and get a bellyful of beer. Then, when there is no more drink to be had, will look for one of the two 'Fs'. Some of us were a bit more genteel and looked for one of the *three* 'Fs', that is, a Female, Food or a Fight. At least I think that is what the 'Fs' were.

Training completed, we were on 125 airfield near Newchurch on the Romney Marshes. There was one pub within easy walking distance. Thinking this would be packed with our lads and army types. I walked a few miles further to Dymchurch. The beer was good and plentiful. Someone told me that the girl who modelled for Jane of the *Daily Mirror* often came in for a drink, but there was no sign of her that night. There was no chance of any of the three 'F's. So it was back to camp for me at closing time.

When I got back the lads told me that I had missed a good show at the local pub. It was packed and overflowing into the yard at the back. When the lads wanted to pee they went to the edge of the concrete and stood there to pee. It developed, of course, into a competition to see who could pee the furthest. A table of Land Army girls had been watching and one of them went over and asked if she could join in. She wanted a table brought up to the firing line. Then dropping her breeches she lay on the table, brought her knees up to her shoulders so that no part of her was over the firing line, and let fly. She beat all the men easily.

Another time and place, I have forgotten where, Jock McMenemy went to London for the weekend. He was picked up by an officer of the US Womens' Army. She took him to the hotel where she was staying and after plying him with drink, took him to bed.

Now Jock was one of our best footballers, with lots of stamina. He said she wanted him again and again all night long. Sometimes without uncoupling. He said there wasn't a dry place on the bottom sheet of their big double bed. In the morning she called room service for break-fast to be brought up to them.

ACTION!

Joe Grainger

I joined the RAF in September 1939, and my first posting, after initial training, was with Units of Bomber, Coastal and Army Co-Op Commands, finally, in 1943, being with a non-operational Unit at RAF

Castle Bromwich in the northern outskirts of Birmingham. Now, whilst the various aircraft involved in these years were in themselves exciting, and working on them was satisfying, life on normal RAF stations could be surprisingly boring and Castle Bromwich particularly so. It was almost a peacetime existence, five-day week, fixed hours, practising against Anti-Aircraft training Units, even billeted at my own home, due to inadequate accommodation on the camp, and this during a most critically dangerous period of the war. I was, to use Service parlance, 'Browned off'.

Then, early in 1943 the Station Engineering Officer, F/Lt. Tinker, sent for me and told me of a completely new type of Unit to be formed shortly with himself as CO. The Unit would be comprised almost entirely of technicians, Engine and Airframe fitters, Riggers, Electricians, Radio Personnel, Armourers, etc. They would initially undergo a period of intensive military training, up to Commando standards, and whilst remaining basically RAF, would fight and work alongside Naval and Army forces in Combined Operations Command, being specifically intended for the coming amphibious operations which would be essential for the invasion of mainland Europe and overseas Japanese held territory.

Volunteers were urgently needed, and knowing through the 'grapevine' of my boredom, he felt that the new Unit would be an ideal move, so 'How about it..?' Thus, with the aid of such arm-twisting, I found myself volunteering, and early in April 1943 was en-route for the new Unit, forming at RAF Sawbridgeworth, my only disappointment being that F/Lt. Tinker did not appear as CO, having been diverted to an urgent posting in the Middle East.

The new Unit, No. 3205 Royal Air Force Servicing Commando, came into existence on 8 April 1943, and I was amongst the first arrivals. So began what would prove to be the most satisfying and exciting period of my six and a half years in the Service.

Combined Operations Training

The training course at Inveraray was varied, and included lectures and demonstrations of weapons and army movements, and of naval vessels and movements. There were practice sessions of loading vehicles into various types of landing craft, including boat pulling on the loch, several weapon-firing sessions on the range, at which all personnel fired each of the Unit's various weapons, rifles, Sten guns, Bren guns and Boyes anti-tank guns, and grenade throwing.

Three exercises were held in which the Unit loaded vehicles onto LSTs

(Landing Ship Tank) and LCTs (Landing Craft Tank), including a beach landing from the latter, which it was explained were the type of landing craft we were most likely to meet with.

During one night exercise, live ammunition was issued and practice firing held against dimly lit targets. The next morning rumours were rife that one of the Duke of Argyll's large herd of deer had been killed by Sten gun bullets, a certain Irish member of 3205 being generally given credit for what would be a very pleasant change of meat. Quite a hue and cry ensued. Everywhere was searched and everyone questioned, but needless to say, no-one knew anything. Eventually the authorities decided that it was just a load of 'bull', it being impossible, in their opinion, for something as large as a deer carcass to be hidden around the camp area. It was overlooked that during the night exercises slit trenches had to be dug when practice firing was held, and filled in later. On this occasion one trench had been considerably larger than the others, yet was filled in by one man, and an Irishman at that. Be that as it may, when the Unit came to depart by road, several trucks had large joints of meat hidden away, and we dined in great style on lovely venison for some time afterwards. Paddy Burns, one of our Southern Ireland men, always denied any part in this shooting, but did admit to being a rotten shot against the official targets and may possibly have missed altogether with one burst from his Sten gun.

Living in Camp

After our training at Inveraray, the Unit lived practically the whole time under canvas. We had ridge tents, eighteen by fourteen feet, accommodating four men each side with their basic kit of side pack and webbing, greatcoat, change of underwear, shirts, etc., and weapons stored at each man's head. We had been issued with large groundsheets – actually waterproof capes – which we used under each bed space, and it was folded and wrapped around the bedding etc during the daytime. Each man had two RAF blankets, with no sheets or pillows, of course, but most of us managed to scrounge additional items to improve the 'comfort'.

On one particular occasion, when we had to pitch our tents down in Kent, on a day of particularly bad weather, we discovered, the hard way, that our ground sheets were barely adequate for such conditions, and, quite unofficially, the Unit decided, practically as one man, that something would have to be done about it. It is impossible to say where they came from, but within a few days every tent, including the Officers', had a proper groundsheet, of heavy waterproof canvas, sufficiently large to completely cover the ground over the tent area.

The cooks had their own tents, one for storage of food stuffs, the other as living quarters. Most of the cooking was done outdoors, in the earlier months on wood-burning fires, and the collection of this wood was one of the daily unpopular fatigues. Each Flight took it in turn to provide a collection party, whose job was to go out around the surrounding countryside and gather sufficient wood for the following day's cooking. There was quite a bit of this, so the collection could be difficult as obviously few farmers liked the idea of several cwts. of their wood being taken every day, so discretion was the password, and quite often the wood party left the job until after dark, having spotted a suitable supply during daylight hours.

At that time most of the airfields in southern England had anti-glider poles over all ground outside the actual runway and dispersal areas. These poles were quite large, six to eight inches in diameter and eight to ten feet tall. They were dug in twelve or fifteen feet apart in all directions. Their purpose had been to create problems for any enemy gliders attempting to land back in the bad old days following the fall of France. It became noticeable that after 3205 had been at an airfield of this type for a few days, the anti-glider poles started to thin out, and eventually the CO had to call a halt to that practice. But, as we eventually received excellent gas–burning stoves, the old wood collecting became a thing of the past.

Paddy on a Charge

Any airman from southern Ireland – which of course was a neutral country, but which nevertheless supplied many thousands of volunteers to help the 'Owld Enemy' – could not go directly home on leave in uniform, or he would be interned. The procedure was for the airman to report to Wembley Depot, hand in his RAF kit, and be issued in lieu with civilian clothes, etc, and the necessary pass for travelling home to the Free State, and on return reversing the procedure.

We had one such volunteer, a real volunteer in the sense that not only had he volunteered to help us in our war, but had then further volunteered to leave the relative comfort of the routine RAF life for the Commandos. It was Paddy whose 'poor' marksmanship with his Sten gun had, to the belief of most of us, provided the venison. Paddy was quite a character, having that special disregard, even scorn, for all authority, which seemed an inherent characteristic of Irishmen, whilst at the same time doing his own job better than average. He had a very broad brogue, which when he became excited became almost a foreign language. Unfortunately, by reason of my own Irish connection, my mother being a native of a small town, Drogheda on the 'Banks of the Bloody Boyne', I could make more sense of Paddy's 'Bloody Boyne' brogue than many, and on occasion acted almost as interpreter.

Well, he went on leave, following the prescribed routine, and returned four days overdue. I was unfortunate in being duty NCO the day Paddy turned up, and had no other course open to me but to put him on a charge for being AWOL (Absent Without Leave). He duly appeared before the CO and it was my duty to march him in under escort, and read the charge out. The CO looked sternly at Paddy and said, in time-honoured fashion 'Well, Burns, you've heard the charge, how do you plead? Have you anything to say in explanation for being four days overdue from your leave.'

Paddy, who obviously considered he had a perfect answer, went into a long tale of reporting to the Embarkation Officer at Belfast, in good time to get back, but being refused a berth, as the ships were all full. He was told to go home and report again forty-eight hours later, which he did, with similar results, and this happened a third time before he got a ship. He then had to divert to Wembley etc. etc, and thus the delay in returning.

The CO must have been in a bad mood, and he glared at Paddy and said 'That may be your story, Burns, but I will not accept it as a proper excuse for being four days overdue, so what have you to say?' Paddy was evidently very puzzled by this response, but taking a deep breath he patiently proceeded to repeat the whole story, again with a few Irish embellishments.

Again the CO responded as before. The Adjutant, Orderly Clerk, escort and I were all somewhat embarrassed but also amused, when Paddy, getting very agitated, once more repeated his story, his brogue getting worse all the time. At the end of this third repetition, and before the CO, who was noticeably getting more annoyed, could respond, Paddy brought out what he obviously believed was his final piece, in a loud voice, standing ramrod straight. 'Mr. Fenton, Sorr, do ye think my name is Jasus Chroist to part the waters and bloody walk oiver, Sorr.'

There was a great hush, whilst the question of whether Paddy got fourteen days 'inside' with stoppages was considered against the possibility of being shot at Dawn, then the CO exploded in a roar of laughter, nearly falling off his chair, slammed his fist down on the charge sheet and shouted at me 'Get that bloody Irishman out of my tent. Charge dismissed. Oh, and Grainger, stand the man a drink from me for the best laugh I've had in a long time.'

Outside, Paddy was still puzzled and indignant, but apparently decided, because of the drink, 'Ah, the old man was having me on, be Jasus.'

Operation Overlord

By the 3 June of 1944 it was very obvious this was to be the real thing, but whether it was to be just a raid or a more 'permanent' affair there was no knowing. Our vehicles were taken away for 90% waterproofing, ration packs issued and, more telling, live ammunition was issued. After the toughest lecture yet on 'security', we moved on the afternoon of 5 June down to park just off Gosport Hards, where the final waterproofing was completed. After a very excited and restless night we moved at first light to embark on four LCTs. It was D-Day, 6 June 1944.

As soon as we were loaded we moved out to join an incredible convoy heading East for the open sea and an enormous fleet, the Battleships Rodney and Renown, Cruisers, Destroyers, dozens of Corvettes and LSTs literally as far as the eye could see in every direction. Hundreds of aircraft were passing or circling overhead. There were fighters, light and heavy bombers and paratroop planes obviously empty and returning. We learned that this was 'Overlord', the largest seaborne attack ever undertaken and mighty proud we were to take part in it.

It is impossible to describe the atmosphere. We were going with cock-sure confidence that we would clobber Jerry and finish him for good. Other operational areas had already shown that given half a chance the 'Invincible Them' could be beaten, and now we would prove it again.

Soon, in growing daylight and a fresh sunny morning, most of us sat on top of our vehicles, having our corned beef breakfasts and, of course, the inevitable brew-up of cha, and thoroughly enjoying the scene. One esteemed character, our technically brilliant signals WO was observed to be quietly absorbed in a book. *No Orchids for Miss Blandish*, or *Lady Chatterley's Lover* perhaps? Investigation showed it to be a complex manual of obstruse mathematical equations, just to pass the time away. All mutually agreed he qualified for the VC!

We now learned we would be landing in Normandy, our job of course to get an Airstrip operational as soon as possible. We could not ascertain whether we would be going for a German airfield or starting our own, but either way it would be hectic.

By early afternoon we began to hear the distant continuous rumble of heavy gunfire, which brought home the fact that we were heading for the real thing. By late afternoon we were running in towards the beach, but it was so congested, every possible type of landing craft, some obviously sunk or stranded, blocking every access that there just was not space for our LCTs to move in and we were obliged to hold off, cruising about half a mile off the beach. The German armour in our zone was heavier than expected, and the urgent demand was for tanks, so vessels carrying them were given priority.

Shortly after dark, we were startled by a sudden outburst of light guns from not only our own Navy ships but also from German intruders. Our invasion Fleet was still immense, and the Navy was at the great disadvantage of being unable to fire low until certain of their targets, whereas Jerry could literally fire at anything and everything with the certainty of doing immense damage.

Soon after it started we heard and saw an immense explosion almost alongside, and high flames showed an LCT sinking fast, and this was followed by two more nearby. Then the Navy's light craft came chasing the German E boats, and several running fights could be seen. Tracer flew around just above sea level, and most seemed to be aimed at us, and it was most frustrating not to be allowed to join in at least with our Bren guns, but we would have been a greater danger to our surrounding friends.

To add to the general free-for-all, Jerry aircraft, which had also been noticeable by their absence all day, now started bombing and strafing. In answer, it seemed as though every gun on every ship opened up, from the big six and four inch Ack Ack guns on the large ships down the line to literally hundreds of lighter weapons, all firing a mix of ball, tracer and incendiary in a never ending stream which lit up the whole sky for miles, sufficient to see the other ships clearly. Ships were hit and sank, and several aircraft were seen crashing in flames, and this went on for hours.

Our convoy had scattered somewhat, and our other three LCTs were no longer with us, causing us dismay and fears that they were amongst those sunk. Very slowly the action subsided, as the German ships and aircraft left off. We were cruising slowly about a mile off-shore, with the only action now being our own big ships firing salvoes inland, to be answered by what appeared to be haphazard fire from enemy big guns further along the coast.

At last there was a lightening of the eastern sky, and we turned landward again, this time to make a practically straight run in to make a

'Ramps Down' dryshod landing near the small village of La Riviera in the 'Juno' Section of the Canadians' landing zone.

It was almost like an exercise, but for one very important difference – long lines of Gascape-wrapped figures lying along the back of the beach reminded us as nothing else could, that this was for real. For some reason, those lines of bodies, faceless, almost formless, only the pair of ammunition boots sticking out at one end of each bundle, remained in my memory for months, indeed years, afterwards. They were of course awaiting removal back to the UK, but were a part of the scene of intense activity, yet taking no part in it.

Early Days in Europe

From the beach we made our way to the rendezvous point, the small village Ver-sur-Mer. There, between the villages of Ver-sur-Mer and St. Croix-sur-Mer, we found that the Army Construction lads had started forming an airstrip on wheatfields. We started offloading and digging in, and by 10.30am the Unit was reassembled. Some of us assisted the Army lads, and others went off in trucks to start the endless task of collecting fuel, all in Jerry cans, ammunition and food stocks from supply craft at the beach. The rest dug slit trenches. It was a case of organised chaos. The biggest job was offloading hundreds of Jerry cans, each containing four and a half gallons of 100 Octane aircraft fuel, and weighing about fifty pounds, from the trucks and forming a number of dumps around what would be the main aircraft dispersal area. Similarly ammunition had to be manhandled and stockpiled – all sorts, from .030 machine gun, through .50, and 22mm. On to sixty pound rocket heads and bodies and 250lb, 500lb and 1,000lb bombs. This was made all the more exciting by the irregular and obviously haphazard shelling.

We hardly had time to look around, but one or two working close to and in the village of Ver-sur-Mer were surprised to find a quite surly atmosphere on the part of the locals, certainly none of the expected 'liberation' atmosphere.

By the evening of 9 June, D plus three, we had finished our preparations, and the airstrip was designated 'B3' and became operational next morning at first light. The 'buzz' was that the first aircraft to land would be the personal Spitfire of Air Vice Marshal Sir Harry Broadhurst, AOC 2/TAF, and we all looked forward to seeing this very popular Commander 'christen' our airstrip. It was not to be. Almost before first light a lone Typhoon, flown by a Canadian of 245 RCAF Squadron, circled, signalled engine trouble, and of course was immediately called in. On inspection we could find nothing wrong, and when the pilot learned of the impending arrival of the AOC he suddenly decided he had been wrong, and took off without more ado. Minutes later the AOC came in, with his personal Spitfire HB. He was greeted formally by the CO, who had warned us that no mention was to be made about the queue-jumping Canadian. Sir Harry addressed us briefly, assured us that everything was going exactly to plan, and that we would be going down in RAF history. (It's taken over fifty years.)

Now our real work began, and throughout this and succeeding days the pattern was unchanged. Aircraft came in, usually Squadrons, taxied to Dispersals, stopped, and refuelling and rearming began immediately. As the days went by, the volume of work increased, and on one day 3205 SC recorded over 1,000 sorties. Every one involved refuelling and rearming and Between Flight Inspections. Every drop of fuel involved carrying Jerricans from the nearest dump to the aircraft. There two or three men stood up on the wing, opened the fuel tank and placed a large steel funnel, lined with chamois leather, in the filler neck. The cans were then lifted six or eight feet up to the men who opened them and poured the fuel in, returning the empty cans back down. They could not be handled roughly for fear of a spark or a bad spillage.

During the day as opportunity arose, or at evening and well into the night, the empty cans had to be taken back to the beach dumps and replacement full cans brought to the airstrip. This was always a hazardous, even a dangerous task. It was only in darkness that the German Air Force could get over the Beachhead, so no lights dare be shown and all travelling, loading and unloading was in pitch darkness, at least until Jerry did fly over, and then the hundreds of AA and other guns firing continuously, with tracer and incendiary ammunition, lit the whole sky sufficiently for all purposes. The trouble was that Jerry strafing and bombing, in addition to the usual shelling, which was mainly haphazard, made the job of carrying hundreds of Jerry cans of 100 Octane fuel and boxes of ammunition in our open three ton trucks most exciting, being very good for the digestion and the soul.

A very disturbing factor entered our little world: we were being sniped at fairly regularly, but could not pin it down. With so many aircraft at the airstrip more or less continuously, plus all the fuel and ammunition in surface dumps, it had to be sorted out once and for all. We started laying traps or ambushes, and found to our surprise that the sniping appeared to come from the general direction of the village. We returned fire with two Bren guns, and whilst we found no casualties, the sniping ceased and we were not troubled again. We suspected, although we had no proof, that the culprits were local girls. Some of the villagers with whom we became very friendly told us that some girls had been friends of, or even married to, German soldiers during the occupation. Those girls who had fraternised had had their heads shaved.

The attitude of the village as a whole was not good, and surly at best. We had neither time nor inclination for social niceties and needed nothing from them really, although inevitably the British Serviceman's seemingly innate desire for eggs did cause parties to tour the small local farms, and 'Avez vous des oeufs' became the stock French phrase, even if it was the only one.

Thinking of shaved heads reminded me that many of us decided to have our hair cut very short, almost shaved. Chalk dust from the subsoil exposed when the strip was cleared was the problem. There were enormous clouds of dust whenever aircraft engines were run or planes took off or landed. Soon everything was permeated by it, clothes, kit, food and stores. We were chewing pounds of chalk every day and in our hair it mixed with sweat, and formed a gooey mix, needing lots of water, which we didn't have, for washing out. So we began the Normandy Crop. It felt great, and when washing you could simply go right over the top. However, there was one snag. We had lived outdoors constantly for months past, usually working stripped to the waist, and all had acquired a deep tan. Now our skulls appeared a horrible dead grey/white, but, worse, all the bumps and scars, cuts and ridges collected during the growing years were still there, and it has to be admitted we looked a right lot of thugs. But we didn't expect to be seeing our wives or girls friends for a year or more, so did not much care.

We were wrong, though. By the end of August we were back in UK, on embarkation leave. I know my wife opened the door to me when I got home late one evening, took one look, burst into tears and '.....if you think I'm going to be seen out with you like that you're mistaken!' So the Conquering Hero returned!

The dust proved to be a much more serious problem for the Typhoon aircraft which we were getting in increasing numbers, and were invaluable as 'Tank Busters', with their powerful and accurate rockets. It was found that many of these, after landing and being serviced by us, were out of action (U/S) the next day because of sticking sleeve valves in the engines. It was not too difficult to release the valves, but took valuable time, and of course the problem would recur the next time they landed in France. The

Germans were starting to recover from their massive initial defeats, and their armour was slowly building up again around our perimeter. Just when they were most needed, the Tank Busters were crippled. An answer had to be found, and it was.

Our factories at home performed miracles, and within a few days had designed, tested, proved and started manufacture of massive air filters for the huge twin air intakes in the nose of the Typhoons. Supplies went to the Squadrons and to us, and the panic was over. The Tank Busters were back in full strength.

Had this happened a few weeks later when the huge tank battles around Caen developed, it is quite possible that the German tanks would have swung the issue and broken through, but the rocket-firing Typhoons were master of the tanks and indeed German prisoners admitted to us they dreaded the Typhoons more than any other weapons.

About this time tragedy hit us. The previous day we had cleaned out a new Spitfire drop-type belly fuel tank and sent it back to the UK on a Spitfire with money to have it filled with beer at our favourite pub in Chichester. Now, as the first patrols came in the Spit was seen, guided to our dispersal, and as soon the prop was stopped the tank was released, dragged clear and the filler removed by the greedy, dribbling 'erks'. 'Whoosh', straight up some fifty or sixty feet went forty gallons of best bitter. We had all overlooked the effect on the beer of coming over at 15,000 feet or so, followed by a bumpy landing. The beer virtually boiled out of the tank, resulting in strong men weeping, trying to catch the descending froth, but mainly watching in frustration as it seeped into the greedy Normandy soil.

We were in France less than two months. On 29 July we moved out, and on 30th embarked on an LST (Landing Ship Tank), disembarking at Southampton, and the European war was over for us. We were puzzled, rather deflated, even angered at the sudden withdrawal. We knew there was lots of work still for us to do in Normandy.

THE GREAT GOOSE THEFT
Frank Rye

At the end of the Normandy campaign we were stationed outside Brussels in a disused factory premises. The owners of the factory also lived on the site and kept ten or so geese. We had strict orders not to interfere with them.

A short time before Christmas there was big trouble as the owners of the factory reported that one of the geese had gone missing. We were all paraded, everything and everywhere was searched, but not even a feather was found. Eventually we were all required to contribute to the cost of this goose, just to keep the peace.

In the early Spring, my friend married his Belgian girlfriend and during the evening celebrations some of the Unit, including the CO, were invited. During the CO's conversation with the new bride, he asked if the lads from the Unit had behaved themselves, as he knew we had visited the bride's home often. She replied that we had all been very good especially at Christmas when a goose had been sent. Two of the lads had arrived with a sack, tipped it out in the kitchen, and the goose, which had only been stunned, got up and flew around the flat trying to escape. There were feathers everywhere. But it had made a good Christmas dinner.

THE UNMARKED GRAVE
Frank Rye

Having just left the beach and after de-waterproofing their vehicles, 3208 Servicing Commando passed a giant crater which appeared to have been made by a large shell from a battleship, something like *HMS Rodney* or *HMS Nelson*, or by a very large bomb. It was massive, and a human limb was showing through the earth at the bottom of the hole. Local dogs were getting at that limb, so some of the lads went down with spades and covered the remains properly.

It was said that there were four horses and five dead Germans in the crater. It looked as if a horse-drawn vehicle had been destroyed by a projectile and what was left of the animals and the men had been hurriedly buried in the crater.

It became fairly obvious, as the Normandy campaign progressed, that for a mechanised army, the Germans used a large number of horse-drawn vehicles. This became even more apparent at the Falaise Gap, when the German Seventh Army was struggling to escape.

MUTINY IN THE RAF
Bryan (Rocky) Stone

As the war in Europe was drawing to a close, 3208 SC was disbanded without a word of thanks or even a parade in front of our CO. The group with which I returned to the UK ended up, as far as I can recollect, at an RAF Station somewhere in Wiltshire. Yatesbury perhaps? It was quite obvious that no-one knew what to do with us, and even young newly-trained aircrew were breaking up air raid shelters with picks and shovels.

In the mornings we were paraded in front of the Station Warrant Officer, a tall, lanky-looking individual, who bellowed and shouted at us and I felt that I had had enough of this treatment. I had been a trades-man since I joined the service and in no way was I ending my war ser-vice as an NCO digging holes, peeling potatoes etc. They could, in fact, have sent us on leave but that would have been too easy.

On about the third day after my little group was ordered to carry out some task or other and when we were dismissed by the WO. I walked off the parade in the opposite direction to my fellow Servicing Commandos. He bellowed out 'Where are you going?' I shouted back 'I am getting on the first ship out of here… Sir!'

I then marched into the Orderly Room and said 'I am volunteering to go to South-East Asia.' The Jap war was still on, of course.

A few weeks later, after a fortnight's leave, I was on a troopship on the way to SEAC. (South-East Asia Command) Unfortunately for me, I did not go to an operational Squadron, as I had hoped, but ended up at a Maintenance Unit at Karachi, on the edge of the Sind Desert. A few months later I was posted to the Maintenance Unit at Cawnpore, the site of the infamous well into which British women and children were thrown after mutilation by the Indian Army mutineers.

After a short while I was again moved, this time back to Karachi, where, after I had been back two or three days, the RAF in SEAC mutinied, and I am sure that Karachi was the first Station to down tools. Seven days later Cawnpore, which I had just left, mutinied and finally fifty thousand RAF men from Karachi to Singapore had downed tools.

Fortunately having just returned to Karachi neither myself nor the other NCO I shared a tent with knew anything about an impending mutiny and certainly would not have wanted to become involved anyway. It was a very unpleasant situation and I was pleased when I was told I was going home for demob. A number of ringleaders were arrested and prison sentences were the order of the day. Apparently one was arrested while walking up the gangplank of the ship which was to take him back to the UK.

Before I embarked to return home I was interviewed by SIB and asked if I knew any of the ringleaders. Because I had only been back at Karachi two or three days I could not tell them anything about the mutiny because neither myself nor my fellow NCO had a single clue that a mutiny was about to take place.

I have since learned why it took place, and it appears that one of the main reasons was that the Government of the day, in 1945, had planned to keep RAF men out in SEAC to police India from the air (as was done before WWII), while shipping Army and Navy men home for demob. Apparently it was cheaper to use the RAF. There were other reasons but it would take too long at this moment to get them down on paper. I have been told that heads did roll amongst the Commanding Officers who had no idea of how to treat their men, and were living like lords, unlike the men.

It was an embarrassing period for the RAF, but I understand it was well hushed up back in the UK and I still meet ex-RAF men who did not know that this great mutiny had taken place in WWII. One thing it did bring about, however, (amongst others) was the shipment of RAF men home for demob.

SMART SERVICE
Bryan (Rocky) Stone

On 7 October 1943, preparations were made at RAF Ford, Sussex, for 3208 SC to take part in a demonstration on the airfield. All personnel were engaged in getting the airfield ready. The preparations continued into the next day, but there were many last minute alterations which prevented the carrying out of the exercise. Four Squadrons of Spitfires (Mark Vb, Vc, IX and Seafires) took off from prepared areas.

The Unit ORB showed that when the aircraft relanded, the men of the SC refuelled and rearmed the four squadrons in 47 minutes from the time the first aircraft was parked. This demonstration gave them their first real test and opportunity of practising under conditions which approximated to those likely to be encountered in actual operations.

During the following four days from 9 to 12 October, preparations for a repeat exercise were made. On 13 October the final rehearsal was held during which the time to refuel and rearm forty Spitfires was reduced to thirty-three minutes. Two of the Squadrons remained behind after rehearsal and the Unit carried out Daily Inspections and Servicing on those aircraft. On the following day the finishing touches were put to the scene.

On 15 October, the Prime Minister, the Secretary of State for Air, the First Sea Lord, the Commander of the USAAF 8th Air Force and the C-in-C of Fighter Command attended the demonstration. The aircraft were rearmed and refuelled in 26 minutes, the best time to date.

DEATH OF A HALIFAX
Bryan (Rocky) Stone

In November 1943, 'D' Flight of No. 3208 was detached to Tangmere which was a very busy airfield. On the night of the 19th heavy bombers returning from Europe in the dark had been diverted and I was standing not far from the Control Tower, near a parked Lancaster. I had heard a 'heavy' approaching and suddenly it came into view, very low. It was obviously having difficulties and appeared to be trying to land with the wheels up, although because of the pitch blackness of the night it was difficult to pick out all the details of the machine. It did not land but roared towards me so low it would have been below the top of the Tower towards, which it was heading. Almost at the last moment it veered away to its left, just passing me on my right, extremely low. Just after it missed the Tower there was an enormous explosion and the machine, which was in fact a Halifax, had flown straight into what was, I believe, the only pre-war hangar still standing at Tangmere.

What a tragedy, to have flown all the way home and then ending their lives like this. All the crew were killed, and six Typhoons and a Spitfire were destroyed in the building by the fire. The men of our unit did a sterling job that night. Apart from trying to get aircraft out of the building, some broke into a locked Lancaster which was in danger of catching fire from the terrific heat, and succeeded in pushing it away.

It was a sad scene when daylight came and the only part of the Halifax which could be seen was the tail turret and tailplane which was hanging from what was left of the outer wall of the hangar. Pre-war hangars were very solid indeed

A few years ago, our Servicing Commando Association Chaplain told me that he had been in the Control Tower that night, and efforts were made to try to talk the machine down, but to no avail.

Our CO or our Adjutant visited us at Tangmere, from time to time, and on one occasion was surprised to find that we had serviced five hundred aircraft in a two week period. In those days we had an air force!

When visiting Tangmere Museum in later years, a brochure described the Halifax as being one from 10 Squadron, and it was thought that the pilot was either wounded or dead, and that the Flight Engineer was trying to land it. An example of the stupidity of not having two pilots in RAF bombers — a whole crew lost. The USAAF always put two pilots in their bombers, light, medium and heavy. They, of course did not suffer a man-power problem, but I cannot believe that we could not have done the same.

One fine day, at Tangmere, we were servicing Typhoons and Spitfires when there was a hell of a long burst of 20mm cannon fire. All the men scattered, as we all obviously thought it was a strafing run by a German aircraft. As I recollect some dived under the parked aircraft which I felt was not a very good idea. I noticed a low brick wall some yards away, which I made a bee line for, intending to dive behind it. A Bedford 3 tonner was going the same way, but to the surprise of the driver I passed him, ON FOOT, going like a bat out of hell. The look on his face was quite something. Apparently the incident had been caused as result of an armourer, who had been checking the Typhoons, one previous to the bubble-hood type, getting out of the machine and shutting the door, probably rather heavily, and every gun in the machine commenced firing until, finally, the magazines were empty. Obviously, there was a fault, but that was the version we heard, anyway. I must say it caught us all by surprise, but the instincts of self-preservation took over pretty damned smartly. It was as well that the 'Typhie' sat pretty high with the tail on the ground, for the 120 shells from each cannon had to end up somewhere.

THE MAKING OF A COMMANDO
Dennis Smith

In 1943 I was serving at 'Stalag 13' in other words 13 MU, Henlow. I volunteered to form some special units along with several other 'bods' who came along as well. I never expected so many, as it was a very difficult Unit from which to get away.

Coltishall, Norfolk, was where we all met and eventually travelled on to Zeals in Wiltshire where apparently the Units were formed. I don't think much of importance happened until we were on our way to

Inveraray, Argyll. Our two DRs were Darkie Davis and Chunky Evans, the latter wore a vertical finger on his helmet with the words '*Digit Exractum*' – very appropriate we thought.

During this journey going south I noticed the route would take us through Worcester City, my home town. And as always I was short of cash and knowing that my father would be working in town I asked Darkie Davis to lend me his bike whilst he would carry on and drive my lorry whilst I visited my father at work and asked for the non-returnable loan of five shillings. Lucky for me he gave it to me, and then I made my back to the convoy where I rejoined my lorry and carried on driving.

We made our way from Inveraray and on to Zeals, then Coltishall without event, eventually arriving in Dunsfold in Essex where we entrenched some distance from the aerodrome, where we stayed for several days doing nothing in particular, until the Station WO found that some of our chaps had not washed or shaved for days. You can imagine what his reactions were – very, very, upset.

However, when we did begin working on the planes, Bostons, they got some quick turnarounds and back into action, the crew commenting that they had never done so much flying.

Soon afterwards we were off again to Odiham. Most of our time whilst we were there we were on Flight Duties. This is where I had a barney with a F.Lt. over his Mustang. I did a DI, checked oil and fuel, but never ran the engine as I was not conversant with the technical terms of the instruments etc. He was going to put me on a charge of neglect of duty etc. I put it to him 'Did you fly Mustangs without instruction?' At this, one of his officers interjected saying 'I can see the mechanic's point of view', at which point he calmed down and I heard nothing further. What was new to me was the starter sequence, one button energised then another engaged the starter. I did get it later on and the Mustang became my favourite plane.

Our next station was Hawarden, Cheshire, again on Mustangs, where we de-rated the supercharger with a smaller supercharger impeller.

From Hawarden we moved to Hawkinge, Kent, where the Unit got along really well with the CO. In fact, do you remember he owned his personal plane, an Airspeed Oxford, which he renamed 'Commando Boy' The emblem was painted on the nose of his plane 'Combined Ops', very impressive. It was painted by one of our lads from 3210.

Now the incident of the electric generator being 'borrowed' from the big house in the woods, and acquired especially for our own home comforts.

I just forget how it found its way on to my lorry, just before we were detached to Lasham to work on Mosquitoes. In the meantime a big enquiry was going on as to where the generator had gone, and what had happened to it, but without success, and there was a complete failure to trace it.

Whilst working on Mosquitoes at Lasham, does anyone remember the Mosquito which crashed there? At the time I was driving one of the trucks along a road, the perimeter, accompanied by a lad named Jones. I saw the plane coming in at a normal speed and height, when suddenly the engines opened up and the plane started to climb at a very steep angle, rising probably to 4-500 feet when it stalled and fell tail first and then turned on to its starboard wing and plunged into the ground and was immediately engulfed in a fireball. It appears the plane was being delivered to Lasham by a woman pilot of the Auxiliary Air Transport Unit and as she was about to land a red flare was fired from the Control Tower and she appeared to abort the landing but had not sufficient speed to get airborne again. A very tragic accident.

Does anyone remember the Mosquito coming back from a sortie with its bombs still on board? Apparently they were delayed fuses, and the bombs were removed and taken to an isolated spot on the drome until they detonated.

During our time at Lasham I was checking my lorry and to my amazement (??) I found a large generator. How did that get there! We then had to return to Hawkinge, where some of our strong arm conjurors replaced it on its concrete block base and bolted it down. It is marvellous how it got on to my truck, but then, miracles do happen.

Our next attachment was to Tangmere. There was a Canadian Squadron at this Station, and there I serviced a Spitfire for a sortie over France. The pilot was a Ft. Lt. Pigg, and he was a gentleman. When the flight returned my Spit. was missing. On enquiry I learned that the pilot had not turned over soon enough from the jettison tank to the main, so he ran out of fuel and was forced to land, which he did and started to run towards the woods. Then the other pilots went in and shot the plane until it caught fire. I never heard the outcome of that episode.

France 6 June 1944
We were loaded on to LCTs, not knowing where our destination was to be. During the crossing I must have dozed off, only to be awakened by a big bang. A German MTB had got into our convoy and fired a torpedo which hit one of our LCTs, which broke in half but kept afloat with a fire on board.

Now the landing. There were nine lorries on each LCT. The first one off on our unit was the Bedford 15 cwt. As soon as it hit the water it was swamped. The next lorry was a 3 ton Bedford which also went down the ramp only to be swamped also. I was the last lorry off owing to the fact that the two swamped wagons were obstructing the LCT and the skipper was forced to take up another position, but they did not let the ramp touch the bottom, so when it came our turn to drive off we went down with a fair bump. I carried extra weight also, having loaded some extra men from the swamped vehicles. And also we were expected to hand over our life belts back to the crew.

At the time I was accompanied by Bill (Jock) Geddes, a Sergeant of the Auxiliary Air Force. However, we were going well for about 70-80 yards, and Jock kept shouting 'Keep her going, Smithy!'. Unfortunately we stopped in really deep water. I tried and tried to get the engine going again, but failed.

I then opened the door and stood on the step waving my arms about frantically trying to get attention from any other vehicle which could tow us out. The tide kept sweeping us back to deeper water, so Jock and I got on to the cab, still waving our arms like mad. It was a good thing there were no snipers about. Eventually an army driver in a heavy gun carriage came to tow us to the beach, and as soon as he got us safely disconnected away he went to another rescue. I pressed the starter, and it fired straight away, and we were left to make our own way up the beach, and it was follow the leader after that.

In France

Our first strip was at Ver-sur-Mer, where we re-named the unit 'Mugs O'Malley's Orchard Rats'. Somehow, we always managed to pitch our tents in orchards.

The next strip was at St. Croux-Sur-Mer. I think it was there that an American pilot came in to land a Thunderbolt. On landing, something happened which turned the plane on to its back, but fortunately this plane had a very strong and tall tail which kept it from crushing the cockpit. Our lads were soon running to help the pilot, who was still conscious. They got under the cockpit, unstrapped the pilot and lowered him down on to his shoulders and then gently pulled him from under the plane. Do any of our men remember this incident, because there were a number of them involved. (Good job, men!)

Beny-Sur-Mer

As far as I remember this strip was much better then the first two as it was situated on the edge of the village.

This is where A Flight was very fortunate to have ME in their midst, because of my fluent French. At that time I used to walk down the lane to a farm with my Sten gun growing out of my shoulder (just in case!) On passing the entrance to the farm there appeared three daughters. Usually one of them could come out into the lane and greet me with 'Bonjour Monsieur' and I would reply 'Bonjour Madamoiselle', then, as I did not really know the French for milk or eggs, I somehow had to make them understand. 'Pardonez moi. Avez vous some (then using sign language: milking a cow and saying 'Moo. Moo. Moo.') She went into peals of laughter, and called her sisters to come and see. Much more laughter from them, especially when I tried asking for eggs, which was much more difficult. I tried making egg shapes with my fingers and cluck, cluck sounds. It seemed to work, and was certainly the cause of much laughter. Anyway, I came away with the milk and eggs, and with the knowledge that 'lait' is milk and 'oeuf' is egg. Or perhaps its the other way round.

The unit returned to UK on 31 July 1944, and we all went our different ways. I had a low demob number and so opted out from being posted to the Far East, but in November 1944 I was posted to Palestine, the land of Milk and Honey, where I really missed the comradeship of 3210.

THE END OF THE AMERICAN CO
Joe Woodley

I was serving with my Unit at Croydon when one morning in the mess hall an announcement was made over the Tannoy system (I understand that this message was given out that morning to all No. 11 Group fighter stations). It was explained that special units were being planned and volunteers were needed in all trades. Ten people from my R&R Party volunteered, and they included Cpl. Don Williams and a tough fellow from Glasgow, Jock Wilson, also an armourer. We subsequently learned we were to join newly formed RAF Servicing Commando Units. Initially they were always referred to as Servicing Echelons in an endeavour to preserve secrecy. Three of those Units were formed, and they were numbered 3201, 3202 and 3203. The unit which was being assembled at Croydon was numbered 3202.

The Unit left Croydon and arrived at RAF Stapleford Tawney, which is close by Abridge in Essex. It was at this station that the Unit was finally assembled and briefed before proceeding to Scotland for our commando training. The strength of the Unit was 147 men, including officers, NCOs and other ranks.

The appointed Commanding Officer was a Flt. Lt. Becker. He was an American who had served seven years with the US Marine Corps. He was a pilot who had seen service with the well-known Eagle Squadron, then serving with the RAF. He was a physical swashbuckling individual and with the entire Unit paraded before him he went to great lengths to explain the dangerous tasks we would encounter, adding that if anybody had second thoughts about staying with the Unit they could withdraw and no questions would be asked. He particularly directed those comments to the married men in the Unit. One married guy with whom I was friendly accepted the offer and was posted off the Unit. When I returned from my overseas service with the rank of LAC he had reached the rank of Sergeant. When one served in a specialised Unit opportunities for promotion were rare.

From Stapleford Tawney we proceeded to Inveraray in Scotland. The journey was made by road in the 12 American Studebaker trucks that were part of the Unit equipment. The Unit was also equipped with a motorcycle. Part of our training was to ensure that people were technically multi-functional. Everybody had to learn something of other peoples' trades, thereby enabling them to carry out daily inspections of aircraft in any trade. Everybody was required to learn to drive, although only specially designated people were truck drivers. Truck drivers were mainly engine fitters who could also maintain the vehicle. Second drivers were invariably airframe fitters who would also ensure the general bodywork of the vehicle was kept in good order. My own main second function was to be that of a Bren gunner. Every trade was represented in the Unit, there was a clerk to look after the administrative duties, a cook, and our medical needs were looked after by one man, LAC Thompson, who, of course, was always referred to as Doc. Thompson. The discipline side of the Unit was the responsibility of a Warrant Officer and a sergeant.

When the Unit arrived at Inveraray we were accommodated on a combined operations vessel named *Etteric* which was anchored in the middle of Loch Fyne. We spent a week on this vessel listening to lectures, which was followed by leaving the vessel by climbing down scrambling nets over the side and embarking into assault craft called R boats which proceeded to the shore and we made a beach landing while navy aircraft made simulated strafing runs over us. Standing on the prow of the first craft to reach the beach was our Armaments Officer FO Crocker. As the craft hit the beach he enthusiastically jumped from the craft to the beach. On hitting the beach he gave a loud yell. The unfortunate man had broken his leg. His place on the Unit was subsequently filled by a replacement Armaments Officer, PO Hatton.

I found the training tough. Some of the more physical specimens amongst us, particularly our American CO, seemed to sail through the exercises. During one simulated attack using our rifles and fixed bayonets through an assault course in driving rain I had an accident. While running through the course you were confronted by uniformed dummies which were placed just around bends and you were expected to bayonet these dummies. At the same time hidden instructors were hurling thunder flashes which would explode with a very loud bang. In addition hidden marksmen were firing live ammunition from automatic weapons. I rounded one bend on the course to be confronted by a sloping drop of about eight feet. I jumped, and on hitting the bottom of the slope took a tumble, finishing up with the bayonet badly cutting my right hand. This wound was stitched in the field with me sitting in a chair being 'supported' by a couple of colleagues. For some weeks my hand was in bandages and at meal times my food was cut up for me, usually by Cpl. Don Williams.

We had various training exercises in Scotland and towards the end of our training were assembled late one evening at the seaside resort of Ayr. The exercise was to board MLCs (motor landing craft) with our trucks at about 11pm, sail, and anchor in the middle of the bay. At first light next day we would make a beach landing on the opposite bay. While we were lined up at the quayside suitably attired with blackened faces the Scots ladies with their usual hospitality were handing out hot drinks and scones. One of the older ladies was crying and I said to her 'Don't worry, Ma, its only an exercise'. To which she replied 'That's what the other lot said, and they never came back'. I can tell you that lady's remark got us all thinking.

We did our beach landing at dawn and were confronted by Polish troops who by my reckoning were a little bit too realistic in their efforts to simulate the enemy. At the end of the exercise we proceeded to the combined operations camp HMS *Dundonald* at Troon.

On this exercise the American Studebaker trucks proved to be unsuitable. Not one reached the beach, and they were eventually replaced by British made three-ton assault type Bedford vehicles

After completing the commando course the Unit moved to RAF West Malling, where we performed various functions, mainly familiarising ourselves with different types of aircraft, and also carrying out route marches and physical training routines.

At this airfield at night they were flying a Boston bomber equipped with a searchlight. The theory was that the aircraft, equipped with radar, would pick up an enemy aircraft on its radar, and at the appropriate range switch on its searchlight illuminating the enemy aircraft which would then be attacked by one of the four-cannon Hurricane aircraft which were flying on either side of the Boston. One night there was an accident when all three aircraft collided. The Boston was blown to bits. One damaged Hurricane was landed by its pilot. The other Hurricane was destroyed. Next day our Unit was given the task of searching the surrounding countryside in an endeavour to locate the remains of the aircraft and bodies. I was in a party that found the Hurricane pilot. His parachute had candled and he had hit the rising ground with some force. We also recovered parts of aircraft.

From West Malling we moved to Ipswich Airport. This was an unused civilian airport, and our main activity was to service 11 Group fighter squadrons who would stay with us for a week engaging in air-to-sea firing. At week-ends from Friday night to Sunday evening we would sleep rough in the field where the aircraft were dispersed (this included the pilots) thereby experiencing conditions which would probably prevail on actual operations. We would parade at about 10 p.m. on the Friday evening after having been stood down at mid-day and given the rest of the day off. Unfortunately a number of the lads spent the evening in the local public house and over-indulged.

One Friday evening we were, as was the usual practice, doubled round to the dispersals with our American CO Ft/Lt. Becker riding the unit motor cycle bringing up the rear to ensure everybody kept up the pace. On reaching the dispersal somebody commented that we appeared to be without water. The practice was to take water to the dispersal in a sort of dustbin on wheels. The CO confronted Cpl. King regarding the missing water. The corporal disputed the COs assertion that he had made the corporal responsible for ensuring the water was taken to the dispersal. An argument ensued which resulted in the CO inviting the corporal to go into the woods and settle their differences. After discarding his peaked hat and tunic the CO accompanied by Cpl. King entered a wooded area. F/Sgt. Cassidy, a Canadian, said to the lads 'I will go and ensure fair play.' Or words to that effect. Whereupon the CO said 'Then take off your tunic. There are no ranks here.' Some time elapsed before Cassidy came back and he made a comment to the effect that the CO was murdering King. This inflamed some of the lads who, you must appreciate had been indulging in some heavy drinking during the evening. Then the CO returned and commenced to put on his tunic and cap when some of the lads made disrespectful comments. This caused the CO to whip off his tunic and cap and say 'Is there anybody else with a chip on his shoulder?', implying he was prepared to take on anybody. This brought forth a torrent of disrespectful and abusive language from many of those present. Whereupon the CO said 'Do I take it you no longer want me as your Commanding Officer?' To which a number of 'tanked up' individuals in the most abusive and blasphemous language told him where they thought he should go. With that F/Lt. Becker replaced his tunic, put on his cap, mounted the motor cycle and departed.

The Unit carried on as though nothing had happened. We carried out our usual routine of servicing aircraft, re-arming and re-fuelling between flights until the week-end exercise finished on the Sunday evening.

It was some weeks before we did get a replacement CO. Everything went on as though nothing had happened. We were also without our technical chief F/Sgt. Draycott who had apparently also had a dispute with the CO, and this had prompted the CO to have Roger Draycott posted off the Unit.

It is fair to say that up to that incident that brought about his departure we other ranks considered the CO to be a reasonable guy albeit very different to the type of RAF officer we had been used to. In anything of a physical nature he could compete with the best of us. He could certainly use his fists, and when firing on the range he obviously knew his stuff. He liked to wear revolvers, and at Ipswich I well remember an incident when Jock Watson (one of my old colleagues from Croydon) was sitting astride the unit motorcycle which was standing outside the CO's office. Suddenly through the office door appears the CO who on seeing Jock sitting astride the machine pulled out one of his revolvers and said 'Get off that machine or I'll plug you'. Needless to say my friend was off that machine in some hurry.

We eventually had a new Commanding Officer posted to us. F/Lt. Wheadon was not a regular but was a trained engineer who I understand worked for a company named Desoutters before volunteering for wartime duty with the RAF.

Another change was made when our discipline Warrant Officer, named Bunn, was posted from the Unit and replaced by another WO. I remember

Mr. Bunn as a very fair, and a kindly, fatherly figure. I guess his posting from the Unit was because of that Friday night incident. Roger Draycott also returned to the Unit. In a book he wrote about his experiences, Roger explains that after the departure of F/Lt. Becker the powers-that-be realised that complaints he, Roger Draycott, had been making regarding the conduct of F/Lt. Becker had some foundation and at the request of the headquarters senior officer responsible for our Unit, Roger agreed to return to our Unit. Quite soon, a new CO, F/Lt. Wheadon, was appointed.

I can never recall what happened to Cpl. King after his fight with the CO I do remember talking to King a few days after the fight. He was upset by F/Lt. Becker's departure, and said we had lost a good CO. He certainly never accompanied the Unit when it went overseas. Somewhere along the line he was 'spirited' away.

There is a school of thought that the main reason we were at Ipswich was because of an intended involvement of our Unit in the Dieppe raid in which there were very heavy Canadian casualties, and which proved to be a failure. Two facts could support this theory. First, there were assault landing craft berthed in the river Orwell close by Ipswich while we were there. Second, the Canadians captured a racecourse at Dieppe which they expected to be used as an airfield. The story goes that two Spitfires landed on the racecourse expecting to be refuelled. The authenticity of this information is open to question, but it makes one think.

The Unit's next posting was to RAF West Kirby prior to embarking on our first operational action. After spending a couple of weeks at West Kirby the Unit prepared to embark. We were divided into two groups. The half of the Unit I was in travelled to Glasgow and we were housed in a building at Langside, a suburb of Glasgow. On arrival our CO was informed by the Army RSM that our Unit would that evening have to supply six men for guard duty. It was decided to select the six men by drawing playing cards. I will never forget the RSM's face when he saw these RAF types drawing playing cards. Two of the unlucky lads were from Glasgow, and to do a guard duty would have scuttled their plans to see their families. Without hesitation two English lads volunteered to take their place.

Eventually we did board a ship on the Clyde. It was a Blue Funnel vessel named *Maron*. I volunteered to assist in the bakery. Initially this proved to be a mistake because being a land-lubber I was to suffer from sea sea-sickness made worse by the smell of yeast used in the making of bread. The ship's baker was a merchant seaman named Jim Sutherland. He had already been torpedoed three times at sea and had survived. I do remember that the day before we made our landing he made me a special cake which exactly fitted the square mess tin with which we were issued, and it proved to be a blessing.

PADRE FOR A DAY
Johnnie Lord

During the War in 1943, 'B' Flight of 3208 Servicing Commando was attached to RAF Bradwell Bay, where we became Duty Flight; and looked after all the visiting aircraft. It was only a flight, about 40 blokes, and we had two shifts night and day. A lot of aircraft were landing there for refuelling because it was the most easterly 'drome in England so they were refuelling when they were going to, say, Berlin, for photography, mainly PRU (Photographic Reconnaissance Unit) aircraft: Spitfires and Mosquitoes.

Whilst there, we had an arrangement whereby one of us corporals went to the mail office and collected 3208's mail, brought it back to the Flight and handed it around to people. One day one of our new arrival corporals, Jock, did this job, and, when he'd finished, he had one letter in his hand and he came to me at the desk and said 'What do I do with this?'. I had a look at it and saw it was addressed to the CO or Padre 3208 Servicing Commando, RAF Bradwell Bay. Our CO was with Headquarters Flight at RAF Ford so I said immediately to Jock 'Send it on to the Old Man at Ford', then I stopped and said 'Hang on, let's have a look at it, I recognise the handwriting'. When I turned the envelope over, I also recognised the address; it was from the wife of one of our lads, Bob, whose wife Betty was in the ATS stationed at Dover on an AckAck Unit.

So, before doing anything, we got Bob in from his job, I gave him the envelope and said 'What do you want me to do with this?' and he went white, looked as if he'd had the stuffing knocked out of him and said 'What can I do?' and I said 'If it was my wife writing to the CO or Padre of the Unit, I would steam the letter open, read it and, if it was OK, onward transmit it or burn it if it was against me'. In the back of our Nissen hut where we operated there was a back half with about ten beds in it for the night shift and there was a stove going there all the time. I said 'Put the kettle on the stove and get a head of steam up and steam it open'.

He came back with it about a quarter of an hour later and was in a terrible state. In his anxiety, he had torn the envelope and I immediately said to him 'I cannot send that on now' and he said 'Read the letter'. It was from his wife, and she was asking the CO or the Padre to interview her husband who she knew was a womaniser. At the ATS Unit she was then on, there was a Captain trying to court her, and wanted her to divorce Bob and marry him. Therefore she wanted the CO or Padre to have a talk to Bob and, if he was no longer interested in Betty, to let her know and she would go ahead with divorce proceedings. She also said in her letter that she hadn't heard from her husband for five weeks.

As the letter was in such a state, we couldn't send it on, so the only remedy was to go down to our billet, get my pad out and write to Betty as though I was the Padre. I said I'd interviewed her husband and his NCO, Corporal Loud, both fine upstanding men (I was laying this on) and I said that, if she hadn't heard from her husband in five weeks, she shouldn't blame her husband but to blame His Majesty's Mail because her husband and Corporal Loud said that he'd been writing regularly. This was a tongue in cheek gesture. Then I had to make it sound like a padre so I started collecting the few biblical pieces that I remembered and stuck these in; such as 'Remember, my dear, that whom God has joined together, let no man or woman put asunder' and I was saying to Bob 'What else can I say?' We added things like 'When you've made your wedding vows, you have to keep them' and so forth and I finished the letter but didn't know how to sign it (we didn't have a Padre), so I signed it Ronald (that sounded like a padre's name) Sprout, Vicar of 3208 Servicing Commando and sent it off.

About three days later, Bob had a phone call from the Orderly Room. She'd taken this letter (I'd never anticipated this) to her CO and showed him that her husband was caring and they gave her seven days compassionate leave to go and sort the marriage out so we had to give Bob leave (we were only an attachment, we had no excuse except that his marriage was breaking down); anyway we got him away and everything was fine.

Later on, when we started a paper for our Commando unit (we called it *Comm Ups)* the Editor, John, came up to me and said 'Would you write on sport or something, just an article to fill a few columns?'. So I did this. When, a few days later, he said they still hadn't got enough people to write articles, I decided to write a weekly article 'From the Pulpit Week by Week' by the Reverend Ronald Sprout, Vicar of Edsdown Beds as a skit on the church. I wrote several comic articles which the blokes had a chuckle about and it became known throughout the Unit. The magazine closed after about four issues, through, I think, lack of support.

Sting in the tail...

In 1945 (two years later) our Unit was disbanded into 15 OCU Harwell where we immediately handed over Harwell to the Atomic people and we went up to Middleton St George, a drome at Darlington, which is now Darlington Airport, and took that over from the Canadians. After several weeks, when it was decided that we'd be settled there, we got digs around and, although I went to Darlington and got several promises, nothing came of it until I went to a little village nearby called Eaglescliff and got digs there.

Unbeknown to me, Bob and Betty (the recipient of my Padre letter) and Angel and Tony had digs there. I arranged for my wife and Derek to come up and they arrived on Eve's birthday (22 August 1945); Bob had mentioned this to the landlady and she decided to have a little spread, like a birthday party although it was wartime rations, so, after getting to the digs, we went for this high tea. It was a good do with Angel and Tony and the lady and her daughter who was in the ATS who'd got on well with Betty who was ex-ATS. We had our tea and sat at the table afterwards smoking and Eve took out what I'd given her for her birthday.

I ought to explain that there were no birthday cards in those days so I'd bought a Patience Strong slip between two glass plates. I'd taken it apart and had written 'Happy birthday ... all my love' etc. on the back. Eve passed this round and everyone commented. Bet was sitting opposite me at the table, and when she turned it over, she made some observation about 'I think you can tell a person's character by their writing.' Now, my writing is awful, backhanded, sloping and with flourishes, and it suddenly dawned on me that she was looking at writing that she would relate, if she thought about it, to the vicar, so I immediately grabbed it and said something like 'You don't want to believe in this muck' and gave it to Eve and told her to put it away. Afterwards Eve said to me 'That was a bit rude'; she knew about the vicar, so I had to explain that Betty might have recognised the handwriting.

Asleep with the enemy

I have a calendar with a January picture of rocket-busting Typhoons at the Falais Gap. At the time of the Falais Gap, we were at Carpiquet (Caen) B17 I think it was called on our numbered airstrips at Normandy. Monty withdraw his armour from in front of us and decided to go round Caen and attack the German divisions behind Caen with two hooks known as Monty's Left Hook. The Americans formed up on the right and he swung his armour all the way round which, he said to us meant 'If you see a tank in front of you, shoot it, it's not British, it's German'. He trapped the German Army in the gap between Falais and Argentan and our Typhoons went in there firing rockets and cannon shooting up all the Germans there. They lost something like six or seven divisions and two armoured divisions; thousands of men were lost and this turned the war because the Germans then turned round and started retreating back to Germany.

However, a few days after this we decided there was looting there and we arranged to go a couple at a time to sort it out. The Gap was filled with dead Germans, dead cattle and horses, caravans obviously orderly rooms on the side, even dead Germans sitting down for a meal we found in one farmhouse. We didn't find much so we came back fairly early. I arranged for several of our lads to do the same if they wanted to go there, have a look round and get German medals that were strewn in the orderly rooms etc.

Two of our lads went two or three days later, Len and Sammy. They were both lighthearted, flibberty gibberty, never concentrating on what they were doing. When they got there they discovered there was a café in which they were fêted being the first English they'd seen and by mid-afternoon they were both pretty drunk. Then they decided they would go and do what they'd set out to do and go into the Gap. On their way to the Gap they saw a ditch with four German dead in it; one peered down and pointed out to the other that there were dead Germans and fell in and, in an attempt to help him out, the other fell in and they went to sleep.

They were pulled out at about 6pm by the French Maquis, the FFI (French Freedom Fighters), and they immediately, seeing one of them move, assumed they were live Germans and were on the point of shooting them. They had their blue RAF uniforms on; I'd assumed that, like us, they'd gone in their khaki working dress. However, Len had the sense to keep on saying 'Anglais, Anglais' until they cast some doubt in the Maquis' mind and were taken to a house and put into a top floor room with the front of the house blown out. They came back several hours later to say they'd sent for the British to come and interrogate them. Next morning an Army Captain came and started talking about England and, of course, they convinced him they were English. They came back about 11am having had a narrow escape.

Porky turned avenger

While we were at Martlesham Heath looking after 'rhubarbs' and 'sweeps', our cookhouse staff had obtained a piglet from the Station's well-run farm. This had made a welcome diversion from our RAF diet of tinned rations. After this delicacy, we were therefore eager to repeat it on a larger scale. One day driving near the perimeter track, we saw an errant pig wandering loose. We braked the lorry and tried to round it up but the pig took refuge underneath a stilted hut. Nothing loath, we got our camouflage net for one end and decided to drive the pig into it with about six lads holding it. Choosing the smallest lad, Joe, we got him to go in the other end to drive the pig into the net. I took up position at the side of the hut to organise the drive. Joe advanced on hands and knees towards the pig yelling like a demented cowboy, driving the pig towards the net. About six yards short of the net the pig sensed danger (or trouble) and turned with a snort and started walking towards Joe. Joe started to retreat as hastily as the cramped conditions would allow, and the pig started to run causing Joe to flop over in his anxiety to get away. The lads with the net came round to me asking what had happened but I was unable to tell them as I was rolling about laughing my socks off. Needless to say, the pig escaped our cookhouse. Joe was nursing his bruises but the rest of us were happy enough at the entertainment!

A RED-FACED ARMAMENTS OFFICER
Bob Breeze

On our journey over to Normandy on 6 June 1944, our Unit, 3210, were on two LSTs. Our Armament Officer, FO Hannaford, or Pretty Billy, was on the same LST as I was. During the trip he spoke to all the drivers, saying that if any driver changed gear while in the water we would have him to answer to.

After a long journey through the night we finally arrived. The ramp went down and the AO in his 15 cwt went slowly into the water and 'Bingo!', he changed gear, and, of course, the engine stopped. The Army Recovery Unit, using a somewhat worse-for-wear Churchill tank, pulled our red-faced AO and his 15 cwt out, and dumped him on the beach, so that the rest of the drivers could get ashore.

The AO never lived it down.

A WORLD RECORD?
Bryan (Rocky) Stone

Whilst in the Normandy Beach-head, 3208 SC was in a tented encampment, in an orchard, as I remember, and we had been withdrawn from air strip operations for a rest. Having had our clothes on for several weeks, apart from washing our bodies occasionally, I thought it might be a good time to change into a set of pyjamas that I had been carrying in my kitbag for ages. Night fell, and change I did, but the Luftwaffe decided here there was to be no rest for the wicked, and I had not been stretched out on the ground for long when we heard an enemy aircraft approaching and heading straight for our patch of Normandy. Every gun in the area opened up and the sky was full of flak. The aircraft passed overhead but at that moment one of our lads, I believe it was Dougie English, an armourer Cpl., had run up to a Bren gun on an anti-aircraft mounting and opened up.

Now I cannot believe that the German aircrew took any particular notice of our peashooter with all the other flak flying about, but I heard the engines roar as the throttles were pushed forward and guessed the pilot was about to make a steep turn. I took off from the tent in time to see tracers leaving the aircraft and coming in the direction of our site and I went like hell across the grass towards the unit water tanker which was some distance away. In seconds I was diving under the vehicle only to find that a Flight Sergeant, I believe it was F/Sgt Duckworth, also an armourer, had reached it before me. He really must have moved, *and* he was fully dressed. Shortly afterwards I made my way back to the tent, but it was not until daylight that I realised that the grass was covered with cow pats, for want of a better description, and my bare feet had missed every one of them. I had held medals for running as a boy, but on that occasion I must have broken all records for it would appear that my feet did not touch the ground!

THE THREE 'F'S
Dennis Munns

Beer was always what we wanted wherever possible, After that, it was one of the three 'F's.

I remember one time we were moving from one airfield to another and I was in the back of a truck with Jos. Williamson in the front. We conveniently had a bit of engine trouble. Nothing serious, just a fan belt slipping or broken. We managed to limp into the car park of a pub. It often happened in 3209, as I suppose it did in the other Units. Jos Williamson was our ACH GD, (Aircrafthand, General Duties) and looked after our stores. He was a very good man for the job. He nipped into the pub first to see if it was open and suitable for the rest of us. He took a new case of cook's and butcher's knives and tools. He came out again and said it was OK. There was two pints for each of us behind the bar. Just enough time to drink them while someone fixed the fan belt. Somehow the case of knives was left behind when we departed.

Jos would be just the chap to tell you about his interesting time in 3209. I don't think he had ever lived in a family home until he joined 3209. We were his family. Now he is married and I don't know how he would feel if his story was published. Getting back to our pre-D-Day time. On our evenings off we would go in search of beer. Some of the lads, Jos included, would look for a dance hall, and preferably one that sold beer. Jos would size up the females and then go up to the one of his choice and say 'Do you fuck, lass?' He never once got his face slapped. Some would leave him and walk away. But others would lead him outside and be really friendly.

We had another character, a Welshman, Taff, of course. He could sing Every Sunday morning, whenever possible he would be in church or chapel. In the front row where everyone could see him, and he would lead the singing. Taff had a lovely Welsh voice and he knew all the hymns. Of course some kind lady would invite him home. Often he would get Sunday lunch, maybe into bed with the lady of the house or her daughter. He usually got his laundry done and his socks darned. Once he had the mother and the daughter, but not at the same time. Sometimes I think it pays to be religious.

In Normandy we were operating from B2. There was talk of Spitfires and Typhoons bringing in beer, but I don't remember getting any. We did get some red wine that one of our drivers got in exchange for some petrol He didn't wash the jerry can out properly, and it tasted horrible. We were drinking it out of mess tins.

A VERY WET LANDING
Ken Garrett

My stay with 3206 was short, but I enjoyed every minute of it. What engaged the minds of many of us before the invasion was how would we cope with the actual landing. In the event, it was indeed spectacular, though admittedly we did not have to storm ashore under a hail of shell, mortar and small arms fire.

We approached the landing area late in the afternoon. I went up on to the bridge to get a better view, and was immediately struck by a huge cloud of what appeared to be brown smoke rising from a field a mile or so beyond the beach. The skipper of our LCT said he thought it was shell fire. Later, when we were operating on B6, our first landings strip, I realised that this had been dust thrown up by aircraft taking off. Dust was the bane of our lives. It got into every aperture in our bodies; when we blew our noses, our handkerchiefs became black; our eye lids were permanently sore as they rode over sharp grit every time we blinked, and we even had to eat it with our food.

As we neared the shore, we were told that the sea was too rough for the landing craft to approach,, and that we would have to lay wallowing at anchor off shore, and hopefully, land in the morning. The navy issued each of us with a tin of soup with a candle in a countersunk hole at one end. The candles were lit, and I opened mine to enjoy the only hot meal we had had on that day, thankful for small mercies. In the failing light I entered a door into a room beneath the bridge. Greeted by a chorus of loud snores, and the stench of unwashed bodies, I decided to risk the night in the back of one of our trucks, shielded by only its canvas tilt cover from the shrapnel that whistled down and tinkled down around the steel decks.. I comforted myself with the thought that during the blitz in London I had never been hit by the showers of jagged steel that came down there, and in any case, here we had an infinite expanse of sea all around for it to fall into.

By this time the scene around the LCT was spectacular. Enemy aircraft were overflying at high altitude and dropping bombs. A little further out to sea, destroyers were laying smoke screens around some capital ships. A gunner in the LCT next to us was firing skywards with what sounded like a 20mm cannon. He was soon silenced by his skipper, who shouted across from the bridge telling him to stop wasting ammunition on an enemy that was way out of range. Around us were hundreds of vessels of all sizes, each sporting a barrage balloon tied to its stern, to discourage the enemy from attacking at low level. All this, with a huge river of tracer welling up screamingly into the sky, the explosions above and below, the balloons and accompanying firework display, reminded me of a fairground back home.

Morning came, and the landing craft glided up to the shore. Down went the ramp, and out drove our CO accompanied by a WO in the Unit's Jeep. There was a splash, and the Jeep with its occupants disappeared and two hats floated up to the surface, to be followed quickly by two heads, whose owners retrieved their hats and swam ashore. Later a tow chain was attached to the Jeep, which was hauled out and a dry replacement issued. The ramp had gone down over a huge hole that had been blown in the sea bed previously by an underwater defence device. Accordingly, the ramp was lifted and the LCT withdrawn and brought ashore further along the beach. The ramp was lowered again, and down went the remainder of 3206.

As I peered over the bonnet of our truck down at the ramp and at the sea beneath, I pondered on how deep it might be, but I need not have worried. Our vehicle had been well waterproofed and we drove through the waves, still fairly high, and on up the beach. Here we were guided between white ribbons from which skull and cross bone flags were fluttering, to mark a path what had been cleared of mines, into an assembly area. A dispatch rider appeared and led us off to B6, the airstrip to which we had been allocated.

FRIENDLY FIRE
Ken Garrett

Our Typhoons bore a superficial resemblance to the German FW190s, and also to the Thunderbolts of the American Air Force. They all had a round nose and blunt wings. Quite frequently the Typhoons were attacked by the Thunderbolts of a Wing operating nearby. Fortunately, the attacks were not particularly successful. One day our Group Captain sent a signal protesting about those attacks to the CO of the nearby American Thunderbolt Squadron. The reply came back quickly, and was posted for all to see. 'You should worry. One of my boys shot me down this morning.'

HAPPY DAYS
Ken Garrett

My mind goes back now and again to some of the camp dances at the various stations in England we visited. On our last night it invariably ended up with 3206 assembling at one end of the dance floor, and forming a rugby scrum, which then moved to the other end of the floor at a rate of knots, sweeping all before it. The final act was to form a pyramid, which was climbed by one of the smaller and lighter members, who affixed a postage stamp to the ceiling and wrote '3206 SC' across it – just to remind people that we had been there – and gone! At our next station we were sometimes met with deductions from pay to meet bills for barrack room damages.

THE LAST REUNION
Bill Geddes

'The Reunion will be held at 8.00pm', the Association letter read,
And it made me think of things I did when it was twenty hundred
   hours instead.
I remembered all those days and nights and early morning calls,
Nissen huts and iron beds and pin-ups on the walls.
Naafi vans, tea and wads and 'Who's pinched me flaming mug?'
Remember Chalky and Lofty, Tinker Bell and Tug?
There were sergeants and corporals and their 'blinkin' ' sons.
Blokes from Leeds and Belfast, Londoners and Brums.
Waafs from Glasgow, Swansea, Newcastle and Roedean.
A priest from Littlehampton, a padre from Aberdeen.
Cooks, drivers, armourers and sparks, fitters, riggers, mechanics and
   clerks.
Merlins and gremlins, magnetoes and throttles, Mae Wests, dinghys
   and oxygen bottles.
Pitot heads and picquets, thumbs up and away.
It looked as though the War might last till Xmas Day!
France and Germany, India, Burma and Malaya.
Remember all those Tomahawks, Kittyhawks, Austers, and Otters,
Buffaloes, Battles, Bostons and Baltimores,

Dakotas, Commandos, Bombays and Harrows, Wellesleys and
   Albamarles,
Whitleys, Wellingtons, Tiger Moths and Ansons.
Swordfish, Gladiators, Hampdens and Hudsons, Fulmars and Barrucudas,
Lysanders, Blenheims, Beauforts and Beaufighters.
Manchesters, Stirlings, Halifaxes and Lancasters.
Flying Forts, Thunderbolts, Mitchells and Marauders.
Whirlwinds, Lightnings, Tempests and Typhoons,
Defiants, Mosquitos, Mustangs and Meteors.
Catalinas, Sunderlands, Walruses and Liberators?
Flying fathers, sons and brothers, husbands and fiances.
Bombers' moon. P.O. Prune, things that went bump in the night.
'It's one of ours', but one of theirs if you dared to show a light.
Spitfires whistling through the air; Hurricanes' Victory Roll.
Aircrews from the Commonwealth, Norwegians, Czechs and Poles,
Pilots and Air Gunners and Pathfinders true,
Wireless Operators, Bomb Aimers, Navigators and Flight Engineers too.
Wing Leaders, Squadron Leaders and Air Aces bold, I read all their
   stories and adventures now told.
There were Yanks, there were tanks, jeeps and Betty Grable.
We all smoked Camels and Capstan, even Passing Cloud, if you were able.
Glass houses, sweatboxes, 'In The Mood' and 'Loving You'.
Church canteens, the blackout and Doodlebugs I and II.
I remember songs that Vera sang, and some she never knew.
I thought of places far away and all those sounds and smells,
Reyjavik, and Normandy, and Far East temple bells.
Charpoys, rickshaws, things I can't repeat.
Paddy fields, monsoon rains and bloody prickly heat.
I remember all the pals I made, and those who never made it back,
But if we had not been there
There would have never been 'The Few.'
I'm glad I served in Air Force Blue,
With you – and you – and you.

REPORT BY FL. LT. A (MUGS) O'MALLEY ON THE OPERATIONS OF 3210 IN NORMANDY.

To sum up, it can be said that the men carried out duties expected of them in a manner which does credit to the Unit, but it must be recorded that they could have coped with at least three times as much work and were disappointed that more could not be found for them. Admittedly, the weather had a strong bearing on this matter, but each man, over a period of months, had trained himself to work flat out for days on end, and naturally there is always the sense of frustration when the quantity of work falls below expectation.

PART III

Background to Operations in South-East Asia

THE WAR AGAINST JAPAN was primarily an American operation, and British participation, after the initial defeats of 1941, was largely confined to the defence of India in Burma, and then the defeat of the Japanese occupiers of Burma.

In truth, Burma was a very minute part of the conflict, and the major battles, after the defeats of 1941, were fought by the American navy and airforces, over the vast distances of the Pacific and its myriad islands. However, some of the war's hardest and most vicious battles were fought by the British 14th Army and by Indian troops.

The roots of the war against Japan lay in the particular geo-physical nature of the Japanese archipelago. Those islands had few natural resources for manufacturing and inadequate land to feed a rapidly growing population. Between 1920 and 1940 the population rose from 55 million to 71 million. Increased foreign trade, or vastly increased emigration, or perhaps both, were essential.

Japan chose to use force to impose the conditions for its own prosperity. The occupation and exploitation of vast areas of China, plus the overthrow and annexation of the British, Dutch, French and American colonies in the oceans surrounding Japan, would provide the essential conditions for overseas settlements and assured sources of raw materials, and also markets for Japanese manufactures. It was simple: they only had to conquer half the world, bend the world to the will of Japan, and live happily and richly ever after. Meanwhile, other great powers in Europe and Eastern Europe were tearing themselves to shreds in a great struggle, and who knows what advantages the result of that struggle might offer to Japan.

Consistently, Japan pressed outwards against its boundaries, especially in China. However, in 1938 and 1939 unexpected victories by Russian troops after Japanese border transgressions shifted interest to the south, and this was especially so after the success of Germany's blitzkrieg war against the colonial powers of Britain, France and Holland.

In September of 1940 Japan began expanding southward by occupying the northern part of French Indo-China. A year later the Vichy French government gave free permission for Japanese forces to enter southern Indo-China and set up bases and airfields. The way to the south was open: Malaya, with its wealth of rubber and tin, and the Dutch East Indies with vast supplies of tropical products plus oilfields were just waiting to be occupied and exploited.

However, America was aware of Japan's hopes and plans, and was stirring. Her own colony of the Philippines could well have been next on the list of Japanese annexations. President Roosevelt imposed an embargo on the export of oil to Japan, an action promptly followed by Britain and the Dutch government-in-exile. Then all Japanese funds in America and Britain were frozen, and Japan was cornered. Her choice was simple; she could abandon her expansion into China and give up her planned 'Greater East Asia Co-Prosperity Sphere' (the Japanese name for the planned empire in South-East Asia), or she could fight. She chose to fight.

At 7.55am on Sunday 7 December 1941, Japan launched a surprise air attack on the American Pacific Fleet moored at Pearl Harbour, Hawaii. An hour latter, Japan made a formal declaration of war against the United States.

Within half an hour of the first bombs falling on the American warships, the US battle fleet had been effectively put out of action and the Japanese were masters of the western Pacific.

On 11 December 1941, Germany and Italy also declared war against the United States. The major pattern of the Second World War was then complete. The British Empire, the Soviet Union and the United States were at war with Germany, Italy and Japan, although the Soviet Union did not declare war on Japan until 1945.

The Japanese war aims were simple and ambitious, and they made no secret of them. They 'intended to seize and exploit a very large and economically self-sufficient area and defend it if necessary.' Attacks on their new empire would be difficult and expensive, entailing travel over enormous distances and therefore long exposure to Japanese defenders. Slowly the will of the Americans and British would be sapped and the will to fight diminish until they accepted Japanese control of Hong Kong, Malaya, Singapore, the Philippines, the Dutch East Indies, Thailand, Burma, French Indo-China and the host of smaller territories littering the Pacific seas.

But they were wrong. In spite of so many initial defeats and losing so many territories, the Allies' will to fight on was never in doubt. Nor was their final victory. The occupation of Malaya and the Dutch East Indies meant that Japan had three-quarters of the world's natural rubber and two-thirds of the tin. More important, the Dutch East Indies produced enough oil for all of Japan's needs, together with vast quantities of palm oil, tea, coffee, and sugar. The problem was conveying that wealth of raw material to the Japanese homeland. It had to be done by sea, of course, and gradually American and to some extent British and Australian sea power grew sufficiently to render that difficult and ultimately impossible.

Although the US had – reluctantly – agreed to British arguments that the war against Germany should have priority, nevertheless the US entered a period of intensive warfare in the Pacific. Gradually, island by island, territory by territory, the Japanese forces were driven back towards their homeland. There were furious battles in places where the climate and the land were a menace as great as the enemy.

As the battles got nearer to the Japanese homeland, so did the ferocity of the Japanese troops increase. The Americans advanced 3000 miles in eighteen months, but it took ten weeks to win the battle of Okinawa. The invasion of the Japanese homeland was expected to bring ever more fierce and expensive resistance. A strategy was agreed for the final battle. In November of 1945 thirteen or fourteen American divisions would invade the Japanese homeland island of Kyushu, and in March 1946 twenty five divisions plus a small British Commonwealth force would attack Honshu and impose unconditional surrender, if necessary amid the ruins of Tokyo.

The British and Indians were scheduled for only a minor role in this scenario. Already they had almost completed the liberation of Burma. When the time came, they would land on the Malayan peninsula and clear that, then accept the Japanese surrender at Singapore.

Although, in the greater picture, the battles in Burma were of less significance than the island re-conquests of the Americans, never-the-less between 1942 and 1945, over 305,000 Japanese soldiers fought in Burma, and 180,000 of them died there. In fact, they fought supremely well, but ultimately they were defeated, and by the time the Emperor surrendered in 1945, they were little more than demoralised, defeated remnants, with no air support, hungry and devoid of supplies, and with no central control or organisation.

However, the planned scenario could not be followed. A new factor appeared in the equation. This was the atom bomb. The arguments for and against its use on a civilian population were long and rancorous, and indeed continue to this day. The final decision lay with the American Commander-in-Chief, the new and untested President Harry Truman. He decided, and early on 6 August 1945 three B29 bombers took off from Tinian in the Mariana Islands, and at 8.15am the bomb was released at 32,000 feet over Hiroshima. Forty-five seconds later it exploded at 2,000 feet, with consequences we all know.

In Washington, President Truman issued a statement threatening the Japanese people 'with a rain of ruin from the air, the like of which has never been seen on this earth.'

On 8 August Russia declared war on Japan, and on 9 August a second atomic bomb was dropped almost over the centre of Nagasaki. The Japanese knew that only unconditional surrender was acceptable by the Allies and this was resisted, mainly by some sections of the army. However, after much discussion, the Emperor used his discretion and his imperial powers to overcome the opposition and on 15 August 1945, in a broadcast to his nation, announced the unconditional surrender of Japan, and thus the end of the Second World War.

Operations in South-East Asia

OUTWARD BOUND
Joe Grainger

On 25 October 1944 the Unit, 3205 Servicing Commando, moved to West Kirby, ready for final preparations prior to embarking for the Far East. We embarked on the ss *Otranto*, bound for Bombay. Our ship sailed first for the Clyde, there to join up with a large convoy of which the *Otranto* was the lead ship. There were about 4,000 troops aboard, and for four weeks we were in almost complete idleness.

Our mess deck was eight decks below the water line, so there was no natural light. It was there that about two hundred and fifty of us would live, sleep and eat. There were tables with fixed bench seats with just enough room between rows to walk. It was well up into the bows, with the walls sloping sharply outwards and the floor and ceiling sloping upwards to the narrowing front end. Two huge steel pipes ran down the room, and we learned the hard way that the anchor chains ran through them.

The atmosphere was terrible, hot, dirty, stinking of bodies and sweat, and, when not long after sailing into the northern seas, it became quite rough, sea sickness added to our pleasures. Those in hammocks had the slight advantage that at least no one could be sick over them.

Once at the Suez Canal we were ordered to put away our UK uniforms and change into the tropical gear issued at West Kirby. This consisted of khaki drill trousers, very heavy and actually heavier than the denim working battle dress we had worn back in Europe. A completely shapeless half-drill aertex material jacket, long sleeved and long waisted, which looked and felt awful, and to finish the 1800s-style uniform, a huge solar topee, heavy, and with a small peak, quite useless for shading the eyes, and with a long square back brim. The whole outfit looked pathetic, but fortunately we found we would not wear it for very long.

On 4 December we began to smell India, and late in the day could see, a strange and warming wartime sight, the lights of Bombay. We docked early the next morning and half a dozen of us were ordered ashore to see our arms and ammunition off-loaded and guarded. This was quite a good scrounge. It gave us a good look at this strange new world, and although most of us had only small change, we found prices so ridiculously low that even we could afford tea and cakes – cha and wads.

At Bombay we had more medicals, more jabs and, thank goodness, a complete issue of new tropical kit, this time in 'jungle green', battle dress, really lightweight uniforms, underwear, socks etc., including two sets of shorts all in jungle green. The despised topees were thrown away and very good bush hats issued. They were of hardwearing felt with a large all-round brim, a sweat band and a 'pugaree' surrounded the hat just above the brim and in this was an RAF flash to distinguish us from the common herd. We had to dye all our webbing and any other items such as spare underwear, handkerchiefs etc. in vats of green dye, evil-smelling stuff which soon dried off.

On 10 December we left Bombay, on our own troop train, for Calcutta. It was a very slow journey, stopping, it seemed, at every station en-route. Whenever it did so, we besieged the engine driver for boiling water from the engine for cha-making, shaving, washing – we must have milked hundreds of gallons of water off the old steamer. The coaches were 'Native 3rd Class', all wood, no glass in the windows, and open 'bog' platform at the rear of each coach (no false modesty here!) It was pretty grim, really, but the journey made an interesting change, with lots of strange countryside and villages to look at.

It ain't 'arf 'ot, Mum
We travelled right across India, skirted round Calcutta, and transferred to a river steamer which took us to the West Bengal port of Chittagong. We moved on from there to Petanga arriving on 18 December, and awaited the allotment of MT vehicles, tents and other equipment, pending the arrival of our own technical equipment from UK.

On 2 January 1945 we set off from Petanga, carrying, in addition to all our men, technical equipment and aircraft spares, fifty tons of 100 octane aircraft fuel, ten tons of 20mm and .303 ammunition, oxygen, aircraft lubricants and glycol etc. The first part of the journey was on reasonable roads as far as Burma, where we paused for food etc, then off again on gradually worsening roads into heavier and denser bush and jungle until at last we broke out on to the beautiful clean wide beach of the Arakan coast of Burma.

Now the last 150 miles was on the beach, good going, but with no cover, and very, very hot. There were the most marvellous mirages in which we could distinctly see our own vehicles travelling continuously toward us but of course never getting closer. At intervals of a few miles the beach was broken by chaungs. These were deep tidal inlets from the sea, some running miles inland. Each of these had to be forded, which with our old and decrepit vehicles, not four wheel drive and not water-proofed, was a dodgy and quite dangerous job. The crossing had to be as close to the sea as possible so as to have minimum depth, but with maximum width as the chaung opened out to the sea. Tidal conditions were highly critical, due to the effect on water depth and flow speed. Men could not be endangered by crossing in the vehicles, which themselves had to be nursed over one at a time with everyone standing by to push or pull as and when a truck started bogging down. The whole process was time consuming and nerve wracking and occasionally stopped for several hours as the tide ebbed and flowed. We had no option but to continue after dark to take advantage of the low tide. It was a beautiful starlit night, but we were constantly in danger of being caught in the open by Jap aircraft, but our luck held.

On 4 January we moved off the beach up a short but steep hill forming a headland. We had reached Foul Point, from which we would go down to a small beach to embark in Landing Craft for the invasion of Akyab Island, some five miles off the Arakan coast.

We now learned much to our surprise and even greater relief that the Japanese had abandoned the island just previously. We embarked, sailed and landed on North Beach at 20.00 hours. We now had another surprise: it appeared that our vehicles were not to come with us, but were to be unloaded and everything was to be manhandled to the airstrip a mile or so inland. It was so utterly ridiculous that our CO blew his top and refused completely to disembark. After some hours delay, with the aid of the Navy sending urgent signals to HQ 224 Group, we were granted permission to retain five of the 3 ton trucks. Even so, it meant hours of unloading, transferring our equipment etc, and ferrying it all to the strip. Had the Japanese stayed and fought, our situation would have been completely hopeless, with the corresponding risk of no aircraft being able to operate for several days, presuming we survived. That episode was one of several which made us realise the hard way that organisation and planning were very, very different from what we had been used to with 2nd TAF.

Fenton's Follies

We were in Chittagong when we learned of the German surrender and the end of the war in Europe. It was decided that we must do something to mark the occasion, and a concert party was formed and named 'Fenton's Follies'. I never learned whether our CO really appreciated this or not, but the name stuck, and became the Unit's own name for itself, and this continued until we were disbanded.

The base for the concert was a large flat clearing which we surrounded on three sides with blankets up on poles to form a back cloth, old balloon fabric stretched across the floor was the stage, and on this were a number of large cases, covered with sheets as tables with smaller boxes as chairs. At the rear was a long case covered with sheets and fixed up with beer pump handles. Those doing turns sat at the tables and stepped up front when ready. The only thing missing was the booze; we had to pretend with orange juice and such – or did we?

Only a day or two before the show, the Unit's liquor rations for the past three months caught up with us, including three gallons of Navy issue rum. The mistake was made of serving real booze at our bar, and the show, intended to run about three hours, in fact lasted more like ten hours. Many of the turns were good, and the Unit band provided background music. There was no question that the best act of all was our 'Awkward Squad'. The idea of course is as old as the hills. A squad armed with rifles who do just about everything possible wrong, back to front, upside down, in reverse and so on during a series of standard drill movements. The lads themselves acted their parts brilliantly, but the masterpiece was Bill Langridge as the Drill Sergeant. It happened that Bill had in fact spent years as a Drill Instructor and it was in his bones. Any sloppiness and Bill automatically reacted, and now it came to the surface. After the first few minutes of 'acting' he started getting annoyed, so of course the lads acted even more outrageously. The crowd were almost in tears with laughter, but Bill could have been heard in Chittagong, and it really seemed he might do the unthinkable and thump someone. One of the squad whilst fiddling with his rifle, was supposed to 'put one up the spout' – a blank, of course – and fire it. That was fine, except that the selected shooter fired a live round which luckily just missed Bill.

That should have ended the concert, but the cast, under the influence by now, carried on. Chiefy Evans, a Welshman with a marvellous voice who had brought the house down with his first batch of songs, was called on to repeat it, which he did, and then there was a general sing-song which went on for hours. Most of the cast slept on the stage and even the mossies (mosquitoes) dare not bite us that night, but next morning it was a case of 'death where is thy sting.'

Malaya

The Unit embarked on 27 August on the Orduna in Bombay, bound for Malaya. We did not know it then, but the war was in fact over. The Japanese had accepted unconditional surrender on 15 August. We did not learn of this until 9 September, when we were at sea, and all sirens on all the ships in the convoy sounded. It is impossible to describe the relief and unadulterated joy. Everyone had a 'tot', but it is doubtful if a gallon each could have had much more effect then the news that the war was over.

So, amid complete pandemonium, we sailed on, and learned that it was intended we should still land at Morib beach, about half way between Port Swettenham and Port Dickson. This was to be Operation Zipper, and it soon began to seem that many of the wisecracks about 'having nothing buttoned up' were remarkably accurate.

Early on 9 September we approached land and transferred into a variety of landing craft several hundred yards off shore. The ships could not get closer because of a multitude of rocks, so our small landing craft had a run-in of four or five hundred yards and the field of fire for well dug-in Japs in jungle only yards behind the beach would have ensured our reception was a very warm one. Even our landing craft had to drop us into some five feet of water, and wading ashore with full battle kit and weapons is dicey at such a depth. Once again Operation Zipper had lived up to its reputation. It is a fair estimate that had there been opposition to our landing, no more than 30 or so men would have reached the airstrip, with no more equipment than they had been able to carry. They would to all intents and purposes have been useless. According to the planning, the very next day they were to have serviced eight Spitfires and three Mosquitoes. However, there was no opposition, and once we were all ashore we headed inland to our destination, a Jap airstrip some three miles from the beach.

On reaching the strip we were astounded and very amused when the large Jap force, several hundreds strong, received us on the entrance road at formal parade and saluted arms. No one really knew quite how to react, but the CO and officers had the Japanese officers surrender formally. Their men moved to their own area and were left to await further orders.

Now the incredible Jap character showed its quite remarkable ways. Only yesterday they were our worst enemy, fighting until killed, no surrendering, completely untrustworthy etc., now the old Emperor having said 'Pack up, lads,' they did so totally and abjectly.

Germans once captured, even after the war in Europe ended, would obey orders from our people reluctantly and would scrounge off, pilfer everything they could and cover up for each other one hundred per cent. The Jap was exactly the opposite, bowing, scraping, grinning. You could put them to the hardest jobs, put their NCOs in charge and they worked their men like slaves. If one tried to skive off his NCO would haul him up for punishment. We now learned that the Jap Army disciplinary system seemed to be based on physical punishment. Offences would be dealt with summarily by a sergeant, say, by anything from a slap across the face to a real two-fisted beating-up depending on the crime. If the man tried to dodge then the lid came off and others would be made to hold him while he was beaten almost senseless. At first we let them do it, having no love or respect for them whatsoever, but eventually we made them cut it out, but then neither men nor NCOs knew what they should really do.

Another most unpleasant facet of the Japs came to light. They were being detailed off for various fatigues, cleaning monsoon ditches etc., but because a few were to be used by our cooks on fatigue in the food stores etc., our Medic, Cpl. Dixon, checked a party of twelve off and he was shocked to find eight had VD. So Dixon reported this to the CO, who reported it to the Chief MO. As a result it was found that something in excess of forty percent of all Jap prisoners had VD. We hurriedly kicked all POWs away from our workings.

On 12 September the CO and myself left by jeep to reconnoitre the road down to Singapore pending the arrival of the Unit's vehicles. I was to return by bike to guide the convoy down. The jeep was loaded with goodies, cigarettes mainly, and en-route we looked for our POW camps. We found two. Amid scenes of terrific pleasure we gave them all the news, promising to advise HQ Malacca to send relief vehicles. It was a most satisfying job, giving all great pleasure, even almost tears. We were appalled to see the state of the POWs and learn of the treatment they had been getting from the Japs. It did more to influence our opinions of the Japs than all previous official propaganda. Indeed, the writer to this day has as little to do with the Nips as possible, even to the extent of being at a disadvantage to himself on occasion.

Whilst travelling through the mountains down central Malaya, the CO and I met a whole Jap regiment on the march. Wondering if this lot knew about the surrender, the CO hurriedly rooted round in the back of the jeep and dug out his cheese-cutter cap. I thought I should do something useful, so unfastened the holster and took out my revolver, only to discover that a colony of ants had nested there overnight, probably attracted by the gun oil. There was much frantic brushing and shaking just before the Japs got to us.

We stood formally to attention, the Japs halted and what was obviously their Officer in Charge marched forward, accompanied by several other officers, one of whom spoke quite good English. They halted a few feet from us, saluted and bowed deeply, hands clasped in front of faces. Bill Fenton also saluted and in a very loud, harsh voice ordered me to go forward, and bring the Jap CO to him. He came quite willingly, stopped when I shouted halt, then I saluted our CO and in a loud voice reported 'Japanese Commander, Sir.' When asked, they said they didn't really know where they were going, but were in fact looking to meet up with the British to receive orders. Bill then told them he would accept their formal surrender. They must remove their officers' swords and leave them with all their flags stockpiled at the road side by our jeep. This they did without the slightest protest or even signs of distress. Bill then laid his map on the jeep bonnet and showed the Japs that we were on the road to Malacca, some sixty miles off. He ordered them to go and report to the military there. More salutes and bowing and away the Japs went, the rear brought up by half a dozen small mobile guns pulled by soldiers. (My revolver would of course have taken care of those!)

We were left with a pile of swords and flags. The CO took the Jap COs sword and I took another very fancy weapon, also a flag each which we buried in the back of the jeep under our clobber. The remainder, seventeen swords and thirty two flags we piled together tied up and dumped on top of the stuff in the back. We were both highly amused at this incident, which somehow was the Servicing Commando Unit thumbing their collective noses at the great Japanese Army.

A STRATEGIC RETREAT
Bill (Jock) Geddes

The first thing I must get off my chest is to apologise to the two lads who did not receive a letter which they might have been expecting while with 3210 SC at Dubbhumqahr in Bihar, India.

I was instructed to proceed to the RAF Post Office in Dalhousie Square, Calcutta (where the original Black Hole was, long before Steven Hawking discovered them.) Among other things, I was to bring back mail for the Unit.

I went by a Harvard plane piloted by an Indian Flt. Lt., a very 'goodness gracious me' type, but a very nice person as I remember. It was on our return journey when over the Howrah Bridge he suddenly dived down towards his family assembled there to greet him. Then he suddenly pulled the nose up, which, according to Newton's Laws one to ten, had the effect of pushing me floorwards and loosing my grip on the precious mail. At least two of those flimsy air mail letters flew out of the rear cockpit in which I was grovelling. I have never forgotten those letters and herewith apologise to whom so ever it did concern. Who knows what news, good or bad, they contained.

I did not inform the CO, Mugs O'Malley, who would have shot me; that's the way he was – he did not like Scotsmen. That was in August 1945. If some young wife had been reporting the birth of a baby, it would be 57 years old now.

My other bad dream concerns a leave in which a number of us, mostly NCOs. I think, had to travel from King's Cross. We had a drink that lunch time in a pub named the Scottish Stores just outside the station. There was a blind oldish male pianist bashing out 'My eyes are dim, I cannot see' etc. A Sergeant Lawton suggested that as the pianist grabbed his free pints off the top of the piano without spilling a drop, then 'he couldn't have been blind; he had eyes in the back of his head.' The pub was crowded with bods who were dead ringers for the Kray twins, the Kray sextuplets etc, and we had to get out of there smartish.

Thus there were six Commando NCOs on the run from the 'blind' pianist and his mates. All that unarmed combat stuff we had learned did not help. We had Japanese strangleholds, spine-stretching grips, head holds and all at our finger tips and ready for instant use, and were 'trained killers'. However, they were trained pianists, so we ran. Sorry, Ft. Lt. O'Malley and WO Ramsbottom, to let you down in that way.

There are probably lots more to tell, but I keep on laughing. I did service in Iceland, Normandy, Malaya and Java, and got my 'comeuppance' just once, at the rout of the NCOs by the blind pianist at King's Cross.

A TALE FROM SAIGON
Eddie Stevens

Tubby was an unusual SP.

A large jovial man, he took a shine to the Commando Unit and became a good friend to some of the guys. The guardroom was a hut at the start of the dirt road which led into Saigon – no doubt the road will be a major highway now. In 1945 there was opposition to the return of the French to Indo-China, and there was a curfew in Saigon, making booking out the order of the day. It was said that if Tubby was on night duty there were no worries provided you were back before his shift finished at 6am.

In Saigon we lived in old 'It ain't 'alf hot, Mum' huts behind the control tower and walked along a track through scrub to a communal site which was shared with the RAF Regiment.

One day Ron brought the attention of Don and myself to a motor bike lying on its side half hidden in long grass. 'It's been there for days. Not moved' he said. It was still there in exactly the same place the next week, and eventually Don said 'I bet I could fix that.'

I heard no more until Ron told me that they had worked on the bike and were going to try it out on the perimeter track at six o'clock. Would I like to come?

I had always wanted to ride a motor bike.

The bike was wheeled down to the perimeter. Don started it up and roared several hundred yards up and down. It was then Ron's turn and I was looking forward to having a go when Tubby appeared from nowhere.

He looked at us and beamed. 'I have never ridden a motor bike,' he said: 'Can I have a go?'.

Who were we to deny him the pleasure?

After suitable instruction from Don, Tubby rode erratically along the perimeter for a hundred yards and stopped. We walked up to him. 'Help me to turn around and I'll go back again.'

Back at the start point he still sat on the bike. 'Can I have another ride sometime?' He went on: 'Funny thing. The Regiment have reported a bike stolen from outside their huts. It was a ...' He paused and looked down. Not a word was spoken. Eventually Tubby said 'Well, I best be off then. I am on duty after all.'

We went as well.

Next day Tubby walked past as we waited for a Dakota to taxi off the runway.

'False alarm' he called. 'They made a mistake. The bike wasn't quite where they thought. It was a few yards away, lying behind a bush.'

Tubby was an unusual SP. And I have never ridden a motorbike.

SAIGON, '45: WITH THE JAPS IN VIETNAM
Phil Kaiserman

We sailed for Bombay late in 1944, aboard the *ss Alcantra*, and from Bombay crossed the country by train to Calcutta. It happened to be the Jewish Festival of Passover, and a number of Jewish British and American Service personnel, including myself, were invited to the home of a local Jewish businessman. His name was Sir David Ezra, and for the eight days of Passover he fed us in a marquee in the grounds of his home.

The contrast between Sir David's obvious great wealth and the hunger and misery all around was something I have never forgotten. He was a kind man, and I remember him with gratitude, but I also remember the poverty and deprivation amongst which he, and us too, lived. We were eating the most marvellous food, and there were beggars starving at the gates. It was so bad that mothers would cripple their children to have more effect when they begged.

Clearly, racism was everywhere, and even the men of my own Unit were infected by it. I remember watching two of our own men making two Indians race with rickshaws, hitting them like animals to make them go faster. The white man was held to be superior, and the coloured made to understand that they were there to do menial tasks. I had spent much of my youth fighting against the rise of fascism in England, and, being Jewish, knew well about racism. There, in India, I felt that I was seeing both fascism and racism in a country for which my own British nation was responsible.

3209 SC arrived in Saigon, in what used to be the French colony of French Indo-China, in October, 1945. This of course was after VJ-Day, and the world was at last at peace again. The General Election of 25 July in Britain had resulted in the election of a Labour Government with an overwhelming majority. Therefore we were in Vietnam, and under the orders of a Government that was supposedly Socialist and therefore anti-imperialist. Yet we, and all the other British and Indian troops in the country, were used to overthrow a popular, anti-imperialist movement, and helped to re-instate French colonial rule. Indirectly, we also paved the way for the later disastrous war between our American allies and the Vietnamese people. It can well be argued that the American defeat in that war led directly to the present day American policy of a threatening neo-imperialism.

We were stationed at Tan Son Nhut airfield, and serviced aircraft there. The Allied contingent were under the command of Major General Gracey, who had arrived in Saigon on 13 September. When he arrived at Tan Son Nhut, the General and his entourage were met by Japanese troops. During the drive into Saigon from the airfield, they found the route decked in British, American and Vietnamese flags and slogans, one of which read 'Welcome to the Allies, to the British and Americans, but we have no room for the French.'

The background to this was that on 19 August the Vietnamese National Liberation Committee took power in Hanoi and the emperor Bao Dai abdicated. The National Liberation Committee was a grouping of about ten different political movements, and undoubtedly represented a very large percentage of the Vietnamese people, and particularly those who had worked and fought against the Japanese occupation. The leader of the National Liberation Committee was Ho Chi Minh, or Nguyen the Patriot, and at a rally in Hanoi on 2 September he announced the formation of the Democratic Republic of Vietnam. He read out the 'Declaration of Independence of the Republic of Vietnam', which began with the same words as the American Declaration of Independence of 1776,

> All men are created equal. They are endowed by their creator with certain inalienable rights, and amongst these rights are Life, Liberty and the pursuit of Happiness.

The Declaration read by Ho Chi Minh went on to quote the Declaration of the French Revolution of 1791, that all men are born equal and with equal rights, and must always remain free and have equal rights.

> Nevertheless, for more than 80 years the French imperialists, abusing the standard of Liberty, Equality and Fraternity, have violated our Fatherland

and oppressed our fellow citizens… They have built more prisons than schools… they have drowned our uprisings in rivers of blood. For these reasons we, members of the Provisional Government of the Democratic Republic of Vietnam, solemnly declare to the world that Vietnam has the right to be a free and independent country and in fact is so already. The entire Vietnamese people are determined to mobilise all their physical and mental strength, to sacrifice their lives and property to safeguard their independence and liberty.

Those were noble words indeed, and certainly they struck a vibrant chord with me, particularly since our own newly-elected Government was at long last a Socialist and anti-imperialist one. Or so we believed.

General Douglas Gracey's orders, so far as we knew, were simple enough. He was to disarm the Japanese troops and ensure their repatriation, free all Allied Prisoners of War and Internees and repatriate them, and maintain law and order. He was instructed to have nothing to do with local politics, but it was taken for granted that Vietnam would once again become a French colony. This the Vietnamese were determined would not happen.

On 21 September, a Proclamation by Gracey was posted up all over Saigon. This was, in effect, a Declaration of Martial Law. It was, incidentally, posted all over the city by Japanese troops. In English, French and Vietnamese, the Proclamation stated that

all wrongdoers… will be summarily shot. That no arms of any description, including sticks, staves, bamboo spears etc. will be carried except by British and Allied troops, and such other forces and police which have been specially authorised by me… The curfew already imposed by the Japanese authorities… will be continued and strictly enforced.

In other words, Gracey was saying that the former common enemy, the Japanese, had now suddenly become authorised to enforce martial law. The Vietnamese had arrested and imprisoned many French men whom they accused of collaborating with the Japanese during the years of occupation. Over a thousand of these were freed by Gracey, who armed them, and allowed them to virtually take over the city. They were the very people of whom Lord Louis Mountbatten wrote, in his report to the Combined Chiefs of Staff, that

The Vichy (French) administration in French Indo-China at all times collaborated with the enemy.

There were far too few Allied – British and Indian – troops to enforce Gen. Gracey's attempts to disarm the Vietnamese. However, there were very many Japanese available, fully armed and very willing. The official history of the Indian Armed Forces noted that

> All the dirty work, to fight and disarm the Vietnamese, was assigned to the Japanese troops.

And this was done under the authority of our new Labour Government, ostensibly socialist and anti-colonialist.

Meanwhile, more and more French troops were arriving, to support the re-establishment of the old colonial system. In a little while, it became clear to me where those French troops were coming from.

On the arrival of our Unit at the airport, the first thing to do was to set up camp, living quarters, cooking facilities etc. The first night we spent sleeping on the concrete floor of a hanger, and the next day was spent organising the building of huts for our use, the same type of 'bashas' that we had used in India. Local labour was employed to do the building and the cooking and all other menial work around the camp, as was usual in the colonies.

Soon after our arrival in Saigon I fell victim to an ear infection and was admitted to hospital for treatment. The hospital was situated in the centre of Saigon, next to the jail. I became friendly with a young soldier, also a patient, who was already in the hospital when I was admitted. As we grew to know each other he felt that he could trust me and said he wanted to show me something he had witnessed.

He took me up to the next floor and pointed out that by looking through the windows we could see into the jail next door. The scene I saw was of a large square surrounded by a high wall. In front of us, making up the wall nearest to the hospital was a long single storey building with barred windows. This proved to be the interrogation block. In the square were about 100 Vietnamese peasants squatting on the ground. They had no shelter from the sun, and the temperature must have been around 100 degrees.

One by one they were taken into one of the rooms with barred windows. From our vantage point we could see into the first of those rooms, and the scene that met my eyes was one which I will remember to my dying day. What I saw was a human being hanging from a hook in the ceiling. His arms were tied behind his back and then hooked over so that he hung suspended by his arms. There were three or four men in the room all armed with clubs similar to baseball bats. We could not hear what was being said, but we could understand what was happening. Torture was being used to obtain information. I don't know how long we stood there observing this obscenity, all I can say is that if we had been armed we would have used our guns against those monsters

And who were those monsters? They were French troops, members of the far-famed French Foreign Legion. More than that, though, as I discovered later. They were in fact German prisoners of war captured in Europe, and given the option: Join the Foreign Legion or stay in the POW camp. Even worse was the fact that these characters were ex-Waffen SS, Hitler's crack troops, and responsible for some of the very worst atrocities committed in Europe. These examples of the pure Aryan 'master race' were using the same methods they had used in Europe against the Vietnamese peasants. They boasted about the raids into the countryside where they burned and pillaged in the name of French colonialism.

Later, in March 1946, Lord Louis Montbatten made a farewell visit to Vice Admiral d'Argenlieu, and was greeted by a Guard of Honour made up entirely of ex-Waffen SS, as, according to the French, 'They are our smartest Legionnaires.'

Not that the Legionnaires were alone in their actions and attitudes. I remember that the French had started an air service from Paris to Saigon using American Skymaster aircraft. On landing they were serviced by French engineers, and Vietnamese labourers were used to refuel and do all the other menial tasks like cleaning etc. On one occasion which I witnessed, an aircraft was being refuelled and a Vietnamese labourer was on the wing of the aircraft putting fuel into the wing tanks. He slipped and fell to the ground, about fifteen feet onto the concrete, and was obviously hurt by the fall. A Frenchman who had been working nearby saw him fall, went over, said something, and getting no reply kicked the man, and, still getting no reply, walked away and left the poor guy lying on the ground. No attempt whatsoever was made to see how badly the man was hurt, and it was left to his friends to pick him up and carry him away.

Not all of my time in Saigon was as traumatic as those incidents were. The city was once known as The Paris of the East, and it was certainly perhaps the most beautiful city I had seen. Wide tree-lined boulevards, the city centre full of fine buildings, with shops, cafes, restaurants and some of the most beautiful women.

Our Unit had by this time been moved from our camp on the airfield to a building in the city that had at some time been a girls' school. It was an elegant colonial building in the form of a quadrangle with the entrance through an arch. Nearby was the home of two men with whom I became friendly. Born in Calcutta, of Greek-Jewish descent, they had lived in Saigon for many years, and had business interests there. They had managed to escape to Calcutta when the Japanese invaded, but were invited back by the British administration to help in re-building the economy. I no longer remember how we met, but I do remember their wonderful hospitality. Their house was beautiful, with cool marble floors and large airy rooms. The many servants were housed elsewhere, of course, and they served us food aplenty. It was absolute luxury in all ways, whilst in the areas of Saigon like Cholon, where the workers lived, the absolute opposite was the norm, and of course out in the countryside the peasant families lived in huts with no facilities whatsoever.

I was in Indo-China for about six months, and was then posted to Burma. It seemed like a very long six months. I was demobbed in 1947, and returned home to a daughter I had never seen.

The Allied Forces had by that time withdrawn from Indo-China, leaving the French to fight a war against the Vietnamese, a war in which they were soundly defeated, and which ended with their submission at Dien Bien Phu in 1954. That was not the end of the sorrows for the Vietnamese, though. Shortly afterwards, they then had to face the American invasion, and a war which lasted until 1975, before the Americans, too, admitted defeat and withdrew from their last foothold in Saigon. But before they left, they had totally devastated that lovely country.

It is easy, when remembering the past, to go down the road of 'if only...' However, I do believe that 'if only' the Allied troops in Indo-China had accepted that the Vietnamese were determined to be freed of the pre-war colonial regime, and that they had every right to that self-determination, our world today would be a much safer and certainly a happier place.

SOME MEMORIES OF SOUTH-EAST ASIA 1945-6
Geoff Hoddinott

As an ex-apprentice (38th entry), I eventually found myself as a Sergeant Flight Commander of some thirty tradesmen in No. 3210 Servicing Commando. We were formed in 1942 and had our commando training at Inveraray in Scotland. We served on several airstrips in Normandy from 7 June to the end of July 1944. We then returned to the UK to prepare for the Far East. An aspect of our training since '42 had been that each man, Fitter IIA, IIE, Armourer or Instrument Repairer, could complete a Daily Inspection on most British and American Fighter aircraft (with the exception of RT) on his own.

India

We made a sea trip to Bombay in December 1944, during which I remember waking one morning after a night in a hammock in a blacked-out troopship in the Red Sea, coming on deck and immediately falling down. Being able to move only my head, I asked the airman sleeping on deck within a couple of feet to tell the sick bay. He replied 'Don't be bloody silly', turned over and went back to sleep. Later I was given a pint of salt water, and immediately recovered.

A four-day rail journey to Calcutta followed, pulling on to a siding to cook our own meals. On an airstrip on the Maidan in the centre of the city we serviced Hurricanes which had been discarded when the squadron in Burma had been re-equipped with P47 Thunderbolt Fighters. As the Thunderbolts weighed some seven tons against the Hurricanes two and half tons, it was found that the latter in the hands of a competent pilot could lob a bomb into a Jap bunker, whereas the former had to pull out at a much higher altitude and was not nearly so accurate.

We lived in tents, nearly all of us had prickly heat, and serviced those old Hurricanes in basha huts. On one occasion a five foot snake dropped on to the wing between two of us and slithered to the ground. On another the Orderly Sergeant shot and killed an Indian intruder in his tent. This Indian turned out to be a Japanese spy.

At Dum Dum airfield north of Calcutta my next task was to change an engine on Lord Mountbatten's personal Liberator. Parked off a hard standing, one wheel had sunk in the soft earth until the propellers were just touching the ground on the port side. No other lifting device being available we used three airbags one above the other, and, after several attempts, managed to lift the wing and pack stones under the wheel.

On a test flight the pilot offered to take a dozen Army NCOs to view Mount Everest. As we neared the mountain, smoke started to fill the cabin and our happy visitors became silent. After reporting to the pilot and being told to 'put the bloody fire out', we removed some decking and found the batteries were overcharging and soon corrected the fault.

Snakes were also a problem at Dum Dum. I was running up a Beaufighter one morning when a large black snake uncoiled from around the port engine cylinders where it had presumably spent the night and exited through the cooling gills and over the wing. When working on the Liberator, we saw a Spitfire take off, do a very rapid turn and land again. Before the aircraft stopped, the pilot jumped out, was hit by the tail plane and suffered a broken collar bone. Apparently, after take-off, he had put his hand down to operate the undercarriage lever, and found a snake coiled round it – quite a shock in the narrow cockpit of a Spitfire.

Burma

In the Arakan in Burma, the main 'rubber' petrol tanks of Thunderbolts were found to be cracking just below the attachment to the overflow pipe at the top of the tank. This was not noticed until the aircraft went into a dive and petrol then flowed down between the front of the tank and bulkhead and hit the hot exhaust pipes leading down inside the fuselage to the turbo supercharger in the rear, with disastrous results to aircraft and pilot.

Crammed with some six tradesmen in a Dakota full of replacement main fuel tanks we flew from Calcutta down to, I think, it was Ratnap, in Burma. We took several days to replace the first tank, but later became much quicker. The last action, after replacing the wooden rubberised strutting inside the tank before climbing out through the top manhole, was to mop up the pool of sweat which had collected at the bottom of the tank. It was certainly hot work!

After some weeks we returned to Calcutta and then inland to Bihar to an American airbase to await yet another deployment (possibly to the Andaman Islands.) We fed on American rations. What a change! All our skin blemishes, lumps and even prickly heat quickly improved or disappeared. Our sleeping hut with open windows was not fenced and one night a tiger lapped from water in an open bath on the verandah. Fortunately it was not hungry.

Malaya

The invasion of Malaya did not appear to be as well organised as the landings in Normandy. Obviously this was due to the sudden ending of the war and many countries having to be taken over from Japanese rule. After embarking in Calcutta we eventually waded ashore minus our vehicles on Morib beach between Port Swettenham and Port Dixon. As we waded ashore the water got deeper instead of shallower until we were almost up to our necks. Detailed to pick up stragglers, three of us SNCOs trooped inland. I could not help thinking, viewing the Japanese pill-boxes along the coast, how difficult the landing would have been against opposition. Inland we came to an as yet unoccupied airfield as it got dark. The three of us, Sgt. 'Happy' Day, Sgt. 'Brig' Lawton and myself tried to sleep in an isolated hut, but with large ants invading our primitive mattresses and rats running over our legs, sleep was constantly interrupted. Next day we reached Kuala Lumpur, met up with our vehicles and were told, after several days, to deploy to Java via Singapore.

Java

Group Captain David Lee wrote a book (now unfortunately out of print) entitled *...and we thought the war was over.* He commanded a Thunderbolt Wing in Java. On the way from Singapore to Batavia our landing craft broke down and our engine fitters managed to get repairs completed while we were towed by a frigate for two days.

We landed at Tanjong Priok and headed inland five miles to Kemajoran airfield on the outskirts of Batavia (now Djakarta). At first we serviced Dakotas of 31 Squadron. As lease-lend had ceased abruptly at the war's end, spares soon dried up and I remember sending little notes to Saigon where 31 Squadron also operated exchanging parts from written-off Dakotas – ailerons, rudders, undercarriages etc. The Dakota originally had three compasses (magnetic, gyro and radio), and we were soon lucky to have the magnetic and one other working.

Three of us SNCOs lived in a nearby empty house – no locks on the doors or windows. We rendered basic medical aid when off duty to the local Indonesians who suffered mainly from deep jungle sores which they tried to treat with tar and leaves. We placed three large containers of water in a row and after removing the tar and leaves, indicated that they should wash in each of the tubs in turn. The water in the first tub became blacker and blacker. The station MO gave us dozens of tubes of aquaflavine which we squirted into the sores, bound them up and told the recipient not to unwind the bandage, and to come back in seven days. It was remarkable how the sores healed – some of which had been down almost to the bone. I like to think that this action helped to save our lives, or at least prevented our weapons from being stolen since some Dutchmen living further down the street had their throats cut one night. As well as our own revolver or Sten gun many of us carried two primed No. 36 grenades in our weapon pouches. As the pouches were hot and heavy I usually strapped mine on the rear of my motorcycle.

One day travelling through a nearby crowded market, I heard a commotion behind and looking back saw two grenades bouncing down the road behind. The street was suddenly empty. I kept going until three seconds were safely past, turned round and picked them up. On another occasion some locals armed with bows and arrows had set up a road block in a lane beside our house. We approached cautiously but they indicated it was the Dutch they were afraid of.

However, one evening on the airfield we were informed that the Black Buffaloes, a local offshoot of the Black Dragon Society of Japan, were planning to attack the airfield. Fortunately, nothing happened, but we spent a long night lying waiting in a soggy ditch on the perimeter.

The main intention of British Forces in Java was to rescue over 100,000 Dutch and other internees in what were Japanese prison camps. It was always going to be difficult as the Japanese had handed over most of their weapons including 40mm anti-aircraft guns to the Indonesians who wanted independence and painted their red and white flag and the slogan 'Merdeka' on almost everything, including hangars, Japanese aircraft and vehicles. There were some ten different Indonesian 'armies', and Dr. Sukarno had indifferent control. We, the British, eventually held four enclaves – Batavia, Semarang, Bandoeng (in the hills) and Sourabaya.

A Dakota taking off from Kemajoran with twenty armed Indian soldiers and RAF crew suffered engine failure and force-landed within five miles of the airfield. The crew and all soldiers were seen to get out safely, but were all butchered before a relieving column could rescue them. It is not known why they did not attempt to defend themselves. The Black Buffaloes were responsible for that atrocity.

From Batavia I flew with a few of my Flight to replace a damaged port undercarriage on a Dakota stranded at Semarang some 200 miles along the north coast. We were dropped off, then were told by the Gurkhas defending the strip that we had until dusk as they could not defend the strip at night. Having replaced the undercarriage we found the brake connection was different. A part from an old DC3 parked on the edge of the strip was no help, so we had to blank off the brake pipe with a piece cut from a cigarette tin. We took off just before dusk, much to the relief of some thirty Dutch internees on board and landed safely back at Kemajoran.

On 9 November 1945, I was in the Dakota that flew to Soerabaya to drop leaflets telling the local Indonesians to lay down their weapons by 10.00 hours the following day or we would attack and retake the town. At that time we held only the docks and part of the airfield near the coast. The background was that part of the 5th Indian Division had landed on

25 October, and their Commander, Brigadier General Mallaby, had been murdered next day trying to arrange a truce. The Indonesians did not wait for 10.00 hours but attacked the airfield at dawn on 10 November, and I was told later that one of the machine gun posts had been over-run by fanatical Indonesians who charged with rusty parangs (short swords) and carrying 'magical' small bamboo sticks which their Mullahs had blessed and which they were told would cause British bullets to bounce back and hit the firer – some 1,000 of them were killed by the defending regiment. Shortly thereafter my Flight was flown to Soerabaya.

By that time a Thunderbolt Squadron was operating on the airfield. There were also a few Dutch Liberator aircraft, but these were not allowed to fly because the surface of the runway was too weak. A large number of 33 gallon petrol drums had been stacked around the airfield and near the slipway which ran down to the sea. As these had been left with the fillercaps uppermost, the heat during the day meant that pressure built up and vapour leaked round the caps. Then, when it rained in the evening and the drum cooled, the pressure decreased and water was drawn into the drums – not a good mixture to put into aircraft.

I was asked to refuel a BOAC flying boat which landed one early morning with the Prime Minister of Australia on board [Editorial Note: This was John Curtin] who was being taken to the UK for a conference. As we had no refuelling lighter we used a lifeboat from HMS *Exeter* which had been sunk in the Java Sea in 1942, and which was in the harbour. It was fitted with an outboard engine. We loaded a number of the 33 gallon drums, and hand pumps, funnels and chamois leathers. When we reached the flying boat the Prime Minister was standing in the rear door smoking a pipe. As a Sunderland on the River Hoogly in Calcutta had recently caught fire during refuelling, I asked the BOAC pilot to ask the Prime Minister to stop smoking. I remember he said 'If I can't smoke I shan't go.' The Station Commander eventually came out and persuaded the Prime Minister to go ashore. I don't know about any-one else but my opinion of politicians reached an all-time low.

Around midday we finished after finally draining some water from the drainage cocks under the wing. (The BOAC pilot was rather suspicious of the quality of the fuel and had some tested in a lab. in the UK on his return – we later heard it was all right.)

Another task my Flight was assigned was the removal of Japanese bombs lying around the dispersals, some of which were exuding, and were therefore dangerous. They were, I think, some 250 or 500lb approx. We carefully rolled them up a wooden ramp covered with rubber tyres and on to more rubber tyres on the floor of a 3-ton Bedford, and took them one by one out into the neighbouring marshes. A Cpl. Armourer in my unit used a one pound slab of guncotton, a 2oz primer and a foot or so of (carefully tested) safety fuse. I stayed on my motorcycle, engine running, while he lit the fuse, and off we went down the track. After several bombs had been dealt with in this way, the hole got deeper and deeper, and once, when he lit the fuse he scrambled up the side of the crater, slid back, scrambled up again, slid down again. I remember saying 'Either get out or pull the bloody fuse out!' Out he came on the third try – but we were spattered with mud some distance away.

A four-engine Jap. flying boat was standing at the top of the slipway close to the hangar apron with some parked Thunderbolts. Three Japanese fitters were making cigarette lighters for the aircrews out of Japanese magnetos in a wooden shack nearby. One day oil was being heated and the shack caught fire. I remember the Station Commander standing in the door of the fiercely burning hut with the fire hose in his hands. The rest of us were busy kicking 33 gallon drums of petrol into the sea, some of them hot and sizzling as they hit the water. The nose of the Japanese flying boat got a little scorched, but eventually, after I left, I heard it flew a short distance. The Japanese method of preventing vibration to metal pipes was to tie them together or to struts with waxed cord – it appeared to be a superior method to the metal clips the RAF used, which could cause chafing.

Once when visiting an internment camp on the outskirts of Sourabaya in a three ton Bedford we missed our way and, when everything became quiet and deserted, we suspected that we had 'crossed the lines'. Returning down a straight road we passed within a few feet of an Indonesian machine gun and crew lying in a shallow ditch. Neither they nor we opened fire until we were some hundred yards away, then they fired and fortunately missed.

A Dakota on the island of Bali (Hindu in a mainly Moslem country) was reported as having a faulty starter motor. With a spare and two men I was taken down in a Dutch-crewed Catalina flying boat and landed on the lagoon of this beautiful island. Instead of an unserviceable starter we found the batteries were flat. By using some car batteries and some tele-phone wire which we pulled down we got the engine started. The aircrew had been enjoying themselves at a nearby hotel, and by the time we got them rounded up, we were getting short of fuel, because we dare not stop the engine. Fortunately, after passing through a thunderstorm we came into the clear and landed back at Sourabaya – one engine cutting out as we touched down.

Shortly thereafter a friend of mine, 'Chick' Taylor and I were leaving for RAF Regiment Officer training in the UK. The only aircraft available was a Mitchell bomber full of refugees, and the only room in it was on boards in the bomb bay. As we did not fancy this, and saw a Dakota about to take off at the end of the runway, we thumbed a lift. Only after we scrambled on aboard and took off did we discover that it had the remains of some eighty humans in rubberised sacks and sandbags on board. Two padres and two assistants had been travelling round SE Asia exhuming bodies and were taking them to Singapore and Saigon for burial. After the three hour journey to Kemajoran, during which Chick sat with his nose to one of the small circular windows, the pilot asked us if we wanted to go on to Singapore with him after lunch. We politely declined and sought another aircraft.

With 50 million inhabitants in an island about half the size of the UK, Java was a beautiful part of the world inhabited by people mainly of Muslim faith, sometimes fighting each other, but determined to obtain independence and not allow the Dutch to return. We, the British, with the Indian Army, had won the war. Our morale was high. Our task was to rescue Dutch and other internees who were at the mercy of fanatics. The Dakota Squadron flew out some 5,000 casualties, mainly Army. The RAF alone lost two Dakotas, and two Thunderbolts were shot down, although one pilot (wounded) was handed back some months later. A total of 30 officers and airmen of the RAF were killed, mostly on the ground. It was reported that the two Army Divisions had more casualties in four months in Java than they had suffered in a year fighting the Japanese in Burma. Eventually, after about a year, peace returned to Java.

THE SPARE PART
Spruce

As my trade in civilian life was the maintenance of typewriters, I was always called upon to attend to the Unit's two very ancient pieces of equipment. They had travelled many miles and had suffered frequent damage, often as a result of bad packing.

It was in Calcutta that a breakdown occurred and it required a part that I was unable to make myself. I needed to obtain one from a local dealer, and that was my first problem. The dealer was in the naughty quarter and was out of bounds to servicemen, I had to get a pass to get past the watchful MPs.

The Adjutant issued me with a pass and I began my quest for this all-important part, keeping my mind on my mission and not what the area was famed for. After many hours of searching I had to admit defeat. The closest I got to obtaining the part was an address of the main agent in Bombay.

So desperate was the Adjutant to get that typewriter working that he obtained a travel warrant getting me to Bombay, and some cash.

Now from Calcutta to Bombay is not a few stations down the line, It is 3-4 days and nights by train.

On arrival in Bombay I sought out the RTO to find accommodation for the night. I was taken to a transit camp, and after a shower and a meal it was time for bed.

Now an Indian charpoy is not the most comfortable of beds, but this one was like sleeping on a bed of nails. It was like hundreds of pins sticking into my tired body, and I was soon to find out why.

The permanent inhabitants of that bed were holding a banquet and I was the main course. I was covered in bed bugs; a hasty dash to remove them did not remove the discomfort I suffered from their bites. My sleeping quarters for the rest of the night was the back of an army lorry.

I journeyed across Bombay to the address I had been given in Calcutta; it proved to be the place I was looking for.

The owner of the establishment greeted me as if I were a VIP, refreshments were laid on, and a tour of the workshops.

I was sent on my way with the all-important part for which payment was refused.

An overjoyed Adjutant welcomed my arrival back in Calcutta especially as the part came without charge.

I wonder how much that part **REALLY** cost?

SEKALI MERDEKA, TETAP MERDEKA
(ONCE FREE, FOREVER FREE)
Tom Atkinson

I don't think I had ever seen a big ship close up until we marched on to a Liverpool quay on 12 December 1944, and were confronted by the *Johan van Oldenbarneveldt*. I don't know her tonnage, but she was big, a Dutch pre-war passenger liner, sailing between Holland and the Dutch East Indies. Nor do I know how many passengers she carried, in considerable comfort, on her peace-time voyages, but now she was to carry about 4,000 men and 200 WAAFs to the Far East.

The men were stowed in the holds, mostly several decks down. They made up their beds on the mess tables, on benches, and on the deck. Some were allocated hammocks, and I was lucky enough to be one of them. 'Lucky', because if you were swinging in your hammock five feet above the deck, there was no-one above to be seasick over you. It was essential to take your boots into the hammock with you, and put them on before wading through the night's accumulation of vomit and other unknown liquids. That all had to be cleared away before breakfast could be served, and the lads on fatigues fought a daily battle as they swept and swilled, while those who had made up their beds on the tables and benches begged to be left alone in their misery. Fortunately, I was never seasick, although I often had to fight nausea when swinging out of my hammock in the early mornings on to a truly disgusting mess deck.

The officers, the WAAFs and, I suppose, senior NCOs were accommodated in the passenger cabins, and fed in the various dining rooms. They were summoned to their meals by Indonesian stewards walking round and playing on little portable gamelans, traditional Indonesian xylophone-like instruments. That was perhaps all that remained as a faint shadow of the *J.v.O*'s peacetime luxury.

We were meant to sail as soon as we embarked, and very soon we felt the vibration as the main engines started. Within seconds there was a loud bang, and the engines stopped. The *J.v.O.* had blown a piston in the main engine. So we were kept tied up at the quayside for a full week while repairs were made. Of course, we missed the convoy, and finally, on 21 December sailed alone, bound for Colombo.

At her top speed, with total black-out and, I understand, a strict radio silence, the *J.v.O.* headed far out into the Atlantic before making a dog-leg back towards Gibraltar. The weather soon improved, and the amount of sea-sickness decreased. The mess decks became less messy.

I really don't remember whether there was any sort of Xmas dinner that year, but I do remember my own celebration. It was a large piece of real cheese, half a loaf of real bread and a lump of real butter. This was a gift from a WAAF, who smuggled the feast out of the WAAF mess hall. I had met her while the ship was still tied up in Liverpool, and we spent a lot of time together. Actually, we still do. We have been married now for almost sixty years, and she still feeds me well.

For me, at least, that trip on the *J.v.O.* was a wonderful holiday. I remember well hanging over the rail watching the sun come up over the Red Sea, the coolness, the empty decks, the happiness of having Rene (LACW Box, R. 462, W.Op) with me. The days sometimes dragged, but my mate Peter Humphries and I spent long hours playing chess in a way of our own devising. We made a chess board on a sheet of brown paper, and used coins as chessmen – halfpenny for a pawn, up to half a crown for the king, and heads and tails denoted black and white.

This provided a lot of entertainment, especially for all those who stood around wondering what on earth we were doing. We were also entertained by the SPs who came around occasionally and had to be convinced that we were not gambling, a heinous offence. Little did they know of the card schools which existed deep down in the mess decks, and continued night and day, and at which as much as sixpence a man changed hands at every game of pontoon.

I remember the singing of an impromptu Welsh choir. One of their favourite songs particularly impressed me, and I was sure it must have some deeply religious meaning. Later I learned that the song was '*Sospan Fach*', 'The Little Saucepan', out of which some Welsh mother had contrived to feed her man and her children.

It was during the sweaty passage down the Red Sea that Harry Schofield, our Adj., came up with the idea of holding a mock election. Anything to pass the time, I suppose. I was persuaded to stand on the Labour ticket, which was certainly not fitting, because my political beliefs were far to the left of the Labour Party. Indeed, I am sure that the Labour Party would have rejected with horror the extreme revolutionary programme I advocated. A couple of other lads from other Units were persuaded to stand as Conservative and Liberal candidates. Perhaps 'persuaded' is the wrong word. The prize for winning was to be 200 cigarettes, and that was incentive enough.

Well, it was a wipe-out and a walkover. The Labour candidate, me, won overwhelmingly, by about 90% of the vote. Perhaps it was all a bit unfair: the other candidates had little idea of how to deal with hecklers and questions, whereas I had mounted a soapbox on quite a few street corners. It was an interesting exercise, and the result meant that I certainly foresaw, and was not surprised by, the overwhelming election of a Labour Government in 1945.

All too soon, for me at least, we reached Colombo and the WAAFs disembarked, and I had to bid a sad, if temporary, farewell to Rene. The *J.v.O.* then turned northabout and we landed at Bombay on 13 January. From there, on 3 February we boarded a train for the four-day journey to Calcutta.

That long and uncomfortable trip marked for me the beginning of a love affair with India and Indians which continues until today. I was fascinated by the country, the sights and smells, the way in which the blue smoke of cow-dung fires drifted in the short twilight, the way the women walked upright over the fields with water containers on their heads. I enjoyed buying tea – chai – at tiny railway halts on the great plains, imbibing the strange spicy milkiness, and then breaking the little clay cup on to the great heap of shards at the side of the chai stall.

What I did not enjoy was the way in which some of the lads had already became infected by the 'Old Sweats' attitude to India and the Indians. Contempt and a sense of innate superiority were common enough: rudeness and cruelty not unknown.

At Calcutta we occupied a tented encampment on the Maidan, just off Chowringhee, right in the centre of that vast city. The great Bengal famine of 1944 was not long over, and its effects were still very clear. In fact, the 'famine' was not really a famine at all. There was plenty of food available, but the distribution system, imposed by the colonial authorities, had completely broken down, and many thousands of people died of starvation whilst the warehouses were brimming with rice. One result of this administrative failure was that countless thousands of people moved from the countryside to the city, where they existed in the utmost, heartbreaking, poverty. It was not easy to accept our three square meals a day in the midst of that morass of human misery, and it would have been worse, much worse, six months earlier.

I enjoyed Calcutta and its people. Not long after arriving there we were re-equipped with transport, and the Wireless Section was allocated a 15 cwt Canadian Ford, which we fitted out as a workshop, this time including fans, which Chick Taylor produced from some unspecified source. Chick was our Wireless WO, and a very proficient scrounger. I had fairly free use of the truck, and travelled widely over the city, and made several good Indian friends, including a Bengali Cultural Group of dancers and drummers, who quite astonished me with their skills and virtuosity.

After various detachments, I applied for leave and got two weeks up in the coolness of the hills at Shillong. However, I had no intention of going there, and with the help of some lads on detachment at Dum Dum airfield, hitched a flight down to Colombo, the idea of course being to spend time with my WAAF friend, Rene.

I have never forgotten her astonishment when she was called to the Guard Room to meet a visitor. Of course I was in jungle green, complete with bush hat and ammunition boots and toting a Sten gun. All the RAF types she knew in Colombo were immaculate in starched khaki and, usually, suede shoes. Quite rightly, she decided that I was too conspicuous in the rarefied atmosphere of the Colombo HQ. – since I had no business being there at all – and that I must immediately get into civvies. A quick visit to the market kitted me out suitably, complete with suede shoes.

We had a very happy and memorable ten days together, including a week up in the hills at Nuwara Eleya, and somehow at that time we became formally engaged, although I have no recollection of how that happened. Then I had to organise a flight back to Calcutta. This was no problem, and I arrived back only six hours late. The Adj. looked at me a bit quizzically when I reported to him, but made no comment. I told him where I had been, and he said that I had shown great initiative. In fact, it was not initiative, but determination driven by frustration.

On 8 September 1945, 3210 SC embarked on *ss Dunera* for Malaya. The war was over, the Japanese had finally surrendered on 15 August, after the final terror of two atomic bombs. It was, I remember quite a holiday-like trip, with the portholes open and a cool breeze deflected into the mess decks.

That landing, on 16 September at Morib Beach, was a real cock-up, and we all thanked whatever gods there be that there was, in fact, no opposition. We were dropped from the landing craft about 400 yards off-shore and into about four feet of water, and had to wade ashore in full battle kit. If there had been only a couple of Japanese in one of the machine gun posts on the beach, I don't think any of us would have made dry land.

Eventually we moved inland to Kuala Lumpur airfield and retrieved our transport from the LSTs, and began operations. Not for long. News came through the bush telegraph that we were bound for Batavia, in the Netherlands East Indies.

It was Chick Taylor who gave me the news, and also informed me that Indonesian nationalists had declared their independence, and were in control of Batavia, and, he believed, most of Indonesia. This had happened on 17 August, just two days after the Japanese surrender.

The ostensible reason for our going into Java was RAPWI – Repatriation of Allied Prisoners of War and Internees. In fact, the cynical amongst us, and there were quite a few, believed that we were likely to be involved in helping to re-establish the Dutch colonial regime on that vast archipelago.

We embarked with our transport at Port Dixon on to LCTs on 8 October, bound for Batavia and arrived there on 13 October. We landed, and drove to Kemajoran, the airport.

The six-mile drive from the docks through the city was strange. There were banners and wall paintings welcoming us as liberators, quoting the Atlantic Charter of Allied War Aims, quoting the American Declaration of Independence, and everywhere the rallying cry of *'Merdeka'* – Freedom, or Independence. There were no welcoming crowds, but people waved at us and smiled.

During the long idle days on the voyage from Port Dixon to Batavia, there had been plenty of time for talking and discussion – as well as pontoon. It was plain that a number of lads shared my apprehension about the real motive, or at least the secondary motive, behind our time in Java. The repatriation programme, certainly, no-one could argue about that, but was there also a hidden agenda? Were we simply going to hold the ring until the Dutch could return in sufficient force to re-establish their colonial regime? If so, we wanted no part of it.

It was actually Chiefy Vipond, an armourer, who came up with the idea that changed my life and laid out, in fact, my whole future. He pointed out that there was a great need for education in the Services. Many lads had joined up virtually straight from school, and had no experience of civilian life. Even in our own Unit there were at least three who were really both illiterate and innumerate. It would be very useful if classes could be organised to help them. I noted the idea and stored it away for the future.

Indonesia, it was clear, was in a very strange condition. Four years of Japanese occupation and exploitation had destroyed much of the infrastructure. However, the Japanese had also encouraged the development of what had already been a powerful nationalist movement for independence. They had dreams of leading a vast association of semi-independent people in their Greater East Asia Co-Prosperity Sphere. And it was not a hopeless dream. After all, their forces had easily defeated and driven out the white colonialists, British, French, Dutch and American. Until such time as the United States gathered together its vast economic strength and reserves of manpower, Japanese control over the whole of East Asia was complete. In Indonesia and other places they trained and gave some arms to the native people. While imposing a rigid and exceptionally cruel occupation, they also encouraged the idea of national independence, basing that on an already strong nationalist movement which had been violently oppressed by the pre-war Dutch government.

It was not surprising that when the Japanese collapse came in August 1945, the Indonesian nationalists immediately stepped into the gap, and on 17 August proclaimed themselves to be a free and independent nation. Obviously prepared to fight for their principles and ideals and independence, they had the slogan:

Sekali Merdeka, Tetap Merdeka!
Once Free, Free Forever!

This was weeks before the British were ready to take over control. In fact, it was not until after the Japanese surrender that it was decided that the British should go into the Dutch East Indies. Up to then, it had been intended that that vast archipelago would be under the control of the Americans. Now the Americans were to concentrate on the occupation of Japan, and the British were allocated the Dutch East Indies, as well as Malaya and French Indo-China.

It was equally not surprising that the Dutch were determined to restore their pre-war empire. The wealth of the East Indies had ensured the prosperity of Holland, and the Dutch had skilfully exploited the timber, the oil, the gold and the agricultural products, as well as the manpower, of their Asian empire. It took five years of bitter fighting and many thousands of deaths before the Dutch finally admitted defeat, withdrew from their Asian empire, and very soon afterwards discovered, to their considerable surprise, that they could prosper even better than before, as a small, hard-working, highly inventive country in Europe.

It was into this morass that 3210 SC descended. It took quite a while before those of us interested in the political situation could make sense of it. There were certainly atrocities committed by the Indonesians. There were reliable reports of the British using Japanese troops in attempts to disarm the Indonesians. There was the great satisfaction of helping the release of the internees. It only really began to make sense when we managed to become friendly with groups of young Indonesian patriots, whose understanding and wisdom far surpassed ours.

One thing was certain. A number of us were determined to do nothing which would help the Dutch to return. We would do anything we could to help the infant Republic of Indonesia to survive. After all, we had just fought a bitter war for certain ideals, and amongst those ideals was the freedom of peoples and the independence of nations. Talks with Indian soldiers convinced us that most of them shared our views. It was plain that the whole great Indian sub-continent was fast heading towards independence, and many of the troops were unhappy and discontented. It was about this time that the Indian Navy mutinied in Bombay, and there was also a wide-spread spate of 'strikes' – they were never called mutinies – in the RAF itself throughout India and Malaya. The situation was indeed delicate and finely balanced.

After much discussion, Peter Humphries and I decided we would try to establish an education centre, a place where we could help our Indonesian friends, perhaps be of help to our own comrades in the Service, and, on a personal level, take us away from any work that might help the Dutch to return to their empire.

There was already an Education Officer at Kemajoran, but he seemed to do little except give an occasional dreary lecture on Post War Britain and the Future. He was delighted to have some positive ideas about education for the troops, and didn't need much persuasion to arrange our secondment from 3210 to HQ. With his help and the enthusiastic support of our Adj., Harry Schofield, we were allocated a large house at the end of the Kemajoran runway, and more or less left to our own devices. Harry, of course, since he was still censoring letters, was well aware of the way our minds were working, and tacitly approved.

Within a few weeks we were ready to roll. Chick Taylor, with his usual skill, had produced a number of desks and tables. By some strange chance I had brought ashore in the Wireless truck no less than fifteen cases of Compo Rations, which no-one seemed to want, and most of them were exchanged on the black market down by the docks for some old typewriters and a clapped out duplicator. These Peter overhauled and restored. Incidentally, Peter was the best shorthand writer and typist I have ever known. He had been a High Court Reporter when he was only eighteen.

We acquired a small library of text books, donated by the Rotary Club of Swindon, and how they ever got to Batavia I have no idea. There was a good supply of note books and paper, pencils and even the very first ball-point pens I had seen. There were blackboards and chalk –

everything we needed was acquired by means both fair and foul. We even had a set of very fine prints of French Impressionist painters which was supposed to have graced the Officers Mess, but was diverted to us by Capt. Sen Gupta, a remarkable Indian officer, and a very good friend.

Jack Nellist, an art student in real life, joined us, and he was to teach drawing and painting. From somewhere he produced a good supply of crayons and paints. Peter and I lived alone in the house, on the ground floor. The class rooms and an office were above, and our private shower – a somewhat modified jettison tank – and toilet – an old wooden armchair with most of its seat removed – in an outhouse. We were a couple of hundred yards from the camp, surrounded by Indonesian houses.

We never locked a door, and never had anything stolen. Our Indonesian friends had put out the word, and we were protected by the pemuda, the youths.

A notice appeared on DROs, and our first students began appearing. Peter taught shorthand and typing, book keeping and office routine. I taught English and current affairs, and also literacy and elementary maths, which was about the limit of my skills. Jack Nellist taught art and art history, but seemed to spend a lot of time persuading students to lie down and have their faces covered in plaster of Paris to make face masks. Well, you had to make allowances for the artistic temperament.

There were some classes during the day, but most were in the evening, and since the lads were in various billets in different parts of the city, we needed a truck to collect and return them. This wasn't a problem, and again, thanks to Harry Schofield, a 3-tonner was put at our disposal.

Of course, after disposing of the students by about half past eight, we had the use of the truck to visit our Indonesian friends and spent many hours in discussions and argument with them.

Very soon, we were able to do what we had really set out to do, and that was to distribute world-wide information about what was happening in Indonesia. Late night hours were spent typing and duplicating a news bulletin, which we called *Indonesian Information*, and addressing envelopes. We collected as many names and addresses as we could of influential people who we believed might help in the struggle for Indonesian independence. They were in Ceylon, India, Australia, America, Canada, Holland and UK. The envelopes were posted in small bundles in the mail boxes of the various billets where we picked up our students. Quite a lot of the envelopes were also posted in other places, especially Singapore, by sympathetic aircrew.

On one occasion we were told by friends that the Indonesian Prime Minister wanted to meet us. We arrived at his office late at night, complete with the 3-tonner, and found him, Sutan Sjahrir, waiting for us. He was a tiny, roly-poly man, with a colossal intellect, and spoke English with an ease and precision we could only envy. He had been prominent in the nationalist movement all his life, in the Socialist Party, and had spent much time in Dutch colonial prisons, and had been released by the Japanese from the hellish jungle exile camp at Boven Digul in New Guinea.

Sjahrir thanked us for what we were doing, and had one request. Could we try to influence the British Government to permit and assist in the return of Indonesian 'romushas' from Malaya, Burma and Thailand. These romushas were young men who had 'volunteered' to help build the notorious Burma railway. There were many thousands of them. Unknown numbers had died, but the survivors wanted to come home. Many were sick, all were very mal-nourished, and, we were told, the British authorities were taking no steps to re-patriate them.

This, of course, was long before the film *The Bridge over the River Kwai.* We had heard of the notorious Burma railway and of the sufferings of POWs building it, but had no idea that many more Indonesians had also been drafted there, to undergo similar hardships and death. We had to tell Sjahrir that there was little we could do, but that we would certainly do what we could. We suggested he ask the shadowy Col. Laurens van der Post (later mentor and friend of Prince Charles, and a well-known writer). Van der Post had some still-unexplained intelligence role in Batavia, after being released from the prison camp. He had been deliberately left behind when the Japanese occupied Indonesia, with the task of organising resistance. He was soon arrested by the Japanese and suffered greatly in the camps. He was reputed to be sympathetic to the Indonesians, and certainly had the ear of Lord Mountbatten, our Commander-in-Chief.

Our next issue of *Indonesian Information* carried the story of the Indonesian romushas, and an appeal for help. It may have been coincidental, but shortly afterwards questions were asked in the House of Commons by Harold Davies MP, one of those who received the bulletin, and measures were finally taken to assist those young men, the ones who were left, to return home.

Sjahrir had served us excellent coffee, and as we were leaving, told us that it was something very special, *kopi lewak*, which was made from coffee beans which had been eaten and then excreted whole by a particular type of civet cat which lived in the coffee plantations of Sumatra. *Kopi lewak* is still available, if you can afford it, and very good it is.

Quite soon the opportunity of some leave came around, and having tossed a coin to choose who went first, Peter Humphries went to Penang in Malaya, where we had some contacts amongst the Chinese whose guerrilla activities during the Japanese occupation had been so successful. I, of course, when my turn came, chose to go to Ceylon. A clapped-out Dakota flew me through a very frightening tropical storm to Singapore, and next day a Sunderland flying boat produced a lift to Ceylon. It was astonishingly easy in those days to hitch flights anywhere around Asia. In fact, there were strong rumours that one of our lads had actually managed to get to London and back during his fourteen days leave.

We made a sea landing at Kogala, the very station where Rene had been working. I say 'had' because two days earlier she had gone off on a posting to Hong Kong. We had both, unknowingly, been in Singapore the previous night. As you can imagine, this was extremely frustrating.

I stayed at Kogala for a few days, relaxing on the beaches, and then went to Colombo, where we had quite a lot of contacts in the Ceylonese independence movement. It was all very pleasant and useful, but not quite the sort of leave I had expected.

There was one scary moment when I was giving a talk about the Indonesian situation in some hall in the city. I had almost finished my talk when the front doors of the hall were slammed open and four MPs appeared. For some reason which I don't recall, I was in uniform, and thus of course breaking all kinds of regulations. Fortunately, the platform was at the back of the hall, so the chairman and I left hurriedly through the back door. The chairman was a young doctor called Peter Keuneman, and his car was close by. We drove through the night to his home in the south of Ceylon, and I spent a couple of very happy days there with Peter and his family, before going back to Colombo and organising a hitch back to Batavia.

So there was a frustrated airman in Batavia, and an equally frustrated WAAF in Hong Kong. But one should never under-estimate the ingenuity of a frustrated WAAF.

A couple of weeks later Peter Humphries and I were taking our ease in the heat of the day when there was a knock on the door, and Peter, in shorts and boots, roused himself to answer. It happened that Peter had a bad case of prickly heat at the time, and most of his torso was coloured bright blue with gentian violet. An astonished airman was faced by an even more astonished Rene. Somehow, by sheer perseverance, arguing and even weeping when necessary, she had managed to hitch from Hong Kong to Batavia, via Singapore.

Batavia was still officially a war zone, and totally out of bounds for servicewomen. There were still firefights almost every night, and bodies floating down the canals. Fortunately, Rene had been met coming off the aircraft by Jerry Stott, our good friend from 3210, and he had hustled her straight away into a truck and delivered her to us. She was our problem, not his.

Of course she had civilian clothes with her, and after getting her fed (by mischance, and to her disgust, it happened to be oxtail and haricot that day), and introducing her to the shower and toilet, she changed into civvies and we went down into the city to arrange accommodation.

There were no hotels, boarding houses or back-packer hostels available then in Batavia (unlike now) and even if there had been, we certainly could not have afforded them. So we asked our Indonesian friends for help, and soon Rene was installed in a very reasonable house. It belonged to Dr. Soebandrio, who was Secretary General of the Ministry of Information at the time, and happened to be going out of the city. He and his wife, also a doctor, were good friends of ours, and subsequently played a very significant role in my later life.

Considering the times and the circumstances, it was a well-equipped house, and very safe, being constantly supervised by a group of 'pemuda', or young men. On her first night there, though, Rene did create quite a bit of consternation. Indonesian bathrooms, even today, are equipped with a large tiled cistern, about 4 feet square and 4 feet high, and this contains the bath water. The idea is that you use a large ladle to pour the water over yourself, and every effective this is. However, Rene, being unfamiliar with the system, went to the bathroom and seeing no shower or tub, climbed into the cistern and bathed there, thus contaminating all the water. Since the water had to be hand-pumped from a well, it was not a popular move.

Apart from being a very welcome visitor, Rene was also a very useful one. One of our problems in circulating our bulletin was getting people to address envelopes. We needed as many different hand writings as possible, in order to divert suspicion, so she was put to work with a pile of envelopes and the address list.

There wasn't much entertainment in Batavia then, but there was pleasure in eating eggs and chips at Rosie's Café in Pasar Baru, and there was an exhibition of Javanese dancing at the Republican radio station. That was our first introduction to Javanese music and dance, and it started an interest that continues to this day.

The days passed quickly, and one very early morning I watched my fiancée board a Dakota bound for Singapore. There had been no problem at all in arranging the hitch, and from Singapore, she had a legal flight back to Hong Kong.

3210 SC had been officially disbanded on 25 January 1946, and many of the lads were dispersed, and many also demobbed. Peter and I were posted to HQ at Kemajoran, and a new young Education Officer was in charge of the school. He knew well what we were doing, and obviously sympathised. He even addressed envelopes for us, asking no questions, and posted bundles of bulletins in the Officers Mess. He also warned us that a couple of Dutch Intelligence Officers were asking questions. Actually, we already knew about that. We had good friends in the Army Field Security Unit in Batavia, and were kept quite well informed.

Ultimately it became clear that if we wished to continue helping the Indonesian struggle for independence, we had to rethink. My own demob number had long come and gone, and we decided that I should go for demob., and we would continue our efforts in UK, with the information passed to me by Peter, whose demob. was not due.

And that is what we did. The rest of the story has nothing to do with the RAF or 3210 SC, but just for the interest I am adding a brief postscript.

Back in the UK I set up a branch of the Indonesian News Agency Antara, and continued sending out the *Indonesian Information* bulletin, using up my accumulated savings and the demob bounty payment in the process. Just in time, Peter was demobbed, and brought with him a sum of money from the Indonesian Ministry of Information – it was £80, I recall. Rene was demobbed. And we were married early in 1947.

When the money ran out, Peter and I supported the continuation of the information service from our own earnings in mundane jobs, and just when we had decided we could not continue, there was a message one day that Dr. Soebandrio (whose house Rene had used in Batavia) was in London and wanted to see us. He had been appointed as Official Representative of the Republic of Indonesia in London.

It was becoming increasingly obvious that the Dutch could not over-come the Indonesians by force of arms, although they continued trying. International pressure on them to seek a negotiated settlement increased by the day. The United Nations was becoming involved. The Republic decided to lay the foundations of a future Diplomatic Service, and Soebandrio was its Official Representative in London. He asked us to join him, which of course we did, and we set up the Indonesian Office in Notting Hill Gate as a quasi-diplomatic organisation.

In 1950 the Dutch were finally forced to negotiate a settlement, and at the *Konperensi Medja Bunda* (Round Table Conference) in Holland – which I attended – Indonesia's existence as an independent State was finally accepted. The Indonesian Office became the Indonesian Embassy, with Soebandrio as His Excellency The Ambassador. To be formal about it, Soebandrio became Ambassador Extraordinary and Minister Plenipotentiary of the Republic of Indonesia to King George VI of Great Britain and Northern Ireland at the Court of St. James. The Embassy was established in Grosvenor Square, very close to the American Embassy. I became Information Officer and Peter Administration Officer.

In 1952 I was recalled to Jakarta, as Batavia had now become, to work in the Ministry of Foreign Affairs. I remained there for ten years, and it was a fascinating time. I travelled the world repeatedly in the entourage of President Sukarno, worked very hard not only in the Ministry, but also in the President's office and various other bodies, and to make financial ends meet, did a lot of teaching. Rene, meanwhile, was working in the Ministry of Information.

It all continued very happily until my health broke down. This was at a General Assembly of the United Nations in 1962, and I think I was simply exhausted. Anyway, Dr. Soebandrio, by then Foreign Minister, arranged for me to be shipped back to the UK, and for Rene to pack up our Jakarta household and join me.

That was almost the end of my association with the Republic of Indonesia, although Peter, who continued working in the London Embassy until about 1980, kept me informed. Thus I missed the horrifying events of 1965, when a military coup in the Republic overthrew the Sukarno Government and led to the slaughter of untold thousands of alleged Communists and Trades Unionists. Estimates of the numbers killed range from half a million to two million, but no-one was counting.

Much later, in 1995, I received a letter from the Ambassador in London, the very first communication I had had since 1962, urging me to attend an Embassy Reception in my honour. I had never made a secret of my bitter feelings about the corrupt military regime of Gen. Soeharto and his clique, and I hesitated long before accepting. Peter Humphries, whose wise advice I would have appreciated then, had, sadly, died quite recently. Eventually I did accept, and must admit that I was made very welcome. Rene and I were then formally invited to attend the 50th Anniversary of the Declaration of Indonesian Independence in Jakarta on 17 August.

Again, after much soul-searching, we agreed, and were greeted there warmly and accommodated well. I cannot say I enjoyed the official proceedings, which were militaristic beyond belief. I could not help but contrast them with other Independence Days, when the atmosphere was gay and light-hearted and full of hope for the future. The oppressive nature of those celebrations in 1995 was hard to withstand.

However, we were able to meet many old friends, and these included Dr. Soebandrio, who had just been released from prison under an amnesty. He had been sentenced to death in 1966 for alleged treason (a truly ridiculous accusation), but the sentence was commuted to life imprisonment, and he served almost twenty years. It was an emotional meeting.

More recently, the barbaric military regime of General Soeharto has been ended, and a new President elected. She is the daughter of the original President Sukarno. Sadly, though, there is little sign that she is able to control the ambitions and greed of the military. However, there is one point that pleases me greatly: in one place in the world there is a President whom I once dandled on my knee and played 'This little piggy' with.

THE OUDENDAY

This was found in the effects of the late Fl/Sgt Jock Stuart. *The Oudenday* (don't ask!) was an occasional newsletter produced in the 3209 SC Orderly Room. The following extract was written by Adjutant F/Lt. Powell on the 2nd 'birthday' of the Unit, in South-East Asia, April 1945.

ADJITORIAL

(On the occasion of the 2nd Anniversary of the Unit's formation)

My greetings to you all on this momentous occasion, and in particular to all you who have borne the heat and burden of the day since the birth of the Unit at Exeter, in the County of Devon, on 5 May 1943. I cannot myself claim to be a genuine original, though. I missed that honour by six weeks buss. Nevertheless I have been privileged to share with you the greater part of your trials and triumphs since first we set forth from Zeals upon our travels and took Inveraray by storm in our first operation, the fires of our enthusiasm no whit dampened by the unfriendly torrents with which haughty Scotland deemed it fit to greet its guests. Thence to the Romney Marsh, where we helped to deny to the Hun the use of his forward air-fields and thus paved the way for Normandy and the momentous events which followed. That year, invasion was denied us, and we retired discomforted to winter quarters, Gatwick, Redhill, Manston, Lasham, Gravesend, Eastchurch, the blizzards and gales of Peterhead, Huttin Cranswick, back to Gravesend, Ford, Redhill once again, Boxgrove, Old Sarum.

D-Day!!! What memories these names bring back! There followed the excitement and relaxation of Villiers le Sec, where we lived among the moles in choking dust and clinging mud; the joyful recrossing of the Channel, Thruxton, Old Sarum, Andover and lachs of leave. And so to West Kirby and the boat, India and Singerbil.

We have seen many adventures together. Some of our numbers have suffered the harrowing experience of being torpedoed. Two others (so they would have us believe) have run the gauntlet of murderous fire to carry ammunition to our forward troops!!! Commando raids we have carried out by the score, and our booty ranges from prize chickens to lavatory seats, from rabbits to motor cars. We have rushed through the length and breadth of England in our thunderous chariots. Everywhere we have left our mark, and in many a town and village the name of '09 is feared, respected, aye, and even loved. Few indeed are the Tavern signs under which we have not drained the frothing tankard, few the rafters that have not rung to our martial cries. Yet for all our swash-buckling manners and joyous carousals, our reputation in the field of aircraft servicing has been second to none.

You have serviced aircraft from the backwoods of Scotland to the battlefields of Normandy, from Spitfire to Lancaster; and everywhere you have earned and been accorded the highest praise. In this theatre we have scarce yet embarked upon our way, yet already you have gained distinction at Imphal and won praises at Khumbergram, and I am confident that you will add greatly to these splendid laurels in the months to come.

To those of you who are comparative newcomers, I say that all this great tradition in no whit less yours. It is your inheritance from those whose places you have taken, handing down to you to guard and cherish so long as you are with us. I know that you are not unworthy of this trust, and those of you who have had the opportunity have already proved your mettle. This is your Unit; its future is in your hands, no less than in those of your veteran comrades. I could not wish it to be in better.

In conclusion I would like to place on record that I consider myself privileged and proud to have been your Adjutant for so long. I have the greatest confidence in you, and I am sure that Sq/Ldr Abbott already feels the same. You have always worked together in a comradely spirit, undivided by petty squabbling, in your Flights and Sections, as teams within a team, in all loyalty and good fellowship. And so now, at the commencement of our third year together, I wish you all success, each and everyone, and more power to your elbow – you'll need it when you get back to the 'Local'! And let us hope that when that day comes it will be possible to raise our elbows all together.
T'ADJ

A WANDERING AIRMAN
Dennis Munns

I was an original member of 3209 SC from its formation at Exeter in Spring 1943, but was transferred to 3207 SC.

We embarked for Bombay on the *Otranto*, after being issued with our tropical kit at West Kirby. This kit included thick heavy wool vests and pants, drainpipe KD trousers that were tight under the arms, and held up by braces, and especially the truly horrible Wolsey helmets. These were the 'pith helmets' beloved of film makers and TV producers who wish to convey tales of the jungle. Altogether, it seemed like kit left over from Victoria's time, and perhaps it was. I also vividly remember the very sharp bee sting of the yellow fever jab.

Our messdeck on the *Otranto* was H1, at the sharp end under the chain locker. It seemed that as we prepared to sail, the anchors were constantly going up and down for twenty four hours, or was it forty eight?

Crossing the Bay of Biscay, as rough as ever, someone spilled the messdeck's porridge on the top step of the companionway. The next mess orderly landed at the bottom of the ladder in a heap of porridge, bacon and tea – and the mess went hungry. Another mess orderly was wholeheartedly sick into the tray of bacon, and another mess went hungry. Jock McMenemy was scrubbing dishes, and, throwing away a bucket of dirty water, saw all the irons (knife, fork and spoon, to the uninitiated) disappear down the chute. I remember working in the galley, right close to the steam ovens, scrubbing what seemed like thousands of greasy tins.

Inevitably, the ventilation fans broke down in the Red Sea. Some of us were lucky enough to be able to sleep on deck. On at least one night I was able to sling my hammock under a ship's lifeboat, and had a good night's sleep, with plenty of fresh air, and did not have to get up very early the next morning when the crew hosed down the decks.

The thing I remember best about Worli Camp in Bombay, where we stayed briefly, was the traditional burning of all the Wolsey helmets and the issue of bush hats. I went to Bombay for a look around, and was disappointed at not being able to explore Grant Road, the famous (perhaps infamous) street of brothels.

The train trip across India was memorable. Two days out from Worli I got a bit of a headache and went to see the train's MO, who was an Indian gentleman. He said that I had a temperature and suspected malaria. They put me off the train at the next stop with my small pack and bedroll, and I was taken to the British Military Hospital at Jubelpur in the middle of the night. The next morning I felt fit, with a normal temperature. Now came the questions. Where had I come from? What Unit? Never heard of them! They told me that mepacrin was not necessary, and anyway, they had none to give me.

They sent me to Jubbelpur Arsenal where there were twelve RAF sergeants and an officer. No Other Ranks, so I was promoted to acting sergeant unpaid. A Sgt. Smith was told to take me around and show me what's what. He had an Anglo-Indian girlfriend, so we went to lots of parties and drank home-made wines and spirits and ate all kinds of native dishes. We met lots of people of various shades of black.

This wonderful life in India lasted only a week. The RAF officer gave me a 2nd class railway ticket to Calcutta and a few Chips (Rupees). Soon afterwards I was at St. James' Transit Camp, and it was the dirtiest, most evil-smelling vermin-ridden place I have ever been to. Weeks later, I was trying to thumb a lift somewhere near Imphal and was picked up by one of our own drivers in a 15-cwt. I often wonder who he was. Anyway, he took me to Palel.

By this time I had a real dose of malaria and hepatitis. I remember waking up in a Field Hospital having my temperature taken, and someone saying 'He'll be alright, it's down to 104.'

Refusing to go on sick leave to a hill station, because I wanted to rejoin 3207, I was sent to Cammack St. Convalescent Home, Calcutta.

After a couple of weeks there, they gave me a bottle of 100 mepacrin and told me to go. So I went off with no money, no pay-book or identity cards, no bits of paper at all, and no help from St. James' Transit Camp.

At the RAF area HQ. I demanded to see the CO or the AOC or the chap in charge. After a long wait an officer reluctantly made me out a Part Two pay-book, which is still in my possession, and gave me a few rupees. They had never heard of 3207.

With much haggling in the market I bought a shirt and a pair of trousers, a road map of India and Burma, which I still have, and a few toilet articles. Calcutta is an interesting place, and I got to know it very well. There was a beautiful house in Ripon Street. It was a pity that I had no spare cash. In Firpo's I bumped into some of my old mates from 3209. They had heard that I had been killed at Meiktilla, and were surprised to see me. We had an enjoyable day or two together, then when I was flat broke I set off to find 3207.

My last four annas were spent on a rickshaw to the railway station. It was easy getting on to the Assam mail train without a ticket, and since there were no British troops aboard that day, I joined some rather strange-looking Indians in jungle green. In fact they were Pathans from Afghanistan. One spoke a little English and told me that before the war he was on the North West Frontier, fighting the British. When asked what he would do after the war, he said he would probably go back to the North West Frontier and fight the British again. A nice chap, he shared his rations with me.

We crossed the Brahmatputra on the ferry, along with lots of hill tribesmen with long rifles, and other strange natives with goats, sheep, cattle, donkeys and one camel.

The next railway was metre gauge, and in the middle of the night, going round the side of a mountain, a few carriages came off the rails. All next day was spent sorting out the mess. One coach was too badly damaged, so it was tipped over the edge, to go crashing down the mountainside. The others were put back on the track and re-coupled to continue, but over a day and a half late.

Off the train at Dimapur, I remember having a meal with some West Africans in a mess at a sort of staging post. One of these black gentlemen said that he was driving a big American truck to Imphal, and that he would take me there. He did. He drove with the finesse of a stock car racer in the Monte Carlo Rally. On the way he told me that one of his tribe, retreating in Burma, had chopped part of the leg off a Japanese soldier with his machete, and eaten it.

At an Army transit Camp at Imphal I met two men from the Manchester Regiment. They told me to keep away from the Orderly Room and RSM and just put my name down for a flight to Central Burma, and to use the Cookhouse with care. We lived away from the main camp, in a basha with the roof falling in. Every morning one of us would check to see if we were booked on a flight and then the days were spent exploring the countryside.

During the following week I managed to acquire another bottle of mepacrin, a bottle of vitamin tablets and a quantity of salt tablets. My Manchester friends 'found' a case of corned mutton in twelve ounce tins and a tin of biscuits. Our basha finally collapsed in a cloud of dust on the day we left.

When we did finally get a flight, the Dakota was loaded with freight. The pilot said that it was well over his limit, and he had doubts whether he would get it airborne. For take-off and landing, we had to sit on the floor as far forward as possible. For most of the day we flew at tree-top level and landed somewhere north-west of Mandalay. The airstrip is not marked on my map, and I can only guess where it was. After unloading, the Dakota took off again.

The drivers of the vehicles who came for our cargo and other passengers were going to Shwebo, not in our direction at all. They said there was an RAF camp about a mile that way, pointing vaguely into the jungle. We picked up our kit and walked until we found it. The camp was very small, unfriendly and even hostile. We were told it was not a transit camp, they had no rations or water or anything for us, and we could go back to where we came from. One sergeant threatened us with violence if he saw us in the camp again.

We wandered away and about two hundred yards into the trees we found a small clearing. Here stood our home for the next few days. It was a basha with no walls, just four bamboo corner poles and a good roof thatched with big leaves. I had noticed a few unattended Indian charpoys (beds) in the camp, so that night we borrowed three of them without any trouble. I even filled our water bottles at their bowser and got away without any trouble. There was a river not far away in the direction away from the camp, and we bathed and did our dhobi there.

Each morning we would pack up and go to the airstrip to meet any planes coming in and see if there was any transport going south. Most days there would be one plane land. Some days there was nothing at all, no planes and no road vehicles.

On about the sixth day a truck belonging to the Manchesters arrived. My two pals were delighted, of course. Their Unit was not where they thought it was. They bade me goodbye and left me wondering where 3207 might be. Getting back to the basha that night I found that a freak whirlwind had taken the roof off. There was another deserted shack, like a big dog kennel, near to a Burmese village. So I carried my charpoy there, where I slept for the next two nights. During the second night I woke up to the sound of rifle fire, shouts and screams. A Bren opened up and then Sten guns with more rifle fire. Some of the bullets were cracking through the trees over my head. It sounded like quite a nice little battle, but it was nothing to do with me, so I turned over and went to sleep again.

The next day three trucks arrived on the strip. One of the drivers was a sergeant who told me they belonged to 17 Squadron, and were going to Meiktila. I could ride with them if I helped them load. We tried to get to Mandalay that day, but with roads blown up or washed away and bridges down, we didn't make it. We didn't even find a protective box before nightfall. In fact, I think we got lost.

That night was spent in a deserted Burmese village. We learned next morning that it was deserted because all the inhabitants had died of cholera. We arrived at 176 Squadron in the afternoon. They gave me a big mess tin full of McConachies stew. It was the first hot meal I had had for weeks. Just as I was starting to eat, a 3207 vehicle pulled up and the driver shouted 'Hurry up and get in if you are coming with me.'

Back with my own Unit at last, no-one asked me where I had been. Someone gave me back my pay book and identity card. When I asked which tent I was in, I was told to join some new arrivals from India in that tent there, but to get a rifle and ammo. because I was on guard that night. My tentmates were Scotty Scott-Richardson, the twins Wally and Bob, and Ginger Simister. I think the twins had been flying as airgunners with the US airforce that day.

Shortly afterwards there came the mad dash for Rangoon. The first stop was near Yamethin, where we formed a box for the night. One lad was stung by a scorpion. The next night we camped near Pyinmana. It was dark when we arrived at Toungoo. The convoy was in a line down one side of the strip, with all vehicle lights on. A twin-engined aircraft flew towards us, and we were wondering whether it was a Mosquito or a Beaufighter, when it dropped a stick of bombs. I believe a few Indian soldiers were killed or wounded.

It was here at Toungoo that we were really short of rations and drinking water. Many men had jungle sores, everyone had stomach trouble, and the cook had dysentery. Our medical corporal used to dose us with castor oil and opium and chalk tablets. There was a big mango tree on the dispersal, with lovely juicy mangoes. Perhaps we ate too many of them! The drinking water was thick with mud and chlorine, but sometimes our section could cadge some water from an Indian looking after some mules.

Then the rains came one night. Everywhere was water. Tents came down and floated away. The strip was out of action and we were supply-dropped. When the Dakotas came over the dropping zone many of the 'chutes failed to open, and the tins exploded on impact. Some tins lay in the sun too long and exploded before they could be picked up. One package came down without a 'chute and landed in the bush some distance away. A couple of the lads raced off to recover it, and after battling through the undergrowth they found a bale of mule fodder.

We were looking after the Hurricanes of No. 6 Squadron. They were armed with 20 mm. Hispano cannons and either eight rockets or two 250lb. Bombs. The guns were in terrible condition, with many stoppages, and the air pressure too low to cock them. We cleared them by having one armourer on the mainplane unlocking the breech with the 'knife, fork and spoon', and another man, in front of the aircraft, pushing the breech block back with a cleaning rod down the barrel.

I was waiting for the ones on the next plane to finish so that I could borrow the tackle when there was a bang and the cleaning rod went flying across the strip like a javelin. We cut up that barrel with a hacksaw and buried the pieces.

Before we left Toungoo we had to move some bombs from where the ground had become boggy. They were stacked three tiers high. We managed to get the top two rows but the bottom ones were sunk deep into the mud and were lost.

I think we were in Toungoo when we heard that VE-Day was being celebrated in England. It was a normal working day for us, except that a party of Japs came through the camp that night throwing hand grenades around. One of the raiding party held a grenade under the engine of a light aircraft and blew off the cowling, but killed himself in the process.

I didn't see many snakes in Burma but there were plenty of scorpions. Some were small and cream coloured, but most were big black ones. Every morning it was advisable to shake them out of your boots before putting them on.

There were many sorts of lizards, too. Some of them were over three feet long and at least nine inches high. Some were in brilliant, almost fluorescent, colours. Once when I was on guard one beautiful moonlit night, a cat came and stood about ten feet in front of me. It was perhaps two feet six tall, and I estimated that it weighed as much as I did. We stood looking at each other for some minutes, then it turned and walked away.

The day before we left Toungoo I was chopping firewood when a chip rebounded and made a gash in my trigger finger. Pat O'Shea, the medic., dressed the wound for me and told me to keep it clean. The next day we struck camp and moved south. The road was in a terrible condition. It was a very hot day. Drinking water and rations were almost non-existent. We made many detours to cross just one river. The bridges were down and the river had to be crossed on makeshift pontoons. The banks were very steep and slippery, and one vehicle, in front of ours, slipped into the water and was drowned. We had to go back up the bank and half a mile down-stream to find another crossing point.

3207's vehicles were all mixed up with others of the 14th Army all going in the same direction. After being on the road for about nine hours we were only three miles from where we had started. I don't remember having anything to eat that day. The bandage on my finger was very wet and dirty, and my finger was beginning to throb. Mosquitoes and flies were troublesome, and I had a headache.

The next day we made better progress. We were told that the road, but not the grass verge, had been cleared of mines. In some places the Japs had used aircraft bombs to make minefields. We passed many heaps of these by the roadside. We also passed many dead bodies, some of them still lying on the road. Where we couldn't drive round them we went over them. The smell was terrible.

Late in the afternoon our truck got a puncture. The milestone informed us that we were 109 miles from Rangoon. We had no spare tyre. A jeep stopped, and it was the last vehicle in our convoy. In it were Ft. Sgt. Lloyd and two others. They said that they would drive on and find a spare wheel to bring back to us. When the jeep had gone on, Scotty said that in the retreat through Burma, someone had buried a case of whisky at the 109 milestone. So, ignoring the warnings about minefields, we all started digging with picks and shovels, and probing with bayonets on both sides of the road for a good distance either side of the milestone. After quite a while the jeep returned with a wheel, but we didn't find the whisky. It was probably buried near the 109 milestone on the Prome road. We were on the Mandalay road.

With the wheel changed, we were on our way again, and it was soon dark. The convoy would have turned off the road somewhere to form a protective box, because there were still thousands of Japs in the area. We drove well into the night without seeing any sign of a protective box or anywhere the convoy had turned off the road. Eventually we pulled into the side of the road and decided to spend the rest of the night there. There were five of us in the back of the truck, Scotty, Ginger Simister, the Clark twins and myself. I don't remember who was our driver and his mate. Then there was the jeep with its three men, making ten in all.

At dawn we were awakened by a heavy machine gun firing over our heads. A British Army officer in an armoured car was checking the road to see that it was safe for the first convoy to move. After a few friendly words we were on our way again.

We saw more heaps of mines, more dead bodies on and off the road. On the way from Toungoo we had passed a few derelict steamrollers of the Aveling and Porter type. Now we were seeing them more frequently. We didn't see any other vehicle until we reached Pegu. Here we found that various units of the Indian Army had occupied a few of the buildings.

We didn't know whether the rest of 3207 was in front of us or behind us, so when we found an empty wooden bungalow that looked inviting, we made it our home for a while.

As soon as possible I went off on my own to find a medic. to get my finger seen to. Within a few hundred yards there was a Red Cross flag flying from a wooden hut. Inside it was a bit spartan. I was greeted by the blackest-faced Indian I have ever seen. He was wearing ammo. boots with no laces, no socks, jungle-green trousers sawn off to mid-calf length, a dirty green vest and a very off-white apron that was covered in filth and bloodstains. I asked if there was an MO around. He didn't speak any English and his Urdu was little better then mine. But I understood that he was the only medic. there was, and he could fix it. He grinned and showed me his lovely white teeth, so I showed him my finger, all red, yellow and green.

I half expected him to produce a butcher's cleaver and carry out an amputation of the finger using the table as a chopping-board. Instead he found a length of cotton gauze, and cleaned it with that. He used no antiseptic or water. He held my hand in a vice-like grip and scrubbed away with the cotton gauze. He removed not only the yellow and green oozing fluid, but all the decaying flesh as well.

I tried not to show that I was in pain, although beads of sweat stood out on my forehead. When he had finished I think I had beads of sweat on my eyeballs. That cotton gauze had felt like wire gauze. The finger certainly looked clean when he had finished. There was about an inch of bare bone showing in the middle of my finger with bits of wire and string, which I suppose were tendons and nerves and things. There was no blood. He filled in the cavity with some orange-coloured paste that he took from a jam jar with a putty knife. After putting on a bandage he told me to leave it on for four days.

I thanked him and went back to the wooden bungalow. There I found that the lads had scrounged some rations from somewhere, and were dishing up a meal of sorts and a brew of tea.

I don't remember how long we stayed at Pegu. It was probably two or three nights. We found a static water tank in the middle of the town, and stripped off for a bath. I managed to keep my right hand dry.

One morning, as we were having breakfast of tinned bacon and new laid eggs, we saw the vehicles of 3207 again. We had to pack our things and quickly rejoin the convoy. The road south was much the same as before with heaps of mines, dead bodies and abandoned steamrollers.

The first night at Mingladon was spent in a red brick building on the perimeter of the airfield. Before the war it may have been a storeroom or a workshop. I was on guard that night, although my trigger finger was still bandaged, so instead of taking my rifle, I armed myself with a few hand grenades.

The next day we moved to Insein, where we occupied a wonderful big brick-built bungalow standing in its own grounds with gardens and out-buildings. It was here that Paddy O'Shea had a look at my trigger finger, which by now was healing miraculously.

Each day some of us travelled to Mingladon to service aircraft, whilst others stayed at the bungalows to look after the camp and repair equipment.

The Home Brew

Something has reminded me of another incident. In Burma with 3207 we were getting no beer, so my mate, Scotty, tried to make some wine. He used an old biscuit tin to make it in, with limes, a few mangoes and other wild fruit, but had no yeast. There wasn't much sugar to spare, and I didn't see much fermentation. After a few days it had grown a thick green furry overcoat, so Scotty stirred it, and left it for a few more days. In the meantime we found some native spirit they called Zuggri. It smelled, or rather stank, of rotting fish. It was so strong that we would nip our noses to take the first sip. After that it was drinkable. But mixed with Scotty's biscuit-tin soup it was even better.

When we got to Singapore we heard that Jos Williamson in 3209 had been promoted to Sergeant. He was in charge of six men to guard the stores, travelling by goods train across India. It was very hot and the train was going very slowly uphill. Jos was dressed in his ammo. boots and nothing else, standing in the open doorway of the wagon. There were some native women scavenging for pieces of coal on the railway track. Jos invited one of them aboard. She accepted, and spent a few hours with him and then, quite satisfied, she got off some miles further along the line.

Rangoon was the next interesting place. Myself and three others were given a jeep and told to go to a tall building next to the cathedral. We had to repair the roof that had some bomb damage, also stop all the water leaks and try to leave at least one working tap on each floor. This was not for our Unit, but for some Headquarters and officers. We were camped in some bamboo bashas on stilts on low-lying ground at Insein. We travelled by jeep after breakfast each day and returned to camp for the evening meal.

Work was progressing well, and towards the end of the week we decided to knock off early and explore the town. We had heard that there were brothels in 22nd Street. We found them, but there were notices on all the doors that said 'Open at 7.30pm' We didn't wait or go back.

I did find a few bottles of 'Fire Tank Brand' whisky. It was aptly named. Nearly as bad as Zuggri.

A few words about my mate Scotty. His full name was John Scott-Richardson. His one claim to fame was that his great-grandfather was hanged for sheep stealing at John O'Groats. Scotty joined our Unit at Meiktilla about the same time as I rejoined it after being in hospital. I weighed less than five stone, but he was even skinnier and a little smaller. But he was as tough as nails. Being an instrument maker he was the one to lead the armourers astray. He had been brought up in the back streets of Glasgow and he enjoyed all the bad habits. He enjoyed life. No-one I know can find out what happened to him after the war.

OLD FRIENDS
Ray Enness

I had just joined 3210 SC, and was sent home on Embarkation leave, and I met a mother of an old school friend. The usual greetings: On leave? How long for? Mentioned I might be going to the Far East – India maybe. 'Albert is out there, you might meet him.' Cutting a long story short, he was stationed at Dum-Dum, and he tracked me down when we were on the Maidan in Calcutta.

Do you remember swimming in the pool at the girls' school? I don't know if the water was the cause but I got ear trouble. (Still deaf in the right ear.) Anyway I was lucky and got picked for hill leave in Assam at Shillong. Being at that elevation gave me trouble in both ears and I finished up in dock for three weeks. From that, I got three weeks' sick leave. In one of the halls in the evening at the camp they held greyhound racing. Dogs made of wood moved by throwing dice (bookmakers included). Large crowd there, all shouting etc. I heard a familiar voice (Essex accent). Another chap I went to school with.

When I got back to Calcutta, the unit had moved to Bihar. Do you remember the tigers roaring during the night?

The next memories are in Kuala Lumpur. How about the four Japs doing guard duty, standing to attention and saluting everyone.

B Flight then moved on near a place called Klang, to refuel Typhoons flying down from up north, and I think on to Singapore.

Next on to Batavia, Java. I became friendly with Jock Kidd. Why I don't know, but he was always in trouble one way or another.

Anyway, we were in Batavia itself. I thumbed a lift from a couple of Indonesians driving a large Buick. Jock asked if we could borrow the car to drive back to camp (he couldn't drive). They said OK, bring it back tomorrow, which we did. Everyone said where the hell did you get that from? So the story was told, whether they believed us or not, I don't know.

The next car we borrowed was a large Fraser Nash, but that broke down and we walked back to camp.

By the way, we were very friendly with a couple of Dutch girls while we were in Batavia.

Another thing I remember was a couple of Indian soldiers turning up at camp delivering what I can't remember. The lorry that brought them returned to town. Later on they asked Geoff Hoddinott (Junior) if he could help them get back to town, so Geoff asked me to take them. I drove a three tonner, one of them in the cab with me to show the way, the other in the back with Jock Kidd. We had to have an armed guard. So 'Kidda' borrowed a Sten gun. When we arrived at the Indians' camp, Jock got in front with me. As he did so, there was one helluva bang. We thought someone was shooting at us. It turned out to be the bloody Sten. It belonged to 'Happy' Day, who had gotten half cut the night before, firing in the air, and had left one up the spout. The bullet went through the cab roof, ripping through the side of the gun mounting, making a real mess of the thing. Lucky for me the gun was pointing upwards.

Another time Geoff asked me if I knew where Meester Cornelus Prison was. I did know, so he asked me to drive there and pick up three Dutch girls, who had been interned there by the Japs, and who did typing and clerical work on the camp. I turned up, banged on the gate, which opened up and out came about thirty women who all climbed on the back of the lorry and refused to get off. So I had to detour through Batavia to drop them off and back to camp with the three original women.

B Flight was then sent to Surabaya. Jock Kidd suggested we keep in touch with the girls in Batavia. We did this. We managed to get lifts in 'Daks' between Surabaya and Batavia at various times.

The first time we went we did it properly and asked (Harry) Schofield, the Adjutant, for a pass, after that we didn't bother, staying the weekend and coming back first thing Monday morning. We came unstuck one time and finished with no lift available, and were seven days AWOL and on a charge when we got back. But we got away with it, since it was nearly Demob time. One time we were in a Dak with no doors – bloody cold – I can tell you.

A PEACEFUL NEW YEAR
Bob Benson

There were three of us from Seletar, Singapore, celebrating the first New Year after the war.

About 2 or 3am we began wondering how we were going to get back to Seletar, about ten miles or so. When the Japanese took Singapore, there were hundreds of cars owned by British civilians, and the Japanese just commandeered them. When the Japanese packed up in August 1945, nobody knew who really owned those vehicles. The vehicles were collected and put into old school playgrounds and areas like that. Some were going missing, and the British forces began doing the odd patrol at night to charge anyone found driving a car that had gone missing.

Jock Keable suddenly had a bright idea. We would take one of those cars and drive back to Seletar. We found one of those dumps and climbed over the fence. After a while we managed to get a car going and off we went. We headed out on the Serangoon Road towards Seletar. Les reckoned we should cut left off the road and go on to 'Ni Soon' (can't spell it properly), the camp where all the Dutch people who had been prisoners in Java etc. were living on their way back to Holland.

Jock, who was driving, thought it was a great idea, and we headed that way. When we arrived, the place was in total darkness, all celebrations were finished, so Jock turned the car round. Suddenly a REME 15 cwt slipped past us and pulled in front of the car we were in. Out jumped a REME Sgt., and a soldier with a Sten gun. The Sgt. spoke to Jock, 'Look here, who owns this car?' Jock looked at him and spouted 'Cpl. So-and So.' The Sgt. looked at him and asked for his Pay Book or Identity Card. Naturally, Jock didn't have any identity, neither did Les or myself – a chargeable offence. The Sgt. told Jock to get out and they would take him to a police station about a couple of miles away for identification. Away they went.

Les and I tried to get the car going, but couldn't. Suddenly there was a burst of Sten gun fire and Les shouted 'Christ, they've killed him!' Shortly the lights of the 15 cwt could be seen coming back, so Les and myself headed for the bushes. They never found us and we eventually made our way back to our billet in Seletar. We kept wondering about Jock, but eventually he arrived. According to him, he baled out at a slow corner and the soldier in the back of the 15 cwt let go with his Sten. Whether he mean to hit him or not is another question.

After the war, I went into the Hotel Management business, and my wife and I managed four different hotels. Eventually, at the age of fifty-one I bought my own pub, not a hotel, just a pub. One lunch time when I was behind the bar, a traveller from a wine and spirit company came to see me. He only bought a half pint of beer as he was driving a car, and eventually got talking to a tall young man who had just come out of the Scots Guards. The lad who had left the Guards asked the traveller if he had ever been in the Armed Forces. The traveller said he had during the war and and that he had been in the REME, I was working behind the bar and I heard most of the conversation.

Eventually I spoke to them both and told them I had been in Singapore when the Japanese packed up. I also mentioned that myself and two others had been stopped by a REME patrol in a 15 cwt at Ni Soon on 1 January 1946. The traveller looked at me and said 'Wait a minute. We stopped a car at Ni Soon around about then and there were three RAF guys in it.' I looked at him and said 'Yes, you took one of us for identification, right?' 'That's right' he said. I looked at him and said 'I was in that car!' 'You're joking' was his reply.

We all had a good laugh about it, and the traveller said he would tell all the others who ran pubs in the area what kind of person I was. We ended up laughing our heads off!!!

Postscript

ON 2 JANUARY 1945, Prime Minister Churchill sent a memo. to the Chief of Air Staff. '...There is another incident which requires your attention, and that is the surrender at Kafissia of about 700 RAF ground forces. These men were mostly of the non-combatant variety, but in spite of several warnings, were left out at this detached station seven miles away from Athens. ...There appears to be a bad arrangement between the military and the Air. ...the military should have recalled this party instead of letting them linger on, with the inhabitants, on a precarious footing. I fear the sufferings of the prisoners may have been very severe... I wish particularly to know how many of those men had rifles and what training they in had in rifle fire. One airman (said) that they were only allowed five rounds for practice per annum. Everybody – and I repeat, everybody – who wears the King's uniform should be capable of fighting, if it be only with a pistol or a tommy gun.'

Nothing better illustrates the importance of the task that the RAF SCUs were trained and equipped to do. Whatever the task those 700 airmen were performing in Greece, it could have been performed, and almost certainly performed better, by a couple of SCUs. And they could also have defended themselves.

Even in the first months of 1945, SCUs were being disbanded although, clearly, there was much work remaining for them to do, and which they were uniquely trained and equipped to do. Therein lies one of the still-unanswered questions of those years. Why did the high command of the RAF show such lack of understanding and even animosity to the SCUs? Beyond question, the Units, when given the opportunity, acquitted themselves brilliantly, completing every task they were given and in terms of speed and efficiency, surpassing all expectations and previous standards. And yet they were, again and again, slighted, ignored and then disbanded at the very first opportunity.

That happened to 3210, my own Unit. In October of 1945, the Commando was fully engaged in servicing and supplying aircraft that landed at Kemajoran, Batavia, and there were many of them, engaged in the repatriation programme, Conditions were primitive and dangerous. We were working right at the sharp end, and well content in performing our proper function again at last. With no warning, on 31 October, the Unit was disbanded.

The scus were unconventional, unorthodox and multi-skilled. They did not fit into the rigidities of RAF organisation. Why, they actually complained at not having enough work to do! And those RAF misfits were imposed upon the rigid orthodoxy of the RAF. Perhaps it is no wonder that they were resented, and disposed of at the first opportunity and certainly as soon as their protector and senior advocate, Lord Mountbatten, went off to new responsibilities in India.

SOUTH EAST ASIA COMMAND HEADQUARTERS.

24th January 1945

My dear Fenton

I am writing to thank you for the
expeditious way you collected the 3205
Servicing Commando for an impromptu
address by me, when I visited Akyab.

Your Servicing Commando has certainly
put up a great show, and it made me feel
particularly proud since, as I told you,
I am more or less the "father" of the
Servicing Commandos.

All good luck to your Commando.

Yours sincerely

Louis Mountbatten

To the Beaches

Flight Lieutenant Frank Tilsley

*Here is the story, written exclusively for the
Royal Air Force Journal, of his invasion experiences with a
Unit of the Servicing Commandos.*

I have been unable to locate the Editor of the *Royal Force Journal* to seek permission to reprint this article. Even senior long-serving Officers have been unable to help. Presumably the periodical has long since ceased publication. After all, the article was published sixty years ago. The article was printed in the *Journal* in August 1944, and won first prize in a competition. I would be happy to seek belated permission to reprint it here if I only knew who to approach. It is re-printed here because it gives a realistic picture of the invasion of France.

Tom Atkinson

I joined the Servicing Commando Unit at their Transit Camp. It was one of those days typical of the first week of the invasion: a cold wind blew about the high and almost treeless plain. Clouds which seemed to be full of rain crowded sulkily in the sky. Occasionally, though, they would disperse and you would get an hour or two of hot sunshine.

The whole countryside appeared to be dotted with these Transit Camps. Each consisted of half a dozen or so marquees in the middle of a field, in which were housed the Orderly Room, Cookhouse, Mess tents, cinema, NAAFI, stores, etc. Surrounding these were flocks of ridge tents in which the men of the various Units lived.

Some of these had been in the camp four or five days: others arrived yesterday. The camp is 'Sealed Off', so there is practically nothing to do but eat and sleep, write letters, yarn with your friends, or improvise a game of football. And listen to the Tannoy.

The whole of the real life of this camp depends on the Tannoy. Whatever else the fellows are doing they are listening to the Tannoy, for it is the Tannoy which initiates the process of movement which will sooner or later deliver us, unit by unit, to the soil of Normandy.

The call to movement begins with a broadcast to the various Commanding Officers to attend a briefing. This will be followed an hour or two later by a broadcast calling on their particular Units to parade. At this parade the troops will be given their instructions, and the time of their departure.

The Adjutant of the Servicing Commando takes me over the Accountant Officer to change my money into French notes – you cannot take any English notes over the water. The Tannoy breaks into life on our way back. We stop and listen. Everybody in the camp stops and listens. It seems the whole of the world stops and listens.

'This is Camp X. The commanding Officers of the following units are to report for briefing at 13.00 hours. No. (blank) Air Information Signals. No. (blank) Transport Section. No. (blank) RAF Regiment. Briefing at 13.00 hours. That is all. Message ends.'

There is a ragged cheer from the men of the Units named: groans from those not named, including from our own Unit. Tonight or at latest first thing in the morning the Units named will take to the road.

I am taken to meet the CO. He comes into the tent and makes me welcome. He is a Flight Lieutenant: I should say in his early thirties, an ex-regular Technical NCO, obviously capable, energetic, experienced, the sort of man who can make a decision and carry it out. I ask him what exactly the Servicing Commando Units are, and he gives me a brief outline.

'There are several Servicing Commando Units. In this country we were formed just over a year ago for the specific job of manning the advanced landing strips so that our aircraft can operate from bases right up by the front line. We don't build these landing strips: that's the job of the Royal Engineers. Our job is to refuel and re-arm the aircraft, to bomb them up and carry out minor repairs. We are the stopgap, holding the landing strip until the squadron's own ground personnel arrive. By the time they do arrive there will be some other advanced strip ready further ahead, and we shall move to that. We have far less men than a regular airfield staff, who have four times as many men to do the same work. Among the officers here are myself, the ADJ. And Dave, the other engineer officer. I'll introduce you to Dave and he'll give you the rest of the gen.'

Dave was in his tent, which I was to share with him.. He was about 25 or 26 years old, of medium height, strongly built, a man of tremendous energy and concentration.

He told me that apart from the fact that almost all the men were volunteers they are also nearly all Group 1 tradesmen. Not only are they experts in their own jobs, but they have also learned to do a variety of other jobs as well as they can their own. They have been trained on a variety of aircraft – Typhoons, Hurricanes, Lightnings, Spitfires, Thunderbolts, Marauders, Beaufighters and Mosquitoes are some examples.

Their training has been intensely practical. Apart from theory, and physical toughening up and combat weapons training, they had accustomed themselves to meeting sudden urgent demands for technical assistance on airfields up and down the country. They have been rushed to these airfields at a moment's notice, not knowing in advance whether they were going to stay for hours, for days, or for weeks, or what sort of job they had to tackle.

They have set up several records. One detachment of 50 men at an Air Practice Camp geared up the serviceability and achieved a 'high' of 60 sorties a day in bitter winter weather. Another detachment of men gave a demonstration, witnessed by the Prime Minister in which 48 Spitfires were refuelled and re-armed in 23 minutes – as quickly as the pilots could park them on the landing ground.

'Of course', said Dave, 'We couldn't do that in active service conditions. All the same we've learned by experience to do things much quicker than they can be accomplished by the accepted methods. We use unorthodox methods and get down to essentials. Re-arming a fighter, for instance, takes an average ten to fifteen minutes. We've got it down to two and a half minutes.'

The whole unit is completely mobile and self-contained with its own medical service, field kitchens, stores and everything else to make it independent in the field. The lorries are fitted out as workshops – one of them is fitted out as an Orderly Room, with tables that are really steady and which fold up into the side of the lorry when the vehicle is taken onto the road.

As we talked the Tannoy broke out again. We stopped in mid-sentence. Beyond the tent a game of football was in progress. One of the men trapped the ball: then everyone stood listening, stiff and silent.

'This is Camp X. The Commanding Officers of the following Units are to report for briefing at 15.30 hours. No. (blank) RAF Regiment. No. (blank Servicing Commandos...' Everybody smiles and tries not to look excited. A cheer comes from the troops at the top end of the field. This is it.

The Tannoy goes again just before tea. I'm talking to a Sergeant from an RAF MT Unit sitting against a hedge: we have seen each other before at some Station or other, years back, and are trying to recall where it was.

'This is Camp X. Attention all ranks. No. (blank) Servicing Commandos are to parade outside the NAAFI at 18.00 hours. Parade outside the NAAFI at 18.00 hours. That is all.'

'Well,' I say, getting up: 'That's us.' I expect it will be our turn tomorrow,' he says. I ask him: 'Are you glad?' He hesitates. 'Honestly, no. One side of me is looking forward to it, of course, and I honestly wouldn't back out of it even if I had the chance. But I've a wife and two children, one of whom is very ill at the moment, and I find myself thinking of them practically the whole time. I wish it were over.'

'I suppose most of us feel rather like that, though the lot I'm going with seem keen enough.' The Sergeant points out that there is a difference between wanting to go because you think it will be exciting, and wanting to go because you want to get it all over and done with. 'I don't know many who are looking forward to it, but yesterday the CO asked for two volunteers to right off away as replacements. Can you guess how many volunteered out of 52?' I shook my head and he told me 'Forty-nine.'

We said goodbye and I went off for tea (which is also dinner – the last meal of the day). I wanted to have this meal right away so that I could get to know some of the boys before the six o'clock parade.

The meals here are good: in the field you have an extra ration of sugar and of meat, the milk is really milk, and there is as much mar- malade as you can eat. And we have white bread! I've never seen anything so white as that bread. I couldn't imagine what it was at first. We ate off tables so scrupulously clean that you buttered your bread without bothering about a plate. One plate, and your own irons, were all you had to provide.

After tea I put my name down for the cinema and Dave took me over to meet the boys.

It is very difficult to generalise about these Servicing Commandos. They are a very mixed bag, of all sorts and conditions of all shapes and sizes. They must be constitutionally strong, because an illness of more than one day's duration results in a posting, unless the circumstances are exceptional. 'The only thing they have in common,' says Dave, 'is that they are keen on their job and will work until they drop. With every one of them the job comes first: everything else takes second place.'

A high proportion of these fellows are regular airmen: almost all the senior NCOs are regulars. The rest of them come from almost every civvy job you could imagine: garage hands, mechanics, clerks, shop assistants – all the usual occupations.

One of them, a comparative newcomer, gives me his impression of the Servicing Commandos. 'They're the toughest looking lot of eggs I've ever seen, and to see them on parade you wouldn't pay them in washers. But wait till you see them on a landing strip! It's a sight for sore eyes. Me? Now I've got used to them I wouldn't leave this Unit for three stripes.'

I must confess that they don't parade like the RAF Regiment when, at 18.00 hours we arrive at the site behind the NAAFI. But they do parade eagerly and it is obvious that they cannot start on the road too soon. Already they have waited too long. They have all told me the same story: that they are the crack Commando Unit and ought to have been landed on D-Day. They have learned that other Servicing Commandos Units got in before them and they are sore about it.

When the CO arrives they form a square, so that everybody can hear what he says. He tells them that they have been allocated a landing strip. This has been pointed out to him on a map. At the moment the front line runs through the site: it is hoped that the enemy will be cleared off it by tomorrow, and that the Engineers will be able to get to work with their bulldozers and level it and lay down the steel mesh runways. We strike camp tomorrow, at 09.00 hours.

The parade terminates rather like a football match: everybody standing about in groups arguing excitedly. There is a great sense of relief. With luck we shall be on the boat tomorrow: that's all we can really think of. We drift to the cinema, and sit on hard forms resting on empty petrol tins. The film is *Tarzan in the Desert* or some such nonsense. Normally many of us would be bored to tears by now, but because we are excited, we laugh and cheer like lunatics. By the noise and applause you would think this was the most brilliant success ever to come out of Hollywood.

Then we go round to the NAAFI and have one or two glasses of ale. The news is on but nobody listens. We lean against the bar, where there are luscious pin-up girls drawn by Petty, and talk and drink and try to tell ourselves that we are not excited, and try not to think of home. You look at your watch. The children will be in bed now, perhaps they are asleep.

'Let's have a game of cards,' says somebody, and you are only too glad to agree. You sleep soundly with a confused impression of rain beating on the canvas of your tent, and one or two sirens which may be alerts or all-clears: then you wake to a cold and surly morning pouring with rain which, in occasional weaker moments dwindles to a thick drizzle.

Breakfast cheers us up, however: there is plenty of sugar for the porridge and for two or three hot cups of tea, fried white bread and an amiable streak of bacon. We go back to our tents, pack up our kit, and at 09.00 hours we are on parade. Then we march off to our lorries, drawn up on the hardstanding ground, beside lines of gliders. We march through the driving rain, whistling and singing, and clattering with our assortment of arms, rifles and revolvers, tommy guns and Commando knives, kit bags, mess tins and so on. The rain is thinning out as we board the lorries and by the time we draw away to the rendezvous the sun has appeared in the sky, full of promise for a hot day.

I sit in the cabin of a three-ton Bedford, beside the driver, trying not to collect too much grease – the lorries have been waterproofed for a wet landing on the beaches, and you get grease over your clothes every time you move. We follow the medical wagon; the medical orderly divides his time between sleeping on the stretcher and endlessly eating sandwiches.

With the other Units moving at this time for our particular transit camp we make quite a long convoy – over fifty vehicles. Small boys raise a cheer as we rumble along the narrow country lanes, moving slowly towards the Reception Centre. In the villages women at gates wave to us, or there is a face at a curtained window, smiling and perhaps giving the 'V' sign. The sun is brilliant now, and the inside of the Bedford cabin is tremendously hot, even though we open all the windows. A halt is called at about 11.00 hours. We climb down from the trucks and sprawl along the wayside of a high green tableland. We eat sandwiches, and are then ordered to burn all our maps. Then we move off again through more country roads and villages, with people who wave occasionally. We are not sufficiently near the Reception centre and the port for people to know that we are on our way over the water, so there are plenty of smiles and thumbs up and V-signs, which we return. A white-haired old lady in a bedroom window catches my eye; she smiles and crosses her fingers and I feel suddenly and deeply moved. I have never seen her before and will never see her again, and she will never know how I made out – how any of us made out – but I feel it was luck, catching her eye in that way.

We reach the Reception Centre at about 15.00 hours. What a sight it is! A canvas city spread under the trees, a vast city through which we can move only slowly, along the winding roads, following the signs. Rows and rows of tents, wedges of transport, hedges of camouflaged lorries, troops of all sorts and nationalities – Americans, British, RAF, white and coloured troops; more men than I imagined all the armies of the world could assemble. And only a fraction, apparently, of the invading army, for nobody stays here more than 24 hours, we are told, and mostly Units are away the same day.

We are allotted to tents, in case we stay the night. Whilst waiting for 17.00 hours we are issued with our Mae Wests, for the boat, and our 24-hour ration packs. The Mae Wests are nothing like their RAF counterparts; they are simple rubber cylinders which you tie under your armpits and inflate (if necessary – let's hope it won't be) with the mouth.

The 24-hour ration packs are square brown boxes of greased cardboard, the joints wrapped round with adhesive taps. They are about six or seven inches square and nearly a couple of inches deep.

We open one out of curiosity – each of us has two packs to keep us going for the first two days. The pack contains about a dozen biscuits, a piece of concentrated porridge and an even bigger piece of concentrated meat. There are four cubes of concentrated tea, three blocks of chocolate, about a dozen boiled sweets of excellent quality and two papers of chewing gum. A rather impressive array taken all round. Certainly nobody is going to starve during the first couple of days, and by the end of two days we shall have the Unit field kitchen going and this will produce hot food for us from the 'compo' rations which have been issued.

In addition to the 24-hour packs we are given a little gadget, and a tin of fuel, for producing sufficient heat to boil a mess tin of water, into which will eventually be ground the porridge or the meat or the tea. Finally, there is a tin which looks at first sight to be a sardine tin, but labelled, ominously, I thought, 'Emergency Ration. This is not be eaten unless there is no other food available.'

We have tea in a marquee under the tall trees – a very good meal, too. The CO is called for briefing, so perhaps we shall be away tonight after all. We go back to the tent and talk. An RAF Regiment officer has been attached to the Unit to organise the defence of the ALG (official name for an airstrip – Advanced Landing Ground) and we talk about the fighting qualities of the Servicing Commandos.

The Commando officers stress the fact that their job is not to fight but to service aircraft. They have all done a combined operations course and have had special weapon training and been toughened up by 30-mile route marches. They have taken part in various exercises, fighting against army detachments and Units of the RAF Regiment in defence of practice airfields.

'We've had bridges blown up under our feet and crawled for days through fields and hedges, glens and dales,' says one of them 'We've practised loading on tank craft and disembarked in the middle of the night with thunder flashes bursting all around us. We've fought for long periods without food, and worked like blacks also without food – just to get us in trim. But even so we aren't likely to do any serious fighting unless there are sudden breaks through by the enemy, or we are faced with recce. patrols by the enemy. Snipers we do expect. In any case, whatever happens, we've been well trained and we've got the weapons, so it' s up to us to put up a good show.'

The CO comes into the tent. 'We move off tonight,' he says, 'at 20.30 hours.'

This time I ride in the jeep. We are the head of our particular column, but as we move into the port there are so many columns that we simply merge into long lines of traffic, crawling slowly along, stopping, moving on again, but all going in the same direction through the gathering darkness, down to the quay. We learn that we are to embark on an LST – a tank landing ship. These are the big ships with the shallow draft and the big ramp doors, so we are rather pleased. It is going to be a more comfortable trip than we had expected.

Midnight arrives, and we are drawn up in the roadway on one of the interminable waits. We are issued with tea from a mobile canteen — very welcome. Troops line the roadway... Americans. They dump their packs on the pavement and sprawl down, resting. Some of them make a meal and we lend them a tin opener. They are full of gratitude and insist on giving us biscuits and cigarettes, chocolate and tobacco. They move away at about 01.00 hours and another batch comes along. Then we move away, to come to another halt a hundred yards nearer the hards.

We doze off, making another move about 02.00 hours. We are given coffee in a mess tin and later a hot tin of M&V (meat and vegetable; you pour it into your mess tin and eat it with a spoon. Very good it is if you don't have too much of it.)

At last about 03.00 hours, we are on the hards. Two LSTs are before us, monstrous in the dark, the lights of their tank deck making brilliant squares in the darkness. What could Jerry do now if only he had the bombers! The jeeps go down first. It is a steep and jolting run down, and an even steeper and more jolting run up into the vessel.

The jeeps and some of the lorries drive right up on to the top deck. Then the remainder drive on to the tank deck. It is now 03.30 hours. A clear half moon rises over the dockyard buildings. The water on the steel decks reflects the searchlights and the barrage balloons. As we load our vehicles in the correct places we sigh with relief and search for blankets to wrap around us: perhaps now we can get some sleep. I fall asleep with my head on someone's tin hat.

We move out to the estuary and drop anchor. We shall have to wait several hours for the tide, we are told. Some of the fellows have swallowed their seasickness tablets already. We line up for breakfast. It is a good breakfast but my inside won't stand it. I have coffee and a piece of bread and butter and go back to the jeep and try and sleep.

I am beginning to realise the true sense of the word in which these Servicing Commandos are tough. A night without sleep has had no effect on them. They eat a hearty breakfast, standing in groups about the top deck, some of them in their shirts, some of them naked from the waist up, although the sun has gone now and personally I am still very cold though wearing a slipover under my battledores and a raincoat. When they sleep, those who cannot find bunks below, or find a comfortable place in the lorries, simply lie on the steel deck. They sleep for hours.

The LST is an American vessel, and the crews are as hospitable as they can be. The officers invite us to share their quarters, where we are given excellent food served by Negro stewards. The troops get exactly the same food, served on the cafeteria principle. There is no liquor here. Nobody seems to miss it; anyway, there is no comment.

We wait many long hours in the roadsteads, first for the tide, then for our position in a convoy. At last we move off. We crowd to the rails of the ship and silently watch the shore of England creep away from us. Somebody plays a banjo very softly. A soldier near me is uninterested in this. He is sitting reading a rather tattered book with the title *Going Places and Seeing Things,* and this absorbs all his attention. The sun is strong now, but cold. The sea is green and somehow magnificent. An erk points out that our ship number adds up to 13, and that are 13 LSTs in line in this convoy. Very shortly, however, we join up with more lines of ships until within the hour we are part of a convoy of big ships which stretch from horizon to horizon. Destroyers, corvettes and even a couple of cruisers move about our lines. I am aware that a faint sense of tension has left my mind. I feel very safe. I sit in the jeep, reading and looking out over the vast green water, and I doze off to sleep.

I have only just realised that there are no Dominion personnel in this Unit. Many of the fellows are talking about their first trip to France in 1939 and the way they had too get out in 1940. 'This is a bit different, eh?' they say, with grim relish. 'Perhaps I'll be able to find the kitbag I left in Boulogne' grins the CO.

Everybody seems to be enjoying themselves now, and I comment to Dave on how they have settled down. 'They'd settle down anywhere,' he says, and I realise that this is the perfect description of the fellows in this Unit. They would settle down anywhere. You cannot imagine any situation would overface them. You feel that if we were wrecked on a desert island they would build a boat, or an aircraft, from odds and ends they found lying about, and would be back in England again almost before you could turn around. Yesterday one of them said to me: 'We take a pride in being able to do every job well, whatever the job, even if it is only a fatigue in the cookhouse.' And he boasted of how on one Station ten of them had peeled 12 cwt of potatoes in some incredibly short space of time. 'They'd thought we would bind about having to peel potatoes,' he said, 'instead we peeled potatoes as they have never been peeled before."

The look-out has just shouted 'Land-Ho!', and there it is, the coast of Normandy, a faint dark line miles ahead of us. The troops crowd to the rails. There is a sense rather of satisfaction than of excitement. We seem to have been on this ship a very long time.

Half an hour passes in silent contemplation of the shore; another half hour. We can see the shipping lying outside the beaches, stretching endlessly, for miles and miles, so that you seem to be looking at a vast industrial town outspread with smoking factories, cranes and derricks.

We are silent with wonder at this great spread of shipping. We expected to see many ships, but nothing like this. It is as though all the ships in the world have been gathered together in one place, as though a World Shipping Convention has been called. There seems to be far more ships than the 4,000 mentioned by Mr Churchill, though of course there cannot possibly be that number. But nobody makes any attempt to guess how many there are, for so many merge into the soft evening distances.

It is about half past seven and the sun shines again, though without much warmth. A voice says we shall have to wait here for weeks if we have to take turns to get on to the beach. 'I've seen convoys in the Mersey,' says one fellow; 'they're like a Sunday afternoon at Rudyar Lake compared with this lot'. We watch the little boats and tenders sailing with the cargoes between the big boats and the beaches.

We are quite close to the shore now, two or three miles. A sandy beach rises to a low green headland. There are sandy scars where bombs and shells have fallen, patches of woodland from which rise what appears to be brown smoke. We think this was shelling; tomorrow we shall discover that it comes from an airstrip, that all Normandy is clouded with brown dust which gets into your hair and teeth, into your eyes and ears.

A motor boat, tossing on the swell, calls us into position. Then we are told by megaphone from the bridge of a destroyer that we will beach at 11.00 hours in the morning. There are groans and shouts from the men on board. 'Make it eleven o'clock tonight' others rub their hands together with satisfaction; we shall get two more good meals on this ship, they say.

We waken up soon after midnight: Jerry is up to his nightly strafe. Some of us go on deck; the Navy is putting up a terrific barrage, with huge cones of searchlights. We hear occasionally the noise of the aircraft engines. So far as we can see no bombs are dropped. It is rather eerie, watching an air raid from the deck of a ship. I've had enough of this after about fifteen minutes and go back to sleep.

We are in position at 11.00 hours, grounded on the beach, but we have to wait a couple of hours for the tide to recede sufficiently to be negotiated by the vehicles. We are given another meal at 12.00 hours, and the Americans make us a present of cigarettes, and tobacco and matches. Their generosity and friendliness kindles inside us the liveliest regards. After lunch we man our vehicles. I go down with a few other chaps to the ramp doors. The ship next to us grounded fifty feet further in, and the vehicles are already pouring on to the beach. One jeep was stuck in the sand and is almost hidden with water: the driver, standing on the seat, is fixing a chain to an adapted tank which will tow him ashore. The wind blows freshly into the ramp doors of the ship; the mid-day sun glimmers on the blue water. Spitfires patrol above us. Convoys of vehicles are creeping up the sand to the dusty road ahead. There is the occasional bang of a gun or an exploding mine. Otherwise everything is as peaceful as you could possibly wish.

All the vehicles are out of the next LST and we have not yet begun. A long ragged line of German prisoners suddenly appears, moving towards the ship, they are going to England.

But all this is forgotten as the order comes to disembark. We rush back to our lorries and away we go. My own vehicle is one of the last, but it is still a steep drop into three or four feet of water. We go in with a splash, and then we are ploughing through the water.

Now we are on the sand, taking our place in the convoy. The driver turns to me, 'So this is France,' he says.

As we drive towards the reporting centre we are all eyes. The country is rather like Kent; smiling fields with pleasant hedges, little houses and bungalows, slightly different from our own. The villages are largely built of stone, and the walls are of stone and very high, sometimes you come across imposing iron gates.

We pass some battered concrete which looks as though it was once part of a fortification system. Along the orchards and cornfields are wooden notices 'Achtung! Minen'. The dust is rising everywhere from the inadequate roads, which our heavy vehicles are grinding into powder. Pioneers are already trying to widen them. We pass one of their camps by which they have erected a sign 'The Muckshifters Army'. Our Report Centre has a notice outside the tent: 'Report here – Wait your turn. No Priorities, No tyres, No spares, No Nothing.'

Everything seems very confused, but in fact we are at the Report Centre less than an hour. A corporal tells me that snipers are their main trouble, that and the flak from the nightly barrage. 'Sleep in ditches,' he says, 'or dig trenches.' I look in some of the tents and see that the occupants have dug a deep pit inside. They sleep down here, covering the opening as well as they can with branches of trees loaded with their kit and anything else they can hold of. The Units here have had small losses, perhaps one or two on landing, one or two with mines or snipers.

We remove the waterproofing from our vehicles and take to the road again. It is a slow and dusty process, with long hold-ups, particularly in the villages. Some of the villagers wave, most of them take no notice of us: some just stare at us. Silently. You can't expect much enthusiasm, I suppose, when we have wrecked their villages and fields. After all, they didn't know what war was until we began it a few days ago. They look reasonably well fed, the children look very well fed and lively and happy. The men all seem to wear blue overalls, with patches of a deeper hue.

Glossary

This short section is not meant for the old-timers. They know exactly what a chore-horse is, for example.

But it is hoped that many others will read this book, and the Publisher has pointed out that even he did not understand many of the terms used in the narratives.

So I have added this Glossary, rather then explaining the unfamiliar terms in the narratives themselves.

ACH GD Aircraft Hand, General Duties. Generally considered to be the lowest form of RAF life. A man without a trade, and one whose life was usually spent scrubbing corridors, or sleeping in the stores. Generally, a good man to befriend .
AIRCRAFT Please refer to the poem by Jock Geddes for an almost complete list of the types of aircraft we handled.
ACK ACK Anti-aircraft guns and anti-aircraft fire.
BODS Bodies, live ones. Personnel, to be polite, I suppose
BOFORS GUN Light quick-firing anti-aircraft gun. A very effective weapon.
BOWSER A petrol tanker, equipped with a pump for re-fuelling aircraft. Usually, but not always, meant to be towed.
BREN GUN A light machine gun. Although needing two men to operate, it was a very successful and popular weapon.
BROWNED OFF Frustrated, bored, even depressed. Could range from a condition relieved by a couple of pints, to suicide.
BRYLCREEM BOYS An insulting description of members of the RAF, frequently used by Brown Jobs – members of the army. Incidentally, the expression 'Brown Jobs' is vastly more insulting than 'Brylcreem Boys', but none of them seemed to know that. The RAF was reputed to use large amounts of Brylcreem, a then-popular hair cream, and so were not tough and really masculine. Little did they know!
BULLSHIT Spit and polish. Unnecessary regulations concerning

behaviour and actions. On one occasion my squadron received orders on how to sit straight and at attention if the truck in which we happened to be riding should pass an Officer. The wearing of collars and ties at all times was thought, rightly, to be bullshit. Obviously the order had been formulated by someone who had never struggled to find a missing collar stud in the total blackness of a crowded tent at two o'clock in the morning when an alarm was sounded.

CHORE-HORSE A two-wheeled trolley, containing a large battery, used in starting aircraft engines. A small petrol engine and generator was mounted on top of the trolley, to charge the large battery.

CIVVY STREET Civilian life. What we all hoped to return to after the war.

DOOLALLY Crazy, insane. Another word from Hindi. Properly Deolali, it was the pre-war mental hospital for all services in India. To go Doolally was to act very foolishly, perhaps by volunteering to do guard duty on a Friday night. It was also applied, of course, to anyone who was genuinely mentally unbalanced.

ERK An aircraftsman: one of the lower orders: The foundations and strength of the RAF.

FAGS Cigarettes. The word was never used with a homophobic meaning, as it is today.

FIGHTER COMMAND The branch of the RAF controlling and operating fighter aircraft. These were usually single-seater, single-engined aircraft, used in combat against similar enemy aircraft. Such combat was known as DOG FIGHTING. The best known of fighter aircraft were Hurricanes and Spitfires. Fighter aircraft were also used as tank-busters, usually firing rockets for that purpose.

FORAGE CAP The peculiar fore-and-aft headgear worn by the RAF. It often meant that the head had to be tilted to one side to keep the cap in place, and gave rise to the rumour that Brylcreem had to be used to stick it in place. Actually, the forage cap could be unbuttoned and unfolded to make a warm and very useful head covering, and one which covered the whole head and neck, and much of the face. It was also very useful for stuffing into the air intake to extinguish a carburettor fire when starting an aircraft engine.

GEN Information or news. There were several types of gen. The best and most reliable (although still not necessarily true) was pukka gen. This came straight from some good source, such as the Orderly Room clerk. Ordinary gen was just wishful thinking or gossip, such as that we were all going on leave. Shithouse gen was in almost cases untrue. It was merely the idle musing or hopes expressed when squatting on the stout pole, trousers around ankles, waiting for the daily relief, and telling your companions that the cook was posted to Wick. And of course assuring them that the gen was in fact pukka.

GHARI A truck or wagon. Another of the Hindi words adopted by Servicemen.

GI. Pronounced Gee Aye. An American soldier. The origin is obscure, but it is generally assumed to stand for Government Issue.

GLASSHOUSE A military prison.

HAIRY Risky, frightening.

JERRYCAN Also Jerrican. A very strong, self-sealing, four and a half gallon petrol can, designed for the German forces, and adopted by the Allies as soon as its advantages were realised.

KITE An aircraft.

LANDING CRAFT Vessels used to land troops and equipment on enemy beaches during an operation. Landing craft were flat-bottomed and equipped with an opening ramp at the bow, so that they could be driven ashore and the troops landed dry-shod. That rarely happened. There were several different types of landing craft. LCI: Landing Craft Infantry and LCT: Landing Craft Tank, for example. LANDING SHIPS were bigger vessels, which carried a complement of troops and LCIs over greater distances.

LUFTWAFFE German Air Force.

MAE WEST A device to support a swimmer. Inflated by blowing into a tube, it had to be worn well up on the chest, and thus was, in the deprived and depraved view of lonely men, similar to the bosomy profile of the film actress Mae West.

MULBERRY The artificial harbour prefabricated from concrete in UK, and towed in sections to the beaches of Normandy.

NCO Non-Commissioned Officer.

PUKKA Another Hindi word, meaning good or reliable.

PRANG An accident. Usually applied to a crashed aircraft.

RAF Royal Air Force.

RANKS The lowest form of RAF life was the ACII: (Aircraftsman Second Class). Just above him was the ACI: (Aircraftsman First Class), and then the LAC (Leading Aircraftsman). Then came the non-commissioned ranks, of which the lowest was Cpl. or Corporal, followed by SGT or Sergeant and Flt/Sgt or Flight Sergeant. Warrant Officer II and I, that is WOII and WOI, completed the non-commisioned ranks. The commissioned ranks began with Pilot Officer: (PO), then Flying Officer: (FO), Flight Lieutenant: (Flt/Lt), Squadron Leader: (Sqd/Ldr) and Wing Commander: (Winco). Above that were the heights with which most of us never came in touch. Strangely, Pilot Officers, Flying Officers and the rest were not necessarily aircrew, and did not necessarily ever fly.

RCAF Royal Canadian Air Force.

SC Servicing Commando.

SCROUNGING The art of picking up unconsidered but desirable trifles which would never be missed. And even if they were, we would be many miles away by that time. One of the fine arts which had to be learned, and quickly, by all members of SCUs.

SCRUMPY Rough cider. Cheapest way of getting inebriated (or, as we would have said in those days of youth and innocence, pissed).

SCUs Servicing Commando Units.

SHUFTI To look at, to explore. Another Hindi word.

SNCO Senior Non-Commissioned officer.

SPROG A new, young and inexperienced airman.

SORTIE One operational flight by one aircraft.

SROs Station Routine Orders.

STALAG Properly, a camp for British Prisoners of War in Germany, but usually applied to any RAF station renowned for its bullshit, boredom and time wasting.

STEN GUN A light, cheap and unreliable automatic weapon. Liable to fire a round if dropped, even with the safety catch on. An unpopular gun.

U/S Unserviceable. Usually an aircraft, but an erk after a pay night.

USAAF United States Army Air Force.

VR Volunteer Reserve. Of the Airforce.
WAAF Womens Auxiliary Air Force. Also a member of the WAAF.

INDEX

Some other books published by **LUATH** PRESS

LUATH GUIDES

Luath Guides are written by authors who invite you to share their intimate knowledge and love of the areas covered. These intriguing guides are not your traditional where-to-stay and what-to-eat books. They are com-panions in the rucksack or car seat, providing the discerning visitor or resident with a blend of fiery opinion and moving description, making them 'a lively counterpoint to the more standard, detached guidebook' (The Washington Post).

The North West Highlands: Roads to the Isles

Tom Atkinson
ISBN 9781913025182 £7.99

The obvious beauty and hidden delights of the mountainous lands from Fort William to Ullapool.

South West Scotland

Tom Atkinson
ISBN 9781913025205 PBK £7.99

The lovely land of hills, moors and beaches is bounded by the Atlantic and the Solway. Steeped in history and legend, still unspoiled, it is a land whose peace and grandeur are at least comparable to the Highlands, and yet it is hardly known. No area of Scotland better repays exploration than this.

The West Highlands: The Lonely Lands

Tom Atkinson
ISBN 9781913025212 £7.99

Inveraray, Oban, Kintyre, Glencoe, Loch Awe, Loch Lomond, Appin, Islay – all the glories of Argyll are described in this book.

The Northern Highlands: The Empty Lands

Tom Atkinson
ISBN 9781913025199 £7.99

The Empty Lands are that great area of northern Scotland between Ullapool and Cape Wrath, and between Bonar Bridge and John O' Groats. It is tru-ly the Land of the Mountain and the Flood, where land and sea mingle in unsurpassed glory.

Details of these and other books published by Luath Press can be found at:
www.luath.co.uk

Luath Press Limited
committed to publishing well written books worth reading

LUATH PRESS takes its name from Robert Burns, whose little collie Luath (*Gael.,* swift or nimble) tripped up Jean Armour at a wedding and gave him the chance to speak to the woman who was to be his wife and the abiding love of his life. Burns called one of 'The Twa Dogs' Luath after Cuchullin's hunting dog in Ossian's *Fingal*. Luath Press was established in 1981 in the heart of Burns country, and is now based a few steps up the road from Burns' first lodgings on Edinburgh's Royal Mile. Luath offers you distinctive writing with a hint of unexpected pleasures.

Most bookshops in the UK, the US, Canada, Australia, New Zealand and parts of Europe either carry our books in stock or can order them for you. To order direct from us, please send a £sterling cheque, postal order, international money order or your credit card details (number, address of cardholder and expiry date) to us at the address below. Please add post and packing as follows: UK – £1.00 per delivery address; overseas surface mail – £2.50 per delivery address; overseas airmail – £3.50 for the first book to each delivery address, plus £1.00 for each additional book by airmail to the same address. If your order is a gift, we will happily enclose your card or message at no extra charge.

Luath Press Limited
543/2 Castlehill
The Royal Mile
Edinburgh EH1 2ND
Scotland

Telephone: 0131 225 4326 (24 hours)
Fax: 0131 225 4324
email: sales@luath.co.uk
Website: www.luath.co.uk